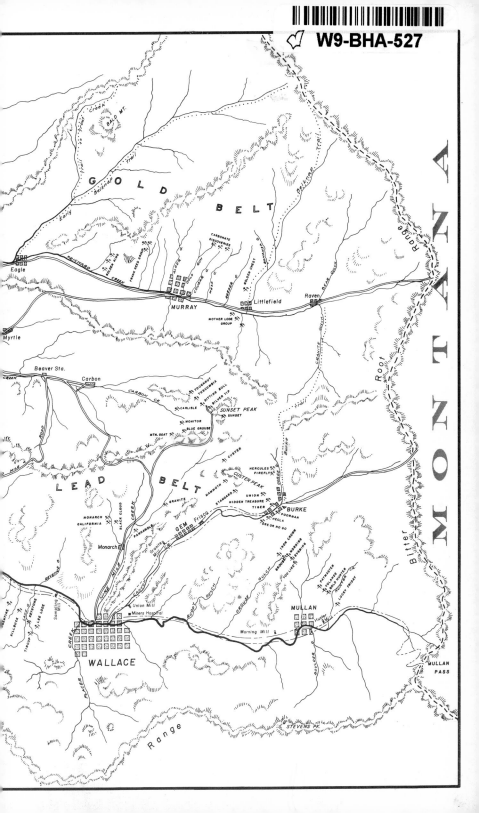

Coeur d'Alene Diary

COEUR D'ALENE DIARY

*The First Ten
Years of Hardrock
Mining in North Idaho*

by

RICHARD G. MAGNUSON

METROPOLITAN PRESS
Portland -:- Oregon -:- 97242

Coeur d'Alene Diary

Printed in the United States of America

FIRST EDITION

DEDICATION

This book is dedicated, in a general way, to the men and women who "pioneered" the Coeur d'Alene Mining District.

In a special way, it is dedicated to my parents, my wife, Elsie, and Rick, Janet and Julie.

FOREWORD

The past seldom intrudes upon the present.

Buildings crumble in decaying towns of the Old West, as defiant and independent in their dying moments as the pioneers they once housed or catered to. And as the wind moans through the moldering boards, one can imagine a ghost from out of the past, not lamenting death, but simply accepting the inevitable.

Such towns are not links with the past, but merely reminders of it. They stand alone, weatherbeaten markers in an old graveyard; or they give way to housing developments, industrial complexes, freeways or shopping centers, and their ghosts are buried in concrete.

But this is not true of the Coeur d'Alene Mining District in Northern Idaho—Here the past mingles with the present, and walks side by side with it into the future.

Mr. Richard G. Magnuson, a lifelong resident of Wallace, Idaho, has detailed the first ten years of the history of this district. His book is fascinating, not because this period is a legend out of the dead past, but because it is a "flashback" that gives meaning to the present.

Some day, when the mineral wealth of this mining district has been exhausted—and no one will predict how far into the future that may be—the stories of this district will become folklore, in the manner of the legends of the Comstock Lode in Nevada and Virginia City, Montana.

But in the meantime Mr. Magnuson has written Act I, Scene I; putting flesh and blood on the dry corporate statistics that have succeeded the passions and the excitement of the early days.

The present is a prosaic parade of statistics, set forth in tabular form for the benefit of accountants and investors.

Coeur d'Alene Mining District

Production for 1967

Value—$57,468,000

Silver—16,293,000 ounces.

Lead—54,791 tons.

Zinc—53,498 tons.

Copper—2,722 tons.

Gold—2,332 ounces.

Total Production
1884-1967

Value—$2,246,950,996

Silver—752,271,499 ounces.

Lead—7,032,926 tons.

Zinc—2,570,313 tons.

Copper—115,483 tons.

Gold—460,440 ounces.

These are dry figures to be swallowed, digested and then spewed forth on command by computers.

Mr. Magnuson has translated them into terms of the men who 84 years ago found the first tiny evidence of ore in the Coeur d'Alene Mining District, and who in their wildest dreams could not have foreseen what they discovered.

Mr. Magnuson tells of the early discovery of the Morning Mine in Mullan in 1884.—In 1968 the Morning Mine is still being "discovered."

It became the deepest lead mine in the world. And now, as part of the Star-Morning Unit operated by Hecla Mining Co. and The Bunker Hill Co., it will be explored to a depth of 9100 feet from the surface. A new shaft in the property, now being sunk, will be the second deepest shaft on the North American continent, with a vertical lift of 7100 feet.

The book describes the first work on what was then called the "dry ore belt from Big Creek to Placer Creek at Wallace." Dry ore is a metallurgical term describing ore with silver but little or no lead content.

The men who dug the first tunnels in this area are responsible for finding what today is known as the "Silver Belt," which produces one-half the silver mined each year in the United States.

Years later, in 1968, S. Norman Kesten, an eminent geologist for the American Smelting and Refining Company stated: "The only foreseeable 'bottom' to the ore in these veins is the limit imposed by the ability of men and machinery to work at great depths."—In the Sunshine Mine in the Silver Belt, the largest silver producing mine in the nation, the depth already is 5200 feet, or 2500 feet below sea level.

Mr. Magnuson cites the work that was being done in 1890 by Corbin and McCormick in the Placer Creek area south of Wallace, then felt to be the eastern boundary of the "dry ore belt."

Little came of this early work. But in 1969, a newly organized company, Caladay Silver Mining Corporation, will begin sinking a shaft to explore at depth veins in the Placer Creek area, now described as a "direct extension of the Silver Belt."

Caladay will be managed by Callahan Mining Corporation, whose Galena Mine in the Silver Belt is the second largest silver producer in the nation. The rich ore in the Galena mine was found at a depth of 3000 feet below the early day workings in the Killbuck property described by Mr. Magnuson.

The author permits the reader to imagine the dreams of the men he describes; and in 1968 these dreams are still being fulfilled. The men he writes about are dead, but their ghosts still walk on every street in the towns that dot the Coeur d'Alene Mining District. These ghosts carry picks and shovels and lead burros beside the mining engineers and geologists who ride Jeeps and carry geo-chemical testing kits and the other paraphernalia of modern day prospectors—seeking ore bodies which eluded the men of the early days.

The reader of this book is told about the 1884 discovery of the Gold Hunter Mine east of Mullan. Sixty years later—and figuratively only a stone's throw away—the Lucky Friday Mine came into production. Today it ranks as the third largest silver producer in the nation. And the Gold Hunter, owned by Day Mines, Inc., once considered worked out, now is to be explored again, through a long tunnel to be driven from the 4000 level of the Lucky Friday Mine. How the ghosts of the men who discovered the Gold Hunter must tremble with excitement at this development!

It is easy to forget, in these days of tenders and takeovers, the heritage of these corporate wars of acquisition.

Mr. Magnuson reminds the reader of this when he describes the discovery of the Bunker Hill in 1885, the litigation that followed before ownership was determined, and the absorption of early day mines and prospects, such as the Last Chance and Stemwinder, by the Bunker Hill.

And one is even more aware of this bridge from the past into the present by the takeover of Bunker Hill early in 1968 by Gulf Resources and Chemical Corporation. Now Bunker Hill is a wholly owned subsidiary of Gulf Resources—part of the nation's corporate infrastructure.

This is progress, but the whir of computers should not be permitted to drown out the voices from the past who say: "This is the way it was."

R. J. Bruning, Publisher
North Idaho Press
Wallace, Idaho

AUTHOR'S PREFACE

Unlike many mining districts of the West, the Coeur d'Alene district still survives. Some had very short lives, and their obituaries were quickly put into print. . . . This was not the case with the Coeur d'Alene. It has already had an active span of 85 years, and shows few signs of being "worked out." Its long life, coupled with a desire for secrecy on the part of some participants in its violent labor disputes, have already served to obscure its early history.

Few books or articles are available on the early years of the Coeur d'Alene, but the newspapers of the last century shed light on the events and the people. Throughout this volume, the reader will find excerpts from the pioneer newspapers. I chose to preserve the style, flavor and humor of their editors without risking the possibility of improper interpretation.

My research was made difficult because the population of the Coeur d'Alenes has been transitory over the years. The "poor" had to move on frequently because of changing economic conditions, and the "rich," with one notable exception, chose to go elsewhere to enjoy the wealth they gained from the mines. Many of the early union miners found it expedient to get out of the district for their own welfare. . . . A good deal of information possessed by these people was therefore taken from the area and lost over the years.

My research was made easier because of the many courtesies shown me while acquiring material for this book. It is impossible for me to specifically credit everyone who contributed. Valuable assistance was given me by the University of Idaho, librarians, historians, and newspapermen, along with other good friends who helped in many ways. Those persons having a deep feeling for the Coeur d'Alenes lent much needed encouragement to this effort, be it big or small.

The research that went into this book was originally done to satisfy my own curiosity as to the first days of the Coeur d'Alene. From the time of my earliest memories, the tales of my grandparents and other "oldtimers" were music to my ears. On occasional Sunday afternoons when I was a young boy, my father took me into Bill Fahle's saloon to show me the historical relics and photos which adorned the back bar and the walls. . . . In later years, miners, lawyers, bartenders and other old friends of the Coeur d'Alene spun me stories to further whet my curiosity. . . . After each story telling session, the words were always the same: "The Coeur d'Alenes have a great history; it is too bad that no one has ever written it up."—This, in its small way, is my effort to chronicle the first ten years of the Coeur d'Alene, a mining camp and its people.

RICHARD G. MAGNUSON

Wallace, Idaho
December 1, 1968

TABLE OF CONTENTS

COEUR D'ALENE DIARY

CHAPTER 1

THE VERY BEGINNING — 1842

If any white man trod the valley floor along the South Fork of the Coeur d'Alene River in Idaho's Panhandle before 1842, he must have walked very lightly, leaving no footprints. Some may have passed through, however, and their excuse would have been to trap fur. The first recorded visitor was not motivated by riches; instead he was interested in the Indian tribes of this inner country of the Northwest.

In 1841, Father Pierre Jean DeSmet had established a Jesuit mission in Montana for the Flathead tribe. In April of 1842, while on a trip from his mission to Fort Colville, in the present state of Washington, he traveled along the Coeur d'Alene River in order to visit the Coeur d'Alene Indians. He spent two or three days giving them religious instruction upon the shores of the lake bearing their name. Two rivers flowed into this lake, and Father DeSmet named the southern one the St. Joseph and the northern one St. Ignatius. The name of the St. Ignatius River was later changed to the Coeur d'Alene River . . . DeSmet's departure was accompanied with his promise to establish a mission with them soon.

The fall of 1842 found Father Nicholas Point and Brother Huet traveling across north Idaho to establish the mission as planned by Father DeSmet. Father Point proceeded to a place on the shores of the St. Joe River where he planted a cross and dedicated the mission to the Sacred Heart. Crude log structures were

1

soon to grace the area, but flood waters caused serious problems every year.

By 1846, it was decided to move the mission to the area drained by the Coeur d'Alene River. Father DeSmet had selected a new site a short distance downstream from the juncture of the South and North Forks of this river. Two years later, Father Anthony Ravalli began building at this site. He had proceeded far enough along with the main building so as to enable its use during the winter of 1849-50. This building was opened for services in either 1852 or 1853.

The advent of white men with different interests grew out of developments in Washington, D. C., where, on March 17, 1853, Washington Territory was organized, and the President appointed Isaac Stevens to serve as governor. This new territory included all of present day Washington and that part of Idaho north of the Salmon River. Stevens was a New Englander by birth and a graduate of West Point, who rose to prominence during his service in the Mexican War. He was thirty-five years old when he received his appointment as governor.

Isaac Stevens knew that Congress had appropriated $150,000 for the survey of railroad routes from the Mississippi to the Pacific Ocean earlier that year. He volunteered his services immediately to survey a proposed route across this part of the nation. He started his trek from St. Louis with 240 soldiers and proceeded up the Mississippi to St. Paul. One of his officers was Lieutenant John Mullan, who was later to gain great stature as an explorer of the Northwest.

Stevens' party came across Idaho through the valley of the South Fork and visited Sacred Heart Mission on its way to the coast. His group followed a trail which was then being used by Nez Perce and Coeur d'Alene Indians on their way to the hunt in Montana. The governor led other parties along this trail during the next few years. His efforts led Congress to set aside more funds for surveys and exploration of that land between the great falls of the Missouri River and Fort Walla Walla.

Congress soon appropriated $30,000 for a survey and $230,000 for the building of a road from Fort Benton in Montana to Fort Walla Walla, some 624 miles apart. The road building duties were given to John Mullan, who had been helping Governor Stevens and also serving the Army in its difficulties with the Indian tribes. The Coeur d'Alene Indians gave these road-building plans as one of their reasons for their being warlike in the mid 1850's.

About that time, the Army had fought battles at Steptoe Butte, near Rosalia, and on the Spokane plains. Colonel George Wright led the troops to victory over several tribes, and in the process 16 Indians were hanged. His conquest of the Coeur d'Alene tribe was complete by September 17, 1858, when he met with their leaders at the Mission on the Coeur d'Alene River and agreed to the terms of their surrender.

The terms of their treaty embodied seven points. First, hostilities were to cease from and after September 17, 1858; and, secondly, the tribe was to surrender all government property taken into its possession during the battles. Third, the chiefs agreed to surrender to the troops the men who commenced the battle with Lieutenant Colonel Steptoe, contrary to the orders of their chiefs, and also to give at least one chief and four men with their families to the officer in command of the troops, as hostages for their future good conduct. Fourth, the tribe promised safe travel for all white persons through its country, which would soon include the Mullan Road. Fifth, the military leaders promised safety for the hostages and to return them within one year. Sixth, it was agreed by both sides that the treaty would be permanent in duration; and lastly, the Indian chiefs agreed that the treaty of peace and friendship should extend also to include the Nez Perce Nation of Indians.

Colonel George Wright signed the treaty on behalf of the Army, and fifteen Indians, designated as chiefs and head men of the Coeur d'Alene Nation, placed their marks on the treaty.

These proceedings were witnessed by twelve of Wright's officers. Three other Indian leaders were to sign the treaty at later times.

This treaty brought peace once again to the Coeur d'Alene Indians. The tribe had been led in its efforts to end the fighting by Father Joset and Father Congiato, who were in contact with Colonel Wright during the fall of 1858. One of Wright's last letters to his superiors, before the treaty, sets out that he was camped sixteen miles above Spokane Falls and that he was engaged in slaughtering 800 horses belonging to the Palouse chief Tilco-ax, who had been very hostile for the last two years. This slaughter was in retaliation for Tilco-ax's rebellious behavior. Wright closed his letter stating:

"This work of slaughter has been going on since 10 o'clock of yesterday, and will not be completed before this evening, and I shall march for the Coeur d'Alene mission to-morrow."

Colonel Wright described his troops' march to the mission, over the terrain later to be traversed by the Mullan Road:

"I marched from my camp on the Spokane River, sixteen miles above the falls, on the morning of the 11th instant (September 11, 1858); after fording the river, our line of march was pursued along its right bank for fourteen miles, when I struck the Coeur d'Alene lake and encamped. Resuming our march on the 12th, we soon lost view of the lake on our right, and struck into the mountains, with a forest on either hand, and a trail which admitted only the passage of a single man or animal at a time. After marching twelve miles I found a small prairie, with a fine running stream of water, and encamped."

"Marching early on the 13th we found the trail infinitely worse than that of the previous day; passing through a dense forest, with an impenetrable undergrowth of bushes on both sides, and an almost continuous obstruction from fallen trees, our progress was necessarily slow, having to halt frequently and cut away the logs before our animals could pass over. The column and pack train could only move in single file, and extended from six to eight miles, but it was perfectly safe, the front and rear were strongly guarded, and nature had fortified either flank. No communication could be had with the head of the column and its rear, and thus we followed this lonely trail for nineteen miles to this place (Coeur d'Alene Mission). The rear of the pack train with the guards did not reach here until 10 o'clock at night. I found the Indians here in much alarm as to the fate which awaited them, but happily they are now all quieted. Father Joset has been extremely zealous and persevering in bringing in the hostiles. They are terribly frightened, but last evening and to-day they are coming in quite freely with the women and children, and turning over to the quartermaster such horses, mules, etc., as they have belonging to the United States."

With peace restored, Coeur d'Alene Valley was about to progress from such Indian trails to the grandeur of the Mullan Road.

CHAPTER 2

THE MULLAN ROAD — 1859

Commencing with the end of the Indian trouble and working until the Civil War halted his efforts, Captain John Mullan undertook to build a road to join the headwaters of the Missouri River with those of the Columbia. The area west of Hell Gate, Montana, could be reached by three different trails. The Lolo was not selected because it was over tough terrain, and the route along the Clark Fork River was undesirable because of periodic flooding. He chose the trail which followed the Coeur d'Alene and St. Regis valleys.

Mullan did survey work near the Sacred Heart Mission during the fall of 1859. He described the Coeur d'Alene River (at a point one mile upstream from the Mission) as having a width of 80 feet, a current of a mile and a half an hour, and a mean depth of two feet, and said it attained an average width of 200 feet and a depth of 15 feet (just below the Mission) with a current so slow as to be imperceptible. This character of the river was the same for its 27 winding miles from the Mission to the lake.

Mullan described the knoll, upon which the Mission was built:

> "Upon its summit are the buildings of the mission, which consist of a large church and two houses for the dwellings of the priests and lay brothers, around which are scattered various tenements, lodges, etc., comprising the Indian village."

6

The country twenty-five miles upstream from the Mission was described by Mullan as having timber of a heavier growth than that near the Mission.

"Cedars from three to six feet in diameter frequently occur. The pine becomes abundant, attaining a growth of from two to four feet in diameter, and from one hundred and fifty to two hundred feet high."

His survey took him to the summit of the divide of the Coeur d'Alene or Bitter Root mountains at Sohon's Pass, which he judged to be 4,932 feet above sea level. From there he proceeded to the St. Regis Borgia River and on into Montana, where the Mullan party camped during the winter of 1859-60.

Mullan's 100-man crew cut the trail across Idaho's Panhandle in 1859 and 1860, and then they spent the next two years improving it. The construction of the road involved 120 miles of difficult timber cutting, 25 feet wide; thirty miles of excavation, 15 to 20 feet wide; the building of miles of corduroy road, and the construction of many bridges. They built about 20 bridges across the Coeur d'Alene River alone.

In 1866, it was reported that no less than 20,000 persons had passed over the Mullan Road to and from Montana during the year, along with mining supplies, freight, horses, mules, and herds of cattle. Over the years the Mullan Road was to serve hunters, adventurers, tourists, emigrants, cattle drivers, Indians, and prospectors. The basic route of the Mullan Road across northern Idaho was later to serve as the main highway between Missoula, Montana, and Spokane, Washington.

Captain Mullan was to recall after the Murray Gold Rush in 1884 that one of the hunters with his road building party, a French-Canadian by the name of Moise, came into camp one day with a handful of coarse gold which he said he had found on the headwaters of the north fork of the Coeur d'Alene River while out hunting. He was not believed at the time because it was thought he traded for this gold with some parties passing up and down from the Fraser River mines. Mullan stated that this happened in 1858 or 1859. Later, another member of his crew was to discover gold on the south bank of the Bitter Root River.

Mullan added that members of this crew were composed very largely of old miners from California, who felt that the entire country from Coeur d'Alene Lake to the east slope of the Rockies was one vast gold-bearing country,

> "and I was always nervous as to the possible discovery of gold along the line of my road, and I am now frank to say that I did nothing to encourage its discovery at that time, for I feared that any rich discovery would lead to a general stampede of my men from my own expedition. . ."

After the Montana gold rush of the 1860's died down, the use of the Mullan Road subsided and it fell into a state of disrepair.

The establishment of Fort Coeur d'Alene (later known as Fort Sherman) upon the shores of Coeur d'Alene Lake in the late 70's brought about renewed usage of the Mullan Road. A military telegraph line was strung along the road in 1876 and this necessitated the building of way stations for repair purposes. The presence of the military did cause some minor repair work to be done on the road in 1879, principally over the Idaho-Montana divide and into Montana.

In later years, Daniel Stresburg, formerly a corporal in A Company of the Second U.S. Infantry, recounted his early experiences with the Signal Service which maintained the military telegraph line along the Mullan Road. He recalled: "I built Swingdoor Cabin, (near Silverton) assisted by others of my company, and we built other cabins along the old Mullan Road in the late seventies. We called them life saving stations, and to a certain extent they proved to be that. . . . They were about ten miles apart."

They built six way-station cabins in the Coeur d'Alenes. One was located in Fourth of July Canyon and another near the mouth of Pine Creek. The third and fourth were built at Evolution (near Osburn) and Swingdoor (near Silverton). The last two cabins were built on Nigger Prairie (Mullan) and on the summit of the Bitterroot Mountains (Idaho-Montana border). Besides being used as temporary shelter for maintenance crews working on the telegraph line, they were used by travelers and prospectors along the Mullan Road.

The road was never properly improved or maintained from its beginning because of the advent of the Civil War. The federal government's interest in the Northwest was not as keen as before. It had been built as a military road, and the Indians were no longer hostile. The telegraph project was abandoned in 1882. Mullan Road was fast reverting to its original natural status when the first mining men appeared on the scene.

CHAPTER 3

THE SEARCH FOR GOLD — 1866

The argument as to who was the first prospector in the Coeur d'Alenes will never be settled, but the early efforts of some of the men shall be set forth.

Perhaps the earliest discovery of gold was made by a colored man whose name is not known. Because of him it is said the colorful name of Nigger Prairie was given to the area now known as Mullan, Idaho. A story printed by a Bozeman, Montana, paper in 1884 set forth that a Negro came into Missoula in the fall of 1866 with a large amount of gold dust, which he spent with abandon, claiming he knew where there was plenty more. . . . The next spring he went out again and in the fall returned with more gold than he had brought in before. The spring of 1868 saw him leaving Missoula once again, with a Flathead Indian. In July of that year, a band of travelers on the Mullan Road reported that the Negro and the Indian were living in a log cabin built in a small opening (in now Mullan, Idaho) along the road. A week later, another group traveling through there found the Negro dead, killed by a gun. They buried his body and went on . . . Late in 1868 the Flathead was seen in possession of the Negro's horses, and it was then supposed that he was responsible for the Negro's death. . . . The people who buried the Negro planted a crude cross at his gravesite.

To the south of the Coeur d'Alenes, there had been a stampede by Montanans to the St. Joe River Country during the 1860's.

Placer diggings were found, but not worked very long. This old camp was nearly south of Mullan, Idaho. Prospectors from the Murray goldfields also went in there on snow shoes in the winter of 1887-1888. They found placer diggings, but the pay was too light to satisfy them, and it was abandoned.

Later John P. Vollmer, a pioneer from the Lewiston, Idaho, area was to write that he and Frank E. Peck, from Boston, led a party from Lewiston to the Coeur d'Alenes to prospect for gold in 1873. He claimed to have traveled to the Old Mission and thence along the South Fork into Montana. On their return trip they looked over the area between the St. Joe and Clearwater rivers. Vollmer and his party spent from June to November on their trek. They returned and did more prospecting during the summer and fall of 1874, but they decided to abandon further search.

One of the members of Vollmer's expedition was George A. Frost, who claimed to have been in the Coeur d'Alenes in 1872.

Andrew J. Prichard, a Civil War veteran, was to receive the credit for leading the first successful party into the Coeur d'Alenes searching for gold. Prichard came in to the Coeur d'Alenes in the fall of 1878 with a William Gerrard, from Montana. They passed through on their way to Fort Coeur d'Alene. Prichard secured a lumber contract for a firm at Spokane Falls, and he soon commenced logging near Fort Coeur d'Alene.

Prichard said he first met Tom Irwin, another pioneer prospector, in January, 1879, at Spokane Falls. At that time Prichard told Irwin of finding a mineral discovery at Evolution (about 4 miles upriver from Kellogg, Idaho) in 1878. Prichard built a cabin at the site of this discovery during the fall of 1879. This made him somewhat of a neighbor to Tom Irwin, who built his Miner's Cabin a mile or so downriver earlier that year. Irwin prospected with a fellow named William Dobson. Prichard stated that his funds at the time he built his cabin consisted of one silver dollar.

The spring of 1880 found Prichard prospecting in a small gulch near Evolution called Prospect Gulch. He set up sluice boxes in

March, and took out what he claimed to be the first placer gold of the Coeur d'Alene. The gulch was small, and he soon ran out of water.

It is believed that Tom Irwin traded his provisions in 1881 for a horse and left for Colorado. Other men were then prospecting in the mountains of the Coeur d'Alenes. W. Edson and Bob Fanning went with Prichard into the mountains to the north. They spent several days on Beaver Creek, but found nothing. - - - Later Edson and Fanning were to prospect in Canyon Creek, but to no avail. . . They became discouraged and took off for civilization.

The following year, Prichard went to Beaver Creek, a tributary of the North Fork of the Coeur d'Alene River, with a man named Gelatt and Phillip Markson. They found nothing and the group continued on to the North Fork of the Coeur d'Alene. Somehow, Gelatt became separated from the rest of the party. He was an older man, being about 65, and described as independent enough to cut himself from his companions whenever he chose.

Gelatt was missing for several days and the others gave up hope of finding him. They continued prospecting and chose to follow a sidestream, which was later named Prichard Creek. Several miles upstream they stopped to look over the land, and they came across Gelatt, who had been doing some prospecting on his own. Their partner, William Gerrard, came into their camp the next day with a small supply of provisions. He had promised them earlier that he would follow them up with food and supplies.

Soon thereafter one member of this prospecting expedition did make a discovery of gold near the site of what was soon to be the gold rush town of Eagle City. - - - Some say it was Gelatt. - - - Which partner made the discovery will perhaps always remain a mystery. . . The last 85 years have not solved that question, and it is not likely to be answered in the future.

This discovery of gold caused a gold rush to Prichard Creek during the fall and winter of 1883, and into the spring of 1884.

During the spring of 1883, Prichard located the Discovery group, in the vicinity of present Murray, which was made up of four claims. He claimed much other land on the creek bank for his friends by using a power of attorney. Gelatt took a claim which turned out to be a big producer. A William Dempsey located placer ground about a mile above the camp at Eagle.

It will not be difficult for any student who researches this gold rush to question several of the foregoing dates or statements. The many versions of the discovery and the prospecting parties differ, and they can not be untangled at this late date. Some of the acts were done quietly in order to keep the discovery a secret until Prichard could bring his friends into this bonanza. Perhaps it did not serve their purpose to completely disclose the sequence of events which led to the discovery of gold on Prichard Creek. In any event, gold was discovered. . . A gold rush soon followed. . . All sorts of men were soon to come to the Coeur d'Alene to "see the elephant." . . . Some would find riches; but that would be a small and select group. Most would find only hardship.

Men came from all over the American West. Gold called them from everywhere. The Forty-Niners were still prowling for gold. Men came from the Black Hills and from the streets of Tombstone. Three of the Earp brothers answered the call. Wyatt Earp, of Dodge City and Tombstone fame, brought his money and threw it into some mining ventures that proved fruitless. He and his brothers set up a saloon in a tent at Eagle City which they operated under the name of the "White Elephant."

The Northern Pacific railroad apparently thought that gold could not call out loud enough on its own. It soon issued a pamphlet describing the rush area in glowing terms, stating a man could make from $25 to $100 a day working the goldfields. Needless to say, this stimulated traffic on their newly laid track across north Idaho. The pamphlet painted a pretty picture for the gold seekers, but time was to show that it took more than desire to get wealth from the bottom of a cold mountain stream.

Men came into the diggings over the Jackass Trail, the North Fork Route, the Thompson Falls Route, the Belknap Trail, and the Trout Creek Trail. Some of these were summer trails, and others were used mainly in the winter. Most of the men came on foot with supplies on their backs. Freight was hauled into the area by horses, mules, and pole-boats, and, during the winter, dog sleds were used.

Eagle City sprang up near where Prichard's party had camped while making the discovery that started the whole golden affair. It really never grew past being a tent city, because its life was short. Some frame buildings went up but were torn down later to provide lumber when Murray replaced Eagle City as the center of gold activity. This took place as soon as the snow left the ground in 1884 and the prospectors found better diggings a few miles upstream from Eagle City.

For some of the placer miners, 1884 was a vintage year, but disappointment confronted others. This last group was faced with poor claim locations, too much water in some cases, too little water in other cases, improper equipment and too little mining talent. Some of them were only summer time prospectors, anyway, having left their farms in Washington and Montana to see what could be gained before the harvest. The miners' committees had adopted district mining rules which made it impossible for the short term prospector to hold a claim. They insisted that one shift be worked on a claim each week during the mining season in order to hold it.

Call it what you wish, but it was disappointment and failure that chased some of the men out of the gold fields near Murray and into the mountains in their search for gold. These men searched in all directions, and some of them journeyed into the South Fork of the Coeur d'Alene. Some of the late comers saw that no land was available in the gold fields, and they scoured the surrounding hills. The original discoverers were not content to sit on their haunches. They continued their efforts into the surrounding country. For example, A. J. Prichard never lost his interest in the area near his original discovery at Evolution, along the South Fork of the Coeur d'Alene.

It was these men principally who did the exploration necessary to "bring in" one of the largest mining districts in the history of the world. In the fall of 1883, Andrew Prichard traveled up the South Fork of the Coeur d'Alene River to the mouth of Canyon Creek. Following up this creek, Prichard claimed to have found good prospects in placer gold at the mouth of Gorge Gulch, near the present town of Burke. April of the following year saw Prichard leading a party of men from his camp about a mile above Evolution to Canyon Creek and Nine Mile Creek. His party included Colonel W. R. Wallace, Theodore Davis, and two men named Gilbert and Kirby.

Travel was quite difficult and took them over deep snow. The party's provisions were scanty, including such necessaries as coffee, bacon, sugar, blankets, a pick, a shovel, and a gold pan. Their first night's camp was on the ridge between Nine Mile and Canyon Creek. The next day found them in the area later to be known as Burke, where they located a tree marked by Prichard during his explorations of 1883. They immediately dug away the snow and found Prichard's sluice box. The depth of the snow prevented them from prospecting at that time. However, the party stayed there for one more day, while each member of the group staked himself a claim.

On the morning of the fourth day, they broke camp and started home. During the next thirty days, these men were instrumental in forming the Evolution Mining District. They recorded their claims and made plans to get supplies.

About this same time Prichard and his group located some claims in the Nine Mile Creek area, and found themselves to be a part of a growing rush to the South Fork of the Coeur d'Alene. On the 2nd of May, John Carten and Almedas Seymore discovered the Tiger Mine on the north side of Canyon Creek, and three days later Scott McDonald and George P. Carter located the Poorman Mine on the south side of Canyon Creek. Colonel

Wallace and others located the Oreornogo claim in the same area on May 10. The Oreornogo became a part of the Hecla mine in later days. - - - The town of Burke was to arise almost immediately upon a site central to these three discoveries.

Soon more prospectors poured over the hillsides from Murray and Eagle, where the gold pickings were proving quite difficult for the miners on a small operation basis. It did not take long for them to locate a good deal of the valley and the hillsides near present day Burke, Mullan and Wallace. - - - May 15, 1884, was to see the location of the Gold Hunter by J. G. Hunter; and the Morning and Evening claims were located on July 2 and 3, 1884, by C. Earle and G. S. Good near present day Mullan. Also located in 1884 were the Black Bear, San Francisco, and Gem of the Mountains claims (near Gem).

The Polaris claim was located near Osburn by W. B. Heyburn and his group in August 1884. - - - The Blake brothers, Dennis and True, located the Yankee claim in Big Creek on September 25, 1884. This claim would later become a part of the famous silver mine known as the Sunshine.

Colonel Wallace and a group of men prospected for gold in Nine Mile canyon during the summer of 1884. The abundance of water thwarted their efforts. During 1885 they attempted to divert the creek away from their workings by way of a flume. Their efforts for gold went for naught, but the Colonel's son, O. B. Wallace, located the first vein structure in the Nine Mile area. He filed his claim under the name of Black Cloud.

The efforts of these earliest prospectors were monumentous during the good seasons of 1884 and 1885. It is amazing to look back and see they had located most of the mining property of great consequence within such a short time. Their claims extended from the Montana border to Pine Creek, along the South Fork, for a distance of about twenty miles.

The most notable of all the discoveries . . . that of the Bunker Hill claim, took place September 10, 1885. In 1884 and 1885, Noah Kellogg was a carpenter and worked in the Murray gold fields. One of his employers, the Coeur d'Alene Water Supply Company, undertook to flume water for sluicing purposes to the claims on the sidehill. The venture was not successful, and the firm had to issue scrip to meet its payroll to Noah Kellogg and others. This scrip was accepted in the gold fields at a value of 35 cents on the dollar; these low wages prompted Kellogg and others to take to the hills in search of wealth.

Intrigue and legend have confused the circumstances of the discovery of the Bunker Hill Mine to a point where the true facts will never be known. In any event, it seems uncontested that Kellogg received a grubstake on August 1, 1885, from Origin O. Peck and Dr. John T. Cooper of Murray. It was agreed that Kellogg was to prospect in the drainage area of the South Fork of the Coeur d'Alene River and that he was to have a half interest in any claims he discovered. Cooper and Peck, as was customary in grubstake contracts, were to have the other half. The grubstake consisted of about $18.50 worth of food and utensils, plus a jackass.

The next day Kellogg traveled over the mountains into the South Fork area, where he prospected in various gulches until his return to Murray on August 27. His grubstake was depleted by this time, and he reported to Cooper and Peck that he had found encouraging prospects, and that he wanted to continue. Kellogg received more provisions from Cooper and Peck and started back to the South Fork on August 29.

Kellogg returned from his second trip on September 13, contending that he had run out of grub on September 9. In any event, he returned the jackass and the tools remaining to Cooper and Peck on September 13 and terminated his grubstake contract with them, without notifying them of any discoveries in Milo Gulch.

Time was to show that certain lode claims were "located" in Milo Gulch on and shortly after September 10: the Bunker Hill, the Richmond, and the Sullivan. These claims were located on behalf of Phil O'Rourke, a miner from Leadville, Colorado; Jacob

Goetz and Harry Baer, partners in Dutch Jake's Saloon; and Cornelius "Con" Sullivan, a friend of O'Rourke's. Goetz and Baer were grubstakers of O'Rourke at the time. Noah Kellogg's name appeared on the location notice for the Bunker Hill claim as a witness for Phil O'Rourke. - - - These claims contained spectacular surface showings of galena, and prospectors flocked to Milo Gulch to take up their claims, such as the Emma, Last Chance, Stemwinder, Tyler and Sierra Nevada.

The unusual activity caused Cooper and Peck to look at their "hole cards." They engaged Major W. W. Woods and W. B. Heyburn as their attorneys, and filed a suit on September 26, against Noah Kellogg, Phil O'Rourke and the others to compel conveyance to them of an undivided one-half interest in the Bunker Hill and the other lode claims. The theory of the grubstakers' case was that Kellogg had actually discovered this mountain of wealth while subject to his agreement with them. They alleged that he had not reported the discovery to them while in Murray, late in August, but instead, had gone to Phil O'Rourke and conspired with him and others to locate the claims in such a way as to leave Cooper and Peck without an interest. They further alleged that Kellogg left Murray at 3 A.M. on August 29, that he met up with Phil O'Rourke at Myrtle (five miles from Murray) and traveled with him to within two miles of the area where the claims were later located. It was alleged that Kellogg and O'Rourke separated at that point in order to allay suspicion of their scheme, and that Kellogg prospected around in the neighboring gulches, while O'Rourke went to work in Milo Gulch. Cooper and Peck further alleged that Kellogg still had some of their grubstake provisions, including the jackass, when the Bunker Hill discovery was made.

The case came on for trial before Judge Norman Buck at Murray in June, 1886. The county seat stirred with interest in the outcome, and the town sentiment favored Phil O'Rourke and his colorful friends. Cooper and Peck did not have many followers in the camp. Judge Buck swore in a jury to render advisory findings of fact. After they heard all the evidence, thirty-six special questions relating to factual issues were presented to the jury for their consideration.

The jury brought in their findings of fact, which were adverse to the claim of Cooper and Peck. This action was rather expected, and the town of Murray was hosted to a lot of drinks during the next few days by Phil O'Rourke, Dutch Jake and Noah Kellogg, the apparent winners of the case.

Judge Norman Buck studied the case for several days and then handed down his decision. This was an equity case and the court was not bound to follow the jury, although a court usually would be so inclined. . . . Judge Buck did his own thinking and adopted some of the jury's findings, while changing and modifying others. The Judge ruled that Cooper and Peck were grubstakers for Kellogg and that they were entitled to a quarter share in the Bunker Hill claim.

The decision was immediately appealed to the Supreme Court for the Territory of Idaho, where Judge Buck's ruling was upheld. . . . Time had worked in favor of all the litigants, including the losers. The Bunker Hill claim became worth more with each passing day, and perhaps it would have been sold earlier if there had not been the legal hassle over its title.

In 1887, Simeon G. Reed, a Portland financier, was subject to the promotional efforts of Jim Wardner, a promoter who held the water rights in Milo Creek. Milo Gulch had many mining properties by that time, including the Bunker Hill claims, and Jim Wardner put together a "package deal" involving some of them. He talked Reed into purchasing the Bunker Hill property, and some other claims, for an announced figure of $650,000. This purchase price was split in many ways, and it is believed that Noah Kellogg received about $150,000 in cash and stock for his interests, and Phil O'Rourke received slightly less. Jim Wardner, Cooper, Peck, Goetz, Baer, Sullivan and others, including the lawyers involved in the grubstake case, received the balance of the purchase price.

Reed's purchase of the Bunker Hill was the first major financial deal in the district, and it laid a foundation for the scene in the Coeur d'Alenes to change from mineral exploration to mineral production.

CHAPTER 4

A TOWN CALLED WALLACE — 1884

A newspaper printed at Eagle City carried the birth announcement, in its May 10, 1884, issue:

> "PLACER CENTER — This is the name of a new town started on the south fork of the Coeur d'Alene, at a point about seven miles up the road from Evolution. This town is situated in a good location and commands Canyon Creek mines and other tributaries of the South Fork, wherein mining in a small way is going on. The town will be a good point for prospectors who intend to put in a summer's work on the range between the Coeur d'Alene and St. Joe, and its permanency is assured from the fact that it is on the Mullan Road, which is the main emigrant road on the Bitter Root divide."

In retrospect, this is a very concise statement as to why, when, and where the city now known as Wallace, Idaho, came into being. The article fails, however, to note the journalistic requirement of reporting on the who's involved. It is the purpose of this writing to tell about the people involved in founding a city and a mining district, which were to become a center for mining for at least the next 100 years.

What starts a town? In the case of Placer Center, it was the building of a cabin by Colonel W. R. Wallace, to serve as his headquarters for mining exploration in the immediate area. He was a leader of men, and his group used the new townsite as their base camp. His cabin was built on the toe of a snow-covered hillside (near the south end of Sixth Street in Wallace). It was not until a year later that the Colonel's wife, Lucy, made her first appearance in Placer Center.

On June 22, 1885, Colonel Wallace drove a wagon to pick her up at the Old Mission. She and her luggage, which included a dog, bird, cats, and chickens, had arrived early in the day by boat. After leaving the Mission they forded the river 14 times before arriving at Placer Center, and this was the cause of some concern. The water was running high, but their only loss was one chicken which drowned when the water dashed over the wagon box. The 25 mile trip took two days, with an overnight stop at Jackass Prairie.

At the time of Mrs. Wallace's arrival, the town's population numbered 14. She was the only woman to "winter" in Placer Center that year. There were two women in Burke, Mrs. F. R. Culbertson, a daughter of S. S. Glidden, and a French woman. The former could not speak French and the latter could not speak English, so there was not much conversation between them. A woman also "wintered" that year at Jackass Prairie. In August, 1886, Lucy Wallace was appointed the first postmistress in town. She later stated that the United States Post Office Department would not accept the name of Placer Center because it was too long. Her husband objected to a town's being named after him because there were many towns of this name already. Lucy Wallace ignored her husband's opinion and filled out the United States Postal Department slip listing the Post Office in the name of Wallace, and so it has remained to this day.

The first merchant to set up in Wallace was Alexander D. McKinlay, who came here in April of 1885, accompanied by Peter J. Holohan. They had been partners for 28 years in Idaho and elsewhere. H. Harrington also opened his store in a log cabin along the Mullan Road nearby, but he was soon to leave for the Kingston area. In 1886, Howes and King opened a general store in a log building, after having purchased the grocery business started by McKinlay and Holohan.

"Business was a little slow with this enterprising firm (Howes and King) the first winter (1886). About all they had to do during the day was to shovel snow to the woodpile and at night varied the monotony by playing chess, checkers, or freezeout with their few, but equally idle, neighbors."

Later in 1886, E. D. Carter built the Carter House and erected the first sawmill, and E. A. Sherwin started a drug store. J. R. Marks, William Hart and E. H. Moffitt set up the town's first hardware store.

About two years had passed and Wallace still did not have a saloon. However, this was remedied during the winter of '86 by John Cameron, who thought Sixth Street was a good location for his saloon. Enough businesses were quickly set up to meet the human needs. Soon to follow were a livery stable operated by Sutherland and White. Billy Haskins came from Kingston and set up a general store, which he soon sold to O. C. Otterson. Most of these early businesses were set up in the area centering around the intersection of Sixth and Bank streets in Wallace. One of the reasons for this was that a large portion of the remaining flat land in Wallace was a large cedar swamp.

A. J. Dunn and J. L. Dunn established the first newspaper in town in Colonel Wallace's building. The Dunn Brothers printed the first issue of their *Wallace Free Press* on July 2, 1887. It is interesting to read one of the feature articles, which states that the early history of Wallace was much too well known to be set forth in their paper. Nevertheless, the early-day newspapers furnish much of the valuable information on any district. Such was the case in the Coeur d'Alene Mining District, which had several papers published bearing the good and bad news of a group of living and loving people.

CHAPTER 5

JULY AND AUGUST — 1887

By the time the first newspaper was published in Wallace the town had grown considerably from Colonel Wallace's original log cabin. Wallace's location, at the confluence of five major canyons, made it a natural trading center for the growing mining district. Mineral production had commenced along the South Fork drainage. In July 1887, 20 men were working at the Morning Mine in Mullan, and the Poorman Mine in Canyon Creek was worked under the management of Simon Healey.

Trains were scheduled to arrive in Wallace within 60 days. D. C. Corbin and his associates of Spokane were bringing in the first line. Their depot was planned on the north side of the river at the north end of Sixth Street.

Cameron's Saloon was doing a good business, as the town started to grow along Cedar Street. Mrs. Lawlor built a two-story lodging house on Cedar, and Holohan and McKinlay started a livery stable nearby. Hart and Doll opened a blacksmith shop. Mrs. A. R. Mills ran the Wallace Laundry. There was a need in Wallace also for the Carter House, Arment's Hotel and McKissick's wholesale liquors.

There was enough business for two butcher shops, a boot and shoemaker, a paint shop, and a dairy. Contractors, notary publics, a doctor, assayer, mineral surveyor, and justice of the peace were also available—it was necessary to travel to Wardner to consult such early day lawyers as Frank Ganahl, Albert Hagan or

A. P. Sharpstein. Wardner also offered such signs of civilization as Dr. Boston, the dentist. Travel to Wardner was not very easy at the time. The Mullan Road was built too low to allow travel all the year, inasmuch as it was under water a good deal of the distance. Wagon travel along the Mullan Road was difficult, if not impossible, but horsemen could travel over it with little problem.

The town of Mullan, with its Morning Mine, was adding to its population all the time. This town got off to an early start with the discovery of the Gold Hunter Mine in May of '85.

The Tiger Mine in Canyon Creek was being worked by 30 men including a few armed guards. A valuable piece of mining land always brought legal problems to its owners. Before such matters could be heard by the court, it was sometimes thought necessary to resort to self help. Such matters also attracted the attention of lawyers. William Stoll of Murray announced his intention to practice law in Burke.

The problem at the Tiger Mine involved water rights. The Tiger management built a dam to hold water for its mining purposes, and others felt they had a prior right to the use of this water. On the night of June 30, a party of men, said to be in the employ of the Poorman Company, destroyed the dam by blowing it up with "giant powder." The Tiger crew quickly went to the dam and ordered those who were still tearing out what remained after the explosion, to stop, and their order was quickly complied with.

The coming years in the District were to see the miners using "giant powder" for such things as "fishing in a hurry," celebrating notable events, blowing up the Frisco Mill in 1892, and extending the same courtesy to the Bunker Hill Mill in 1899; they also found it useful in blowing up railroad bridges, especially ahead of trains bringing federal troops into this district to regulate labor negotiations. . . . And a lot of it was used underground for mining purposes.

Until July 28, no death had occurred in Wallace. On that date the question arose as to where to bury Captain Fayette Place, who had died after a long illness. Place had been a resident of the district for about two years and was a native of New York. He was 56 years old and had been one of the first men into the Black Hills. . . . A suitable spot was selected on an elevated tract near where Canyon Creek empties into the South Fork—now known as Buena Vista Heights. The newspaper stated that it offered "sufficient space for the silent city which time will surely build." However, it served as a burial ground only for the next five years, when it became necessary to establish a graveyard in Nine Mile Canyon.

At the end of July, E. D. Carter announced that he was going to build a three-story hotel at the east end of the Carter House. His hotel would have a depth of 60 feet and a frontage of 35 feet.

The area surrounding Wallace was showing signs of progress. Preliminary steps were being taken toward laying out the town of Davenport (later changed to Gem), in the neighborhood of the Gem group of mines and a short distance below the San Francisco Group.

Thus far, this narration has set forth the legitimate efforts of men searching for wealth. There were others, however, who did not choose to work for a living. Early on the morning of August 5, E. J. Catleff, the freighter, was held up by three highwaymen on the Glidden Summit. He left Burke on the preceding afternoon and camped near Summit. In the morning, he awoke intending to go to Thompson Falls, but he was approached by a man who stopped his wagon and demanded his cash. Catleff was held at gunpoint by the other two men, and $135 was taken from him. The robbers took off on the divide between Prospect and Canyon Creeks, and nothing was ever heard of them afterward.

A young town trying to get started showed signs of both the old and the new at every turn. Within the same week, a number of Indians came to Wallace trying to sell some of their ponies to

the miners, and the Silver Palace Saloon presented Wallace with
its first billiard table.

August of 1887 was a busy month. . . . S. S. Glidden had
acquired the Tiger Mine and was shipping ore by way of Thompson Falls. About one-third of the Tiger ore was shipped without
concentration. The Tiger was building a mill, which was to have
a capacity of 125 tons daily.

At this time, the town of Burke recalled that a month before
it had less than half a dozen frame buildings. Most of its business was conducted in log cabins and many tents. Every building
fronted toward the creek, and there were no clearly defined
streets. With the opening of the new trail from Wallace in
August, much lumber was made available. Tents were rapidly
being replaced by frame buildings. The growth of the Tiger
Mine caused great activity in Burke for years to follow.

The new town of Georgetown (Osburn) was laid out by the
surveyors at the junction of the Murray Road (via Two Mile
Gulch) and Mullan Road. The railroad had reached this site and
was progressing toward Wallace. . . . In 1885, Seth McFarren
and Samuel Norman became that area's first residents, when they
located a ranch in the bottom of the valley and erected a house
and other buildings on it. On March 18, 1886, they sold their
160 acres to S. V. William Osburn for $2,000. "Billy" Osburn
built a hotel, barn, stables, ice house, cellar, fences and cleared
and cultivated some 60 acres of land during the next three years.
For a short time, the property was known as the Buckhorn Ranch,
but the more familiar title of Osburn's Ranch was to last over
the years.

Mullan also had something to crow about. . . . Its correspondent for the *Wallace Free Press* cited Mullan as:

> ". . . the one town in the Coeur d'Alene which is not yet
> afflicted with those individuals of the feminine gender who
> build their houses on the way to hell, those beings who have
> been forsaken by the purity of the angels and who flaunt
> their festering identity in the face of public decency. . ."

While Mullan was concerned with such serious matters, Col. Wallace was fishing in Placer Creek. His one day catch was 247 trout. . . . He did not fish all the time, though. One week later he got into a fracas with Theodore Anderson, who pulled a knife on the Colonel, who reciprocated by firing one barrel of his shotgun at Anderson. Some of the shot hit Anderson, and Wallace was charged with an attack with intent to inflict bodily harm. The case was later dismissed as the shooting was held justifiable.

Things were starting to get busy for Hanley, the Sheriff of Shoshone County, as another highway robbery occurred. On August 14, on the Murray-Thompson Falls road, three men were robbed by one highwayman. C. W. O'Neill lost $40 and a gold watch and a package of currency belonging to the Bank of Murray, which contained $2,000. John Hachett lost $500 in currency and a watch and ring. The Bank of Murray immediately showed its concern and its sense of values. It offered a reward of $100 for the robber and a reward of $500 for the return of the stolen money.

Wallace was to concern itself with a proposal for the establishment of a water system for its business district. Nothing concerning water passed the talking stage at that time, but some enterprising man opened a saloon in a tent at the mouth of Canyon Creek. L. J. Fowler opened a store at the junction of Canyon Creek with the South Fork. It seemed that they wanted to shortstop all the business which might come out of Burke or Mullan before it got to Wallace.

Although Mullan had been settled for about three years, there had not yet occurred a birth, a death, or a marriage. - - - It must have been a healthy place, if you wanted to stay single.

Transportation remained one of the district's biggest problems. The railroad had not yet come to Wallace, but D. C. Corbin had let a contract to the Willamette Iron Works for the building of a steamer to run on Lake Coeur d'Alene. It was to be 110 feet long and 23 feet wide, and run by a 480-horsepower engine. The steamer was to have hydraulic steering and the motive source was an eight-foot screw wheel. The steamer was to be built of iron so that it could navigate the lake during the winter's ice season. The contract called for completion by December of 1887. All the woodwork and machinery were to be done in Portland, Oregon, but the ship was to be put together on the lake. It would furnish the connecting link between the planned narrow-gauge railroad line from Wallace to the Mission, and the railroad line which connected Coeur d'Alene with the outside world.

CHAPTER 6

SEPTEMBER, OCTOBER AND NOVEMBER — 1887

With the coming of September in '87, Wallace held a town meeting to formulate plans for welcoming the railroad to town. The railroad would provide the avenue through which all the valuable ore could be transferred elsewhere for processing. In Wardner, the Bunker Hill and Sullivan was making plans to start hauling its ore in October to the railroad depot at Wardner Junction, where the Bunker Hill purchased ground upon which the stockpile of ore awaited shipment. The Bunker Hill was also setting up a large stable at that site for its stock, and other buildings for the company's use. Wardner Junction was located in the present Sunnyside section of Kellogg, which is approximately a mile north from the town of Wardner.

Wardner was on the threshhold of a new existence. From a rustic headquarters for mining exploration and development, it was to change into a bustling center for mineral production, and later mineral processing. Only two years had passed since Noah Kellogg had made his original discovery in Milo Gulch, but that time was sufficient to show the outside world the magnitude of the mineral wealth available. Soon money was to be poured into the Bunker Hill by the big investors from the West Coast.

By this time, Wardner was sporting many signs of civilization. In fact, Wardner progressed so far as to have a minister which the town shared with the surrounding area. It was not reported how Wallace took the news of the preacher, but Dave Cox took the opportunity to open a new saloon on the corner of Sixth and Cedar.

O. C. Otterson, a merchant who was to stay at Wallace for years afterwards, started clearing his lot on East Bank Street, next to J. R. Marks & Company. Otterson was still a postmaster at the Mission Townsite, from whence he came. He had offered his resignation from that office repeatedly, but it was not duly accepted, so he just packed up and left Mission Townsite.

In September Coeur d'Alene City acquired the legal status of a town, after a majority of its male inhabitants petitioned the Kootenai County Commissioners. At their organizational meeting, they elected Major Warner to serve as Chairman of the Board of Trustees. The military installation there, originally known as Fort Coeur d'Alene and later as Fort Sherman, had been occupied since the late 1870's by an average of five companies of soldiers, four being infantry and one of cavalry, Including women and children, the Fort probably had as many as three hundred people living there most of the time.

The fort at Coeur d'Alene and the new town were to provide a transportation center for the Coeur d'Alene Mining District for years to come. They were to figure in boating upon the lake, travel along the Mullan Road and later with the railroad shipments of ore in the Coeur d'Alenes. The coming of all this modern transportation would cause some difficulties, however. - - - Billy Haskins, who ran the stage between Wallace and Osburn, announced that he would be out of a job as soon as the trains commenced running. Older transportation was still avaiable. Another band of Indians passed through Wallace late in September, with several hundred horses for sale. They kept moving into Montana until they had sold all of their herd.

Mining in the east end of the county was progressing all the time. . . . Rumors were rampant that the Morning Mine was being sold to Eastern interests. Such rumors were highly publicized, but usually did not materialize. Every time a group of

investors came into the area it served someone's interest to spec-
ulate upon their intentions. The Poorman Mine in Burke was
working a day and night shift and would increase its force
as soon as there was room for them. Pat Clark, its manager, was
in the area to push further developments and to erect suitable
buildings.

One of Burke's classic legal battles was about to unfold. On
September 17, a Thompson Falls peddler named Stiles came to
Burke with a lot of cabbages to retail from the tailgate of his
wagon. One of Burke's merchants, P. P. Weber, had Stiles
arrested for violating the peddling law. Stiles was immediately
brought before Justice Byrnett, and a jury was impaneled.
William T. Stoll appeared for the defense and after a quick
trial, the jury decided in favor of the defendant, Stiles. Merchant
Weber was assessed for the cost of the proceeding.

Then it was discovered that one of the jurors was not a citizen
and Weber demanded a rehearing, which demand was speedily
complied with. The second trial resulted in the same decision as
the first. The arrest, trial and dismissal of Stiles proved to be an
excellent advertisement for his cabbage, which he sold out
shortly. Stiles undertook to "gin up" the town, which he succeeded in doing, even invading the chamber where justice had
been dealt out to him. Although Stiles left the following day, he
was not forgotten by a number of Burke citizens who were living
on a plain diet of cabbage soup three times a day. . . .

It was a rainy day on Friday, September 30, when the first
train arrived at Wallace. A large contingent was on hand from
all over the area to welcome the Iron Horse. At 4:00 P.M. when
the train pulled into town, Colonel Wallace and the Honorable
Albert Hagan delivered speeches of welcome. The celebration
was originally planned for the open air, but because of the rainy
weather it was taken to the first floor of the Carter Hotel.
Among the other speakers were the Honorable Dubois and Adam
Aulbach. That evening a grand ball took place in the Carter
Hotel.

A narrow-gauge train and the steamer, *Coeur d'Alene*, at the Old Mission landing
in the late 1880's.

Early-day street scene in Wardner, Idaho, showing Noah Kellogg's jackass, which figured in
the discovery of the Bunker Hill Mine. Note the water barrels on the roof for fire protection.

Mother Lode "Boys," near Murray, Idaho, in the 1880's.

Placer mining operation at the Gillette Placer Claims
on Prichard Creek in the 1880's.

Both the Tiger and Poorman at Burke were eagerly awaiting the arrival of the railroad there. If the crews did not get all the track laid before cold weather set in, it would be necessary to close both mines down during the winter. Ore was being sacked at that time for shipment and was awaiting transportation. . . . However long the delay, the railroads would provide an improvement to the existing transportation system.

*   *   *

The fall season brought other troubles: Deputy Sheriffs Bill Pain and Jack Waite were transporting ex-sheriff Teddy Guthrie to jail for disturbing the peace, when Matt Guthrie became incensed and commenced shooting at the officers. Pain suffered powder burns on his face, and Matt Guthrie got shot in his left thumb. A bullet hole was found in the ex-sheriff's clothes but he was not wounded. Later that year both Matt and Teddy Guthrie were brought before Judge Buck who fined Matt the sum of $500 and fined Teddy $1,000.

The cry of gold was still to be heard from the diggings on the north side of the county. Syd Mills had purchased a solid block of placer ground on Eagle Creek four and one-half miles in length, commencing at the mouth of East Eagle, and he planned to work it on an extensive scale. Workings such as this one were to continue on the north side for years to come, but the gold diggings were never to see any renewed interest of gold rush proportions.

Wallace had progressed to the point where it could furnish its children with their first school. Fifteen children were expected to attend the first session. Miss May Peterson of Portland had been hired to teach for a three-month term. She had had several years' experience on the coast and came well recommended. The community had rented a building from E. G. Arment to serve as a school house. The school opened on Wednesday, October 19, with Miss May Peterson at the helm. Two days later the first school teacher was asked to resign, which she did.

"Rumors have been afloat concerning the present teacher which were not calculated to raise her in the estimation of the public."

No other explanation was ever offered by the press. A week later, a newspaper carried an announcement of the wedding of George Fitzgibbons and Miss May Peterson on October 27. . . . Mrs. Hall then undertook the teaching duties and conducted the school term until January 27 of the following year.

The town of Wallace was having a problem with fire protection for its wood frame buildings. A well was dug in front of the Morris Brother's Feed Stable and another on the corner of Mrs. Lawlor's block. A force pump was put on each well and a long hose attached to the pumps, by means of which a stream of water could be thrown to the top of the highest building on Cedar Street. Such was fire protection in 1887.

Burke was once again suffering growing pains. It seems that two Irishmen had found themselves in a fracas. Oscar Shay was killed by a pistol shot fired by Pat Flynn. Flynn had been drinking and became abusive. Shay made the mistake of throwing a glass of beer into Flynn's face. Flynn fired but one shot. At the time, Shay was sharing some beer and a lunch with Prosecuting Attorney Walter Jones and Judge Byrnett in a tent saloon at about 2:30 a.m. Jones came from Murray during the prior afternoon, and had just finished a jury trial before Judge Byrnett in the wee hours of the morning. Flynn was arrested and was to be tried about a month later. The *Wallace Free Press* commented:

"Guns have been displayed and threats have been made on numerous occasions lately where no cause is given to warrant such action. This should serve as a warning to others that firearms are not necessary to the settlement of ordinary disputes in this country."

Transportation was once again a primary subject of public interest. Donations were made by Wallace parties in the amount of $595 to complete two miles of road up Nine Mile Canyon. It was thought that this sum was sufficient to complete the job. Ultimately it was intended to proceed as far as Sunset Peak when sufficient money was collected. Most all roads that were built in the county at this time were built by public donation rather than by the county government, which suffered from the pangs of poverty. G. W. Marsh operated his stage known as the "Cannonball" between Wallace and Mullan. Billy Haskins was having difficulty with his stage which operated between Wallace and Osburn. The road between those two towns became impassable late in October and caused Haskins' stage to break down.

By November, 1887, Wallace had a population of about 500. Burke was boasting at that time that its population was greater than Wallace's. All this growth had been made by Burke in only one year. Burke's Post Office was a curiosity in itself. It consisted of a candle box divided into two compartments (incoming and outgoing mail) standing on the counter in a store. Every Burke man was his own postmaster and letter carrier. He helped himself to whatever bore his name. The mail was brought up daily from Wallace by anybody who happened to be coming over the trail. There was no red tape about postal matters in Burke, but it was expected there would be, as Delegate Dubois had promised them a Postmaster.

D. C. Corbin, the Spokane railroad builder, stated: "From the town of Wallace to Burke we shall go over the distance with our railroad in 30 days, and Burke will be the only mining camp in the world to get a railroad before it gets a wagon road."

The rumor was started that Mullan's Post Office was going to be moved from its existing location, where the mail was handled out of whiskey kegs. " . . . the same being in defiance of the postal laws."

One of Mullan's pioneer residents, B. P. Potts, was one of the owners of the Evening Mine. He was later to attempt to set up a competing town a few miles upstream from Mullan which was to bear the name of Pottsville. Later, around the turn of the century, he sold his one-quarter interest in the Lucky Friday mine for $750.

The paper reported that J. H. Jackson, Mayor of Davenport (Gem) ran a first class saloon there, and that all trains would stop fifteen minutes at his establishment for refreshments on their travels between Wallace and Burke. . . . Not bad; one saloon stop on a seven-mile run.

Bishop Ethelbert Talbot, the Episcopal Bishop for the Territories of Idaho and Wyoming, came to Wallace to hold religious meetings during mid-November. The Bishop was a cousin of the Dunn Brothers of Wallace.

He later recalled the green posters which advertised his coming to the Coeur d'Alenes:

"The Bishop is coming. Let us all turn out and hear the Bishop. Services in George and Human's Hall to-morrow, Sunday, at 11 A.M. and 8 P.M. Please leave your guns with the usher."

On the evening of his arrival, Bishop Talbot secured a promise of a satisfactory lot for a church from Colonel Wallace. - - - At an earlier date a Philadelphia resident, Lemuel Coffin, gave Bishop Talbot a check for $500 on condition that he raise an additional $1,000 to build a church in some western town. The Bishop asked the Wallace citizens if they would raise the $1,000, for the building of a church. He was very pleased to find that almost a sufficient amount had been pledged at the services.

As Bishop Talbot was about to leave Wallace on the next day, two men approached him and asked that he accompany them for a short time before his train was to depart. They wished his help in soliciting more funds for the church. - - - Within that time, the Bishop and the two men collected between three and four hundred dollars in the saloons of Wallace. - - - The money was later used to erect Wallace's first church.

In November of 1887, the Postal Department took another look at its Burke Post Office and decided that the name should be changed to Bayard. The Burke public was properly indignant as the town was originally named to honor John M. Burke, one of its pioneer founders. For the forthcoming weeks, Burke was to revolt in its own way against this name change. The public refused to use the new postal designation, but instead addressed all its mail as having come from Burke, Idaho and encouraged outsiders to write them in care of Burke, Idaho. Public indignation was a powerful force. November was coming to an end as Colonel Wallace tore down his first log cabin, and The Red Front Stable, formerly owned by the Morris Brothers was sold to George P. White and Angus Sutherland.

The closing note for November 1887, was a turkey shooting match which took place the day before Thanksgiving in the outskirts of Wallace.

"A turkey's head was the mark, 60 yards the distance, and we are told that a dozen marksmen, more or less, did the shooting. When finished, the turkey's condition was no worse than when the engagement began. As a last resort, the turkey went off at a raffle."

The newspaper suggested that a rifle team be organized.

CHAPTER 7

DECEMBER — 1887

Wardner's public school opened for classes early in December, 1887; there were no regular seasons of the year for conducting schools. Most educational sessions were geared to the needs of the community and to the availability of someone to do the teaching. These sessions usually lasted as long as the community's funds.

In December, Pat Flynn was acquitted of murdering Oscar Shay in Burke, and the *Wallace Free Press* editor was incensed at the outcome of the trial. The newspaper's tirade started off by stating that the killing was done in the presence of the Prosecuting Attorney (Walter Jones), and a Justice of the Peace (G. V. Byrnett), and yet a conviction could not be had. The editor continued that the causes of Shoshone County justice consisted of the following components:

> "First, a lawless element; second, an imbecile judge; third, a pair of unscrupulous tricky lawyers; fourth, some heavy actors who can pick a jury, intimidate witnesses and generally 'fix' things, and the piece is ready to be played. The County Courthouse . . . is the Theater, the taxpayers the audience and the murderer the beneficiary." - - -

The year of 1887 was to end in Wallace and the surrounding district with transportation as the main topic. The iron steamer of the Coeur d'Alene Railway and Navigation Co., built to break

ice on the river and lake, was launched at Coeur d'Alene City
on December 11. She was named the *Kootenai* and drew eight
feet of water without a load.

The day after the *Kootenai* was put into service, the first railroad shipment of ore was made from that part of the mining
district east of Wardner. This shipment consisted of one carload of nearly 13 tons of ore from the Granite Mining Company, on Canyon Creek. The narrow-gauge ore cars carried loads
varying from 10 to 15 tons.

Burke welcomed the coming of the railroad on December 22
in grand style. Burke had good reason to shout as both the
Tiger and Poorman Mines were increasing their payrolls. The
Tiger employed 100 men and the Poorman worked about 70
men. The Tiger Concentrator had just started up with the coming of the train, which travelled up Burke Canyon within convenient reach of both the Tiger and Poorman properties.

The Poorman Mine, more formally known as the Coeur d'Alene
Silver-Lead Mining Company, shipped the first ore from Burke
on December 31 in two railroad cars. The shipment was destined
for the smelters in Omaha. The Tiger Concentrator was running
well, and it was reported that 25 tons a day would be the average
shipment from that source.

The railroad announced its rates, which were considerably
lower than those charged by the previous freight haulers. The
railroad charged 85¢ per hundred pounds from Coeur d'Alene
City to Burke; and 10¢ per hundred from Wallace to Burke. The
rate from Coeur d'Alene City to Wallace was 80¢ per hundred.
Lastly, the passenger fare from Wallace to Burke was 50¢, one
way.

Yes, Burke had a big year in 1887. Everything had gone its
way except for the U. S. Postal Department changing its name
to Bayard. The new name was never accepted by the townspeople, and it caused them to engage in their first of many
battles with "big government." The Burke miner has always
resented domination from whatever source, including his em-

ployers, the county, state and federal governments. At the end of 1887, they had won their battle . . . the U. S. Postal Department relented and changed the name of their post office back to Burke.

The year had seen the settlement of Placer Center grow into the town of Wallace. The drifting prospector and the unemployed men who roamed the West, looking for a livelihood, had found a place to set down roots; and they wrote their wives to come along and bring the kids. From a miners' camp it was growing into a place families could call a home. - - - It was time for Wallace men, women and children to gather at their first Christmas tree, set up in the Heller House, where a ball was held on Christmas Eve.

CHAPTER 8

JANUARY AND FEBRUARY – 1888

The year 1888 started off by trying to knock the bottom out of the thermometers. On January 6, the temperature fell to 8° below zero. H. E. Howes, who had wintered in Wallace the previous year, reported that it had snowed or rained 49 consecutive days during January and February in 1887. Such good news must have been encouraging to those trying to brave the winter in their crude homes.

It was so cold that the new iron steamer, *Kootenai,* which was made for cutting ice, failed to arrive at the Mission on the 6th. She had become disabled on the lake while breaking ice six inches thick. This was the beginning of serious trouble for the mines and miners, as there were then over 300 tons of ore at the Mission waiting transportation on the boat. It was necessary for the shipments to continue in order for the mines to get enough money to keep working.

For two weeks the cold continued, and the town of Wallace suffered. On January 14, the temperature dropped to 26° below zero. The news came into town that the steamer *Kootenai* had blown out a cylinder head and was still disabled in the ice. Meanwhile, the incoming mail from the West was being carried by pack train from Coeur d'Alene City over the Mullan Road through Fourth of July Canyon. Two pack trains were kept moving on this route bringing in supplies during the cold spell.

The winter was hard. Toward the latter part of January,

the river and the lake were still blockaded by ice. Oil and potatoes were in short supply within the district, especially in
Burke. In previous years, the people had always stocked up as
much as possible for winter because they anticipated the ice
blockade. They were not so well prepared in 1888, however,
because they had thought the new ice breaker *Kootenai* would
prevent them from ever being blockaded again.

January brought other problems to the area. Colonel W. R.
Wallace had located the Oreornogo claim in Canyon Creek in
1884, after finding float in the creek bed. He traced it up the
mountainside and made the location of this claim. He then
opened a trail from the Mullan Road to the mine and spent about
$4,000 of his money developing the property. The latest news
to hit Wallace was that someone had jumped his claim.

It must have been a close winter, for the people started to get
cranky. . . . The paper carried stories pointing out the imperative
need for public bath tub facilities in Wallace as none existed.
. . . Many were complaining that too many dogs were running at
large about town. And it matters were not tough enough, the
newspaper printed, for all to see, the academic and deportment
grades of all the students in the Wallace school.

Another problem was starting to jell for the mines of the
district, and it revolved around the freight rates charged for
hauling ore and concentrates from Coeur d'Alene City to various
places around the country. Some of these charges were as follows:

Coeur d'Alene City	to Portland	$10.40 per ton
"	" to Tacoma	10.40 per ton
"	" to San Francisco	13.40 per ton
"	" to Omaha	17.00 per ton
"	" to Newark, N. J.	21.60 per ton
"	" to Wickes, Montana	5.00 per ton

One of the mine owners, Van B. DeLashmutt announced that
he would go to Newark, where the largest smelter in the country
was located, and endeavor to get a more profitable market. The
Portland Board of Trade was considering a boycott of the North-

ern Pacific Railroad to break what is termed "discrimination" against Portland. The same groups in Spokane and Tacoma were interested in the matter also. Some charged that Jim Wardner, a mining promoter of old, was working with a group which had set up a scheme whereby Wickes, Montana was to be favored and that they were to share in the profits resulting to Wickes, Montana, because of the favorable freight rates.

The ice blockade remained until January 26, when Capt. Sanburn brought the steamer *Kootenai* up river to the Mission landing. It was the first boat through for twenty days, and its trip was not easy. The captain had loaded the boat very heavily so that her propeller would ride a safe distance below the ice. Many times during the trip the boat became stalled, and it was necessary to back her up and take a run at the ice in order to break through. The ice attained a thickness of 18 inches at some places in the river channel. Sometimes the *Kootenai* would have to back up for 75 to 100 yards to come at the ice and then would make no more than 15 or 20 feet in headway. The blockade had caused great hardship to the mining district, as well as great loss in mining income.

In Wardner, the Stemwinder mine put the first aerial tramway in the district into operation. It transported ore for a distance of two miles from the mine to the concentrator.

Many of the early inhabitants of the Coeur d'Alene Mining District could neither read nor write. Some were poorly educated and others were immigrants from foreign lands, who had only mastered their mother language. This problem was overcome by district merchants and craftsmen by placing some sign or standard in front of their place of business which indicated the nature of their goods or services. Druggists advertised by placing a mortar and pestle on a standard in the walkway in front of their store. Shoemakers hung a big wooden sign in the shape of a boot; the jeweler set up a clock in front of his place of business. The barber had his striped pole, and the livery stable could show a picture of a horse. . . . One old photograph of Wallace shows a street scene presenting most of the foregoing examples, but adding one marker of unusual interest. On the top of a post about eight feet high located in front of the Hathaway House was a replica of an old-fashioned bathtub, which advertised the public bathing facilities within . . . at last!

It appeared 1888 was to be a banner year for the district. Those claims which had been regarded as promising prospects now were developing into richly producing mines. New strikes were still being made. Everyone looked to spring for increased production. The Poorman had contracted with Small & Colby for 200,000 feet of lumber to build a concentrator and other buildings at its mine. The Shoshone County Commissioners advertised for bids to be opened on March 16 for the building of a County Hospital at Osburn in accordance with plans filed with the County Clerk. The commissioners advised that the cost of said hospital building was not to exceed $1,000.

Happy days were on hand for the investor. The Granite Mine declared what is believed to be the first corporate dividend by any mine in the South Fork drainage. During mid-February, Van DeLashmutt, the manager, received $6,000 from the smelter in San Francisco as return for over 100 tons of ore shipped there, which netted about $53 per ton after deducting transportation and charges. He also received $9,000 as an advance on 19 carloads of ore from the Granite, which were then on the road to the smelting works at Denver. The cost of operating the mine under the existing management had been about $8,000, so a dividend of 1% on the capital stock of $500,000 was declared, which amounted to $5,000.

Because the steamer *Coeur d'Alene* was unable to make any trips through the ice on the river to the Mission, the ore continued to pile up at that point. It would be quite some time before that ship could get through.

In mid-February, 1888, a miners' union was organized at Burke. Such an organization had already been formed in Wardner. . . . Labor difficulties were beginning. A worker at the Tiger

Concentrator was ordered fired because he did not buy his groceries at the company store. The employee lived with his wife and family in Burke. Mr. Abeling, the Superintendent of the Tiger Concentrator, refused to fire the man for this cause and tendered his own resignation for the reason that he would not carry out such instructions. The Tiger management refused to accept Abeling's resignation. As a result, the laborer kept his job at the Tiger Concentrator, under the protection thrown around him by Abeling.

At the end of February there were two immense stockpiles of Bunker Hill ore at Wardner Junction and the Mission. The railroad started moving it from the Junction at the rate of 10 cars a day. On February 23, the steamer *Sherman*, with a barge, made her first trip and thereafter was to make the run regularly from the Mission to Coeur d'Alene. The Sherman moved 10 cars of ore per trip, but took two days for a round trip. The *Kootenai* moved 4 cars of ore per day, which made a daily average of 9 cars (about 150 tons) over the water route. The stockpiles at the Mission and Wardner Junction would be cleared away by mid-March. The railroad moved about 100 tons per day, and the boats moved about 150 tons a day.

CHAPTER 9

MARCH AND APRIL — 1888

Early in March, Sheriff Hanley, armed with a court order, went to Burke with Colonel Wallace and evicted the claim jumpers from the Oreornogo claim. Colonel Wallace's Oreornogo had been jumped on the first day of the year and worked by the claim jumpers since that time.

A March shipment of ore from the Poorman Mine netted over $70 per ton. Four or five months earlier, the Poorman was bought for $136,000.00 and stocked for $500,000.00. Several of the original owners took stock at 27 cents a share in payment. The stock in the Poorman was selling at $1.00 a share in March. The corporate stock certificates bore a beautiful steel engraving of Miss Maggie Daly, the daughter of Marcus Daly, the financial wizard of Montana.

Business was improving all through the district. The railroad announced that it was purchasing 20 new freight and box cars which would arrive in the area during the middle of the month. Up until that time there had been a shortage of railroad cars, and some of the shipments were delayed for this reason.

On March 8, lead was quoted in New York at $5.30 per hundred, the highest price for the last ten years. Metal prices were improving, and the Gold Hunter at Mullan shipped its maiden car of ore on the railroad, March 5. The Emma and Last Chance Mines, lying between the Stemwinder and Tyler were sold for $75,000.00 to A. M. Esler, representing a Helena syndicate,

Charles Sweeney of Wardner and Frank Moore of Spokane Falls. Business was so good that two stage lines were operating between Wallace and Mullan. Fare for either line was $1.25 for a one-way trip. Each stage line made one round trip per day.

Farther west from the district, some interest was being shown in mineral locations at the head of Wolf Lodge Bay, some ten miles away from Coeur d'Alene City. About 120 mineral locations had been made there, most of them being on the Indian Reservation. Coeur d'Alene City acquired a newspaper known as *The Herald*, which put out its first edition late in March.

At a meeting of mining men in Portland, the speaker urged for early action on the Coeur d'Alene Indian Reservation. He was eager to restore a portion of it to the public domain, suggesting that the reservation was as rich in minerals as the Coeur d'Alene Mining District and that it contained much good timber. The meeting adopted a resolution to this effect and forwarded it on to Congress.

Senator Dawes, of the Committee on Indian Affairs, reported that the bill authorizing the Secretary of Interior to permit miners to prospect and develop, lease and own Indian land upon any Indian reservation was meeting with adversity. The Secretary of Interior opposed the Bill because the Commissioner of Indian Affairs said it would be extremely difficult for the Government to preserve peace and quiet among the Indians if the miners were to come upon the reservation.

The problem of encroachment upon the Indian Reservation had already begun. A few weeks before it was reported that some people had settled on a portion of the land near the Mission which had been considered a part of the Reservation. Troops were sent over from Fort Sherman to remove the settlers and to hold the land as part of the Indian Reservation.

The County Commissioners postponed further action on the hospital question as Doctor R. S. Harvey had made them a proposition. He agreed to attend the sick and indigent poor of the county, both medically and surgically, furnishing medicine and including post mortems, for $150 a month, with an addition of $1 per mile one way for all cases off tributaries of the South Fork, for one year. . . . The Commissioners hastily accepted this offer.

March closed with the announcement that work was being pushed on the upper and lower tunnels on the Killbuck Claim (part of the present Galena Mine in Lake Gulch). The Killbuck Claim was leased to Mr. Cox. It was predicted that with small expense this property could ship a considerable quantity of ore.

The coming of spring brought increased activity at the Polaris Mine near Osburn. Mr. Heyburn, an owner, reported that a wagon road would be built immediately from Osburn to the mine.

*　　*　　*

The first session of the Wallace school ran for a little more than three months and incurred expenses in the amount of $364.30 for the teacher's salary, house rent, wood and supplies. The district still had a balance of $163.48, with $100 more being anticipated as revenue. It was felt that there would be ample money for three months of summer school. The *Wallace Free Press* called attention to the fact that $80 had been spent thus far for rent for school purposes, and it would not take long at this rate to pay for constructing a school house for Wallace.

Bitter spring weather brought many new faces to the Coeur d'Alenes, and not all were welcome. Early in April a Wallace citizens' meeting was held, at which time it was reported that over $200 had been subscribed for the purpose of erecting a jail. The county had promised to match these funds. Jack Waite was appointed in charge of this fund and for building of the jail.

Another visitor to Wallace was William Buzzard, of Spokane Falls. He came to the district and visited Wardner and Burke also. He was in the business of booking theatrical performances. It was his desire to secure a hall in each town in which to give occasional shows. He planned to return within two weeks with a first-class entertainment company. Buzzard was one of the early miners into the gold rush at Eagle City where, early in

1884, he participated in a gunfight over a town lot in Eagle. There were several different versions of this gunfight, but one version has it that Wyatt Earp was the leader of his opposition, and another (perhaps the most acceptable) has Wyatt Earp serving as a peacemaker in bringing an end to the dispute. In any event, he had participated in the gold rush and was engaged in many mining ventures in the mid '80's.

On April 14, Burke was the site for a prize fight of ten rounds which was held at the Black Diamond Hall between Jack Martin, weighing 152 pounds, and Charles Keikeritz, weighing 175 pounds. Lawyer Stoll was the referee. In the first round Martin knocked his opponent down, but he in turn was felled in the fifth round. Both fighters carried on through the tenth round and the fight was announced as a draw. Later that evening it was learned that Martin broke his wrist in falling his opponent in the first round and had fought the whole battle in that condition.

CHAPTER 10

MAY, JUNE AND JULY — 1888

The summer of 1888 brought the easiest living that the citizens had had for quite some time, and it was filled with many civic enterprises. E. H. Moffitt and other town citizens petitioned the County Commissioners to incorporate Wallace as a town. On May 2, the Commissioners granted their petition and appointed the following town trustees: Colonel W. R. Wallace, Horace King, C. W. Vedder, C. M. Hall and D. C. McKissick. All of the trustees were businessmen and property owners. This action made Wallace the first town in Shoshone County to incorporate.

Colonel Wallace was instrumental in setting up a company for the purpose of supplying the town of Wallace with water. A ditch was then being dug through his property at the south end of Sixth Street to conduct water from a large reservoir in the gulch on the southerly side of his home, to a hydrant on the corner of Sixth and Bank streets. This arrangement gave the water a fall of about two hundred feet. One thousand feet of four-inch pipe was ordered. It was proposed that mains would be laid from Sixth Street to Cedar and on Bank Street east from Sixth.

It was said that but one murderer had received punishment for a murder committed in Shoshone County since the beginning of the gold rush—and he had served only a few years in prison. That would have been Murray's early newspaper man, Henry Bernard, who killed his printer, John Enright, in 1884. He was sentenced to the Idaho State Penitentiary. There was an impera-

50

tive need for the proposed jail in Wallace. Angus Sutherland, the Wallace Marshal, made an arrest which necessitated his keeping two prisoners jailed in stable stalls at his livery stable for safekeeping. Working under such difficult conditions apparently caused Mr. Sutherland to resign; W. A. Morris was appointed his successor. . . . Colonel Wallace took the opportunity to donate one lot for a city jail, and another for a school. Plans commenced in June for a study of possible routes for a wagon road over the Dobson Pass area. Prior to this time all travel to the North Side had passed over the Two Mile road from Osburn. Colonel Wallace was a leading advocate for building a road to Murray by way of Dobson Pass. He stated the trip from Wallace to Murray took six hours and that a road over Dobson Pass to Murray would reduce the time to three hours.

Plans were being made for the forthcoming Fourth of July celebration. The big event of the day was to be balloon-ascension test trials. The ascensions for 30-foot balloons were planned for every hour during the celebration.

Another grand event was announced for the celebration; Wallace was to have a baseball game and the men of town were kept busy clearing the field of stumps. The site selected for this game was a level field at the westerly end of Bank Street. It would be in the area of the modern day Catholic School.

On July 4, 1888, Wallace engaged in a mighty battle with the baseball team from Burke. The game was called in the sixth inning with Burke leading by a score of 16 to 13. The reason for calling the end of the game was not inclement weather, nor darkness, but the fact that there were only two baseballs in town and both of them had been lost by that time.

About one year had passed since the newspaper had started its publication in Wallace. During this period the town's population had doubled and there had not been a business failure.

The town of Wallace enacted its first dog tax, which went into effect on July 1, and license No. 1 was put on "Coeur d'Alene Jack." This dog came to the north side with the original gold rush during the winter of 1883 and drifted into Wallace in 1887. The fee for his license was paid by public donation.

The Wallace water works were being operated and a $3 tax per year was put on each residence and business house for water.

Meanwhile, Kingston had seven saloons, three bakeries, four restaurants, two livery stables, three barber shops, three general stores, plus a hotel and lodging houses.

July in the Coeur d'Alenes has always been a wonderful time for fishing. William Gaughan and William Fitz went fishing up Placer Creek and returned the same evening with 178 fish. One of the fishermen had four flies on his line, and he said that several times he landed three trout at a time. It was nothing unusual for him to hook two; in fact, he joked that one fish was no inducement for him to pull up his line.

CHAPTER 11

AUGUST THROUGH DECEMBER – 1888

The last five months of 1888 passed in very orderly fashion. Payrolls were ever increasing throughout the district, and in August, the Bunker Hill & Sullivan announced that its profit for the prior 12 months was $400,000. At the time, the price of lead was $4.32½ per hundred. Each newspaper carried news of ore shipments from the district, most particularly from the Tiger, Poorman and Granite Mines. At the west end of the county, the Bunker Hill Mine and the Sierra Nevada Mine of Wardner were also shipping.

The question of moving the county seat to the South Fork drainage arose, but the opinion was generally held in Wallace that the County could not afford to move the county seat. It is interesting to note that this opinion was held at a time when Shoshone County could afford to support 94 saloons.

A large number of Italians landed at the Mission in mid-August to work on the railroad line to the east end of the mining district.

The County Commissioners accepted the five miles of road built up Nine Mile on October 1. - - - A meeting was held in Osburn, backed by Wardner and Milo people, which advocated the moving of the county seat from Murray to their area.

November of 1888 brought the election season. Two co-owners bet each other a 1/6th interest in the Bob Lee, a claim which was an extension of the Maud S. mining claim, on the outcome of the Hawley-Dubois election race for Congressional delegate.

Arthur McKenna bet on Hawley and Jake Turner bet on Dubois. Each of the 1/6th interests were worth between $1,000.00 and $1,500.00. The election was held and Dubois was the winner. The list of votes cast shows that Wallace was not the largest center of population at the time of the election.

Wardner	400
Burke	244
Murray	226*
Milo	127
Wallace	201
Delta	70*
Myrtle	22*
Littlefield	23*
Eagle	56*
Osburn	74
Kingston	94
Wardner Junction	59
Mullan	118
Carbon	36*
TOTAL	1,750

*Mining camps on the north side of the district. It will be seen that the north side cast 433 votes, or less than a quarter of the total.

A Burke saloon was the site in November for a gunfight between a Negro, Charlie Garrett, and a white man, Joe Morgan. The casualties amounted to two wounded innocent spectators. Within a week, the townsmen of Burke had scheduled a benefit for the two bystanders who had been seriously injured.

The last big news for November was that a new iron barge, named *Barge Number 3*, was launched at the Mission under the supervision of Captain I. B. Sanburn. It was constructed for the railroad company at the Mission and was to be used during the winter in transferring ore with the steamer *Kootenai*. The barge was 120 feet long with 24 foot beam, having a hold six feet deep. It had a capacity of 200 tons.

Much effort was given in December to construction work throughout the district. In Wallace, Bank Street was extended in an easterly direction to meet the county road to Mullan and a bridge was built across the river at the east end of Wallace. This bridge was a big improvement on the road to Mullan. Of the 22 crossings of the Coeur d'Alene River between Wallace and Mullan, this bridge reduced the number to 21.

In Burke, S. S. Glidden started building the Tiger Hotel to house Tiger Mine employees. It was to have 35 sleeping rooms, and acquired quite some fame in future years. The canyon at the building site at Burke was so narrow that it was necessary to build the hotel so that Canyon Creek flowed under it, and the Burke Highway and the railroad traveled through the building instead of around it. Woe unto any tenant of the hotel who did not close his windows, when the wood burning locomotives passed through the building.

The city jail for Wallace was being built by J. D. Smith upon a contract for $400.00. The jail building was to be 16 foot by 28 foot, and this space was utilized for a courtroom for the justice of the peace, a corridor and three cells for prisoners. The cells were to have walls 4 inches thick between them, made by spiking 2 x 4's together, and the outside walls and floors were 6 inches thick. In mid-December, the jail still was not finished and the Wallace police had two prisoners in custody. They were confined in a box car in the railroad yards pending completion of the jail.

The year of 1888 ended in Wallace as the Wallace residents petitioned the Supreme Court of Idaho Territory to hold sessions of the District Court in Wallace at least twice a year. It worked a great inconvenience to transport all the litigants and witnesses to Murray for the hearing of all the cases.

CHAPTER 12

JANUARY AND FEBRUARY — 1889

The year of 1889 was ushered in as one promising unequaled prosperity for the district. Weatherwise, the prior winter was the best the district had ever seen. More men spent the winter working than ever before, and the payrolls were larger, accounting for more money in circulation. This was not because of any boom, but it represented steady development of the area's resources. In each prior winter, the population had more or less fallen off. Many of the men left the district and wintered in Spokane or Portland. Some of them traveled back east to their families. The town had progressed to the point where it was habitable in wintertime and the mines could keep working.

One of the early entertainments of the year was a prize fight between Conroy and Liverpool who fought in a glove fight at the City Hall in Wallace for a purse of $100. Liverpool gave up after the 22nd round.

Wintertime still provided some difficulties for the industry. On January 7, nine cars of concentrates were sunk in Coeur d'Alene Lake when a barge ran into trouble with the ice. Only three or four cars of the ore were recovered. This was the same barge that was launched at the Mission late in 1888, known as *Barge No. 3*. It sank off Sandy Beach, between the Farmington Landing and Coeur d'Alene. The steamer *Kootenai* had the barge in tow and the floating ice probably knocked a hole in the bottom of it. When it started sinking the *Kootenai* pulled the barge toward the shore, but it sank anyway, with one end out of the water. The barge was raised later in the day, but the concentrates fell to the bottom of the lake. Efforts were made as late as 1960 to recover these concentrates from the waters of Coeur d'Alene Lake.

In January, the Burke citizens were clamoring for a wagon road to Wallace, but the Shoshone County government could not help them. The county was in financial trouble, and its warrants were worth only 50 cents on the dollar.

Elsewhere in the district, William Worstell, of Murray, announced he was moving his furniture store to Wallace. This move was looked upon with approval as it took many other businesses to bring balance to the business community of Wallace, which had sixteen saloons at the time.

Mullan was the site of a killing in one of the saloons. John Oland, a Negro, shot and killed a white man, Charles Porter. Oland was promptly taken into custody and held for trial.

Valentine's day saw the opening of a new hotel at Beaver Station. The hotel served as a halfway house upon the stage line joining the towns in the North Fork drainage with those in the South Fork drainage of the Coeur d'Alene River.

The hills and valleys of the Coeur d'Alene have always been filled with game. Carl Trowbridge trapped a beaver between Wallace and Mullan which weighed 60 pounds, and he caught an otter which measured five feet five inches in length. He was an experienced hunter and trapper and said the otter was the finest he had ever seen. The firm of J. R. Marks & Co. at Murray, Wardner, Wallace, Mullan and Burke, merged with Holley-Mason & Co., of Spokane Falls, and was to operate in all of these places under the name of Holley, Mason, Marks and Co. It formed one of the strongest hardware firms in the northwest.

The Coeur d'Alene Mining District was lending great impetus to the growth of Spokane Falls by 1889. The city by the falls then had 17 dry goods stores, 25 grocery stores, 15 hotels, 44 saloons, 11 meat markets, 13 cigar stores and 41 realty firms, along with many other types of businesses.

* * *

On the lighter side, Justice of the Peace Michael Maher of Mullan heard a case calling for tolerance and logic. Two Italians entered the saloon of A. Susman and while there became very drunk. So much so that one Italian had to remain there to sleep it off. The other one, very worried about the safety of his partner, took the latter's money and went home to sleep. The first Italian later awakened and found himself in a strange place, minus his money. He promptly threw a tantrum and accused the bar owner, Susman, of taking it. This enraged Susman and prompted him to enter into an argument. Soon the rumor started that a fellow had been rolled in Susman's place and the barkeeper found it necessary, in order to maintain his reputation, to have the second Italian arrested for theft.

The level-headed Irish Judge saw from the evidence that there was no intention of theft on the part of the second Italian, and he ruled that he could not separate them by sending one to jail in Murray in order to vindicate the good character of Susman. . . . So he bade the sons of Italy depart in peace, and permitted, by judicial order, A. Susman to pay the court costs involved.

The foregoing story is a good example of how immigrants were looked upon and treated throughout the West and particularly in the Coeur d'Alene Mining District at that time. It should be pointed out that the newspaper article which reported this case did not find it necessary to use the names of the two Italians. There were no set rules as to how one nationality or another should be treated, but those who could trace their ancestry to England, Wales or Ireland, enjoyed an enviable position on the social ladder. The merchants and craftsmen who immigrated from mid-Europe received a certain amount of respect. The Nordics occupied a somewhat lower position. Of all the European immigrants, those from Southern Europe received the roughest treatment by and large. The newspapers, when writing stories involving a Negro, usually included his name, but it was a rarity when the name of an Italian or a Slav was used in an article. The Chinese received the roughest treatment of all.

*   *   *

Elsewhere in the district the business climate was steadily improving. There were 18 men then employed at the Gem Mine in Burke Canyon. Charles Hussey was busy planning construction of a concentrator at his mine, the Morning, but work would not begin on that project until the railroad's location in Mullan was definitely established.

Once again, the transportation of ore in wintertime was a problem. The ore accumulated at the Mission in tremendous quantity. It was not possible to estimate the amount of the stockpile in mid-February, but it would be a long time before the steamers could catch up even when all were running again. Captain Sanburn was making repairs on the steamer *Coeur d'Alene* and it was out of service. Captain Nesbit was then in command of the *Kootenai*, which was the only boat on the route at that time. She took only 50 tons a trip and the water was so low in February at the bar at the mouth of the river that it was impossible for her to carry a full load. In a short time all boats would be running—the *Coeur d'Alene*, *Kootenai* and *Sherman*. With these boats and two barges, they would be able to carry 1,340 tons of ore per week, a capacity more than equal to the output of the mines then working. When the Hunter Mill did start up, it was expected that it would tax the full capacity of the railroad and steamer company, and that a new barge would have to be built.

CHAPTER 13

TOWNSITE TROUBLE – FEBRUARY – 1889

On February 19, Wallace was going about its usual business, when, late in the afternoon, word reached the town of a new ruling by the Secretary of the Interior. This ruling touched upon the title to the townsite of Wallace, which had been purchased by Colonel Wallace with Sioux scrip. The scrip had been issued to Walter Bourke, an Indian, whose whereabouts were then unknown. The Secretary of the Interior had ruled that Bourke's Sioux scrip was not subject to sale. By way of explanation this scrip was issued to persons, in the instant case Sioux Indians, who had been dispossessed of their lands by the federal government, and it entitled such evicted persons to go elsewhere upon the public lands and secure title by purchasing the land with scrip.

Immediately men began jumping property all over town. Notice of new locations and claims were posted everywhere, and many lots were crudely and hastily fenced in. By 2 a.m., everything was located and the rush subsided. One excited citizen posted his claim on the city jail. Many claimants spent the night on the lots, and the next morning a citizens' meeting was called. The Wallace Townsite Company claimed the Secretary of Interior's ruling did not affect their holdings, which they claimed were the same as patented land.

On the following day, at the citizens' meeting, a committee of five was appointed to check the title to the Wallace townsite. The meeting then adjourned. Three of these members went to

Coeur d'Alene. They soon returned to report that the original location of Wallace townsite was made on June 5, 1886, by W. R. Wallace, that he had used Sioux scrip, and that duplicate scrip had been issued upon the same scrip used by Colonel Wallace. The duplicate scrip had been used in locating land in Dakota Territory in 1880. They reported that the government considered Wallace's scrip as void, that the U. S. government canceled the Colonel's notice of location on January 24, 1887, and that he had been so notified by letter dated February 3, 1887. Colonel Wallace had never told the citizens of Wallace about the government's cancellation.

After hearing the committee's report, another citizens' meeting was called for 7 p.m. on February 22, 1889. No one wasted any time in getting action on this matter, which affected the ownership of their homes and business property. They adopted the following town rules:

1. Existing streets were to be recognized by all.
2. Every U. S. citizen or one who had declared his intentions to become one, of over 21 years, was entitled to four 25 x 100 foot lots and no more.
3. Lots were to be staked in legal form and recorded within 5 days, and fenced within 10 days after location.
4. The city recorder was authorized to collect a $2 recording fee.
5. All disputes regarding ownership of Wallace property were to be settled by a committee of 7 citizens.
6. A building placed on a lot before February 19, 1889, would hold the lot for the owner of the building without the necessity of his having to relocate said lot.

Lot jumping was the sole topic of discussion for the days to come. The citizens' rules were strictly followed and enforced. All lots were assessed $1 each to be used in obtaining a patent. There was considerable fencing being done about town.

News of the lot jumpings in Wallace spread throughout the

nation. The *Chicago Tribune* mentioned it in an editorial, March 1, 1889, which praised the local handling of the situation.

About a week after the furor started, Colonel Wallace made his first extensive explanation of the townsite problem. He explained that he had first located and fenced land in Wallace in the spring of 1884 for agricultural purposes. Later he and Richard Lockey had bought Sioux scrip from the First National Bank of Spokane with which to pay for the 80 acres.

In 1887, the Colonel was called to Coeur d'Alene by the U. S. Land Receiver and informed that the scrip he used to buy the land with was no good. Wallace claimed he then paid the land officer $50 "for advice" and was told the government's letter informing the land officer about the scrip would not become a part of the Land Office records. Wallace then went to Spokane Falls to buy other land scrip so he could cover his purchase, but he found it was too expensive. He claimed the land officer told him to sell the land and no one could injure him for it. The land officer said he would protect him as his attorney. . . . Wallace contended the entry or issuance of the duplicate scrip was fraudulent, and that he would fight to establish his rights.

On March 7, the town council met to consider ways to raise money to get a patent on the town land. Colonel Wallace asked that nothing be done for 30 days, as a land officer was on the way to investigate his land problem. His request was not complied with.

S. S. Glidden, an owner of the Tiger Mine in Burke, said that he had the same trouble with Sioux scrip as did W. R. Wallace. Glidden put his scrip upon Thompson Falls land, and it turned out to be worthless. He investigated his case and determined that it was useless to proceed with any protest.

Colonel Wallace became very upset over the land turmoil. He wrote a letter to the publishers of the *Wallace Free Press,* scorching the Dunn Brothers for their stand on the problem. Wallace made public a contract in which he had guaranteed the Dunns $1,800 in receipts for their first six months in the newspaper business in Wallace, plus six months' free rent on their building. It was pointed out that the business took in more than the guaranteed amount; at the end of the six months the Dunns bought the building.

Toward the end of March, a test case on the Wallace land problem was filed in the district court. It was filed under the title of Wallace Townsite Company vs. C. W. and F. P. Vedder, but much time was to pass before the problem was solved. . . .

CHAPTER 14

MARCH THROUGH JULY — 1889

Big as the townsite problem may have been, it did not stop many other things from happening in the area. On March 2, the *Wallace Free Press* reported:

". . . a Dago employed on the railroad between here and Mullan . . . was crushed to the ground, and 30 rails (standard gauge) crashed down upon him. They had fallen from a car that had left the track."

Luckily the ground was very wet and soft and it eased the blow. He was bruised from head to toe but his injuries were not thought to be necessarily fatal. This is a good example of the journalism of those times; it reflected the attitude of many people.

At the Morning Mine, John Waters was killed by a premature blast of six holes. Until then, the papers did not report many accidents in the mines, but eventually there were to be many of them. No explanation is offered except that more men were being put to work in the mines, and probably they were not skilled to the degree of the early miners.

The Northern Pacific Railroad Company was doing work in the Mullan area, and its station there was called Ryan. The railroad completely ignored the town name of Mullan. Instead, it chose to honor Dennis Ryan of St. Paul, the principal owner of the Hunter Mine.

In a very magnanimous way, the Wallace merchants announced late in March that they would start closing their stores

Wallace, Idaho, in 1887.

Wallace, Idaho, in 1888.

Left: Burke, Idaho, in August, 1887. *Right:* Early gathering at the Hercules Mine near Burke, Idaho. From left: Mr. Markwell (seated), Mrs. Markwell, H. F. Samuels, Mrs. L. Hutton (seated), Jerome Day, Mrs. A. Paulsen, Miss White, and August Paulsen (on woodpile).

Wardner in the early 1890's.

at 1 P.M. on Sundays, in order to give themselves and their employees one-half day off per week.

In March, 1889, the Poorman Mill was shipping about 40 tons of concentrates per day. Its mine and the Tiger were the largest in Canyon Creek, but progress was being made in the San Francisco, Gem, and Black Bear mines also. Time was to make all of them good producers.

The San Francisco Mine, located near Gem, was owned by A. M. Esler. A new tunnel was being run below the old workings at this mine and it was calculated to tap the ledge by running in 160 feet. In March of 1889, they were in the process of building a concentrator which would be in operation in May. The concentrator was 500 feet directly below the main working tunnel and the ore would be brought down to the concentrator by a gravity tramway. The water for the mill was to be taken from Canyon Creek almost a mile upstream and then flumed along the sidehill to the Frisco Mill.

At the Gem Mine work was being performed under the supervision of A. B. Campbell, one of the principal owners. The lower tunnel was now in over 300 feet and they had over 100 feet left to go before they expected to strike the ledge. Between 40 and 50 men were employed at this property.

These mines were all near Gem, and it was expected that this town would grow quickly as these mines progressed into production. At that time Gem had a post office, a telephone office, a general store and two saloons. Its most prominent citizen was J. J. Ullman, who owned the store and saloon and was the postmaster and telephone agent. - - - It was suggested that the railroad company immediately build a depot at Gem in recognition of its growing importance.

The Iron Horse came to Mullan on Sunday the 24th of March. Everything and everyone in Mullan was startled by the sound of the first locomotive that ever blew its whistle in Mullan.

". . . Web Leasure's old cow, Lil, with tail erect, tore down Pine Avenue to the barn for shelter, and every dutiful cock corralled his flock under the nearest cover, as if to ward off some impending danger. Hats were thrust from shop windows, men were hurried hither and thither, and even Lawyer Lydell Baker, who has seen nearly every railroad in christendom was seen to make a bee-line in the direction from whence emanated this unusual noise in Mullan. . . ."

Before long nearly the entire population of Mullan was wending its way down Mill Street at the foot of which stood Engine No. Three, with Engineer Al Matheson in charge. It was not known when the first passenger train would roll into Mullan, but it was expected in the near future.

April brought interesting litigation to the district. In District Court, the Wallace townsite case came up for a hearing and Lawyer Stoll asked that Al Dunn of the *Wallace Free Press* be excluded from the courtroom because his articles in the paper were adverse to his client's interest. The judge denied this request. Not content with this ruling Stoll subpoenaed Dunn as a witness and then Stoll moved to exclude all witnesses from the courtroom—and the judge was obligated to grant this motion.

At about the same time, Colonel Wallace was charged with shooting toward Henry Ford's house. Ford was then the attorney for the town of Wallace, and had been offering legal opinions on the townsite situation. Four bullet holes were found in the post on Ford's porch. It was claimed that several parties saw Wallace fire the shots. The Colonel obtained a change of venue to the court at Wardner Junction, and was soon declared not guilty by the jury, which was made up of men from the west end of the county.

Some mining was being done in the Nine Mile area. Ten men were on the payroll at the California Mine, and Oscar Wallace, the Colonel's son, was planning to resume work at his Black Cloud Mine. Mark Hewitt ran a saloon and hotel to serve that district, which also had the Monarch, Panhandle and the Yankee

Girl mines. The growing mining industry made demands for new businesses all the time. The mine owners were anxiously awaiting the arrival of telegraph lines into the district, to speed their communications. The Cameron Brothers were building a new sawmill about two miles east of Wallace to help service the mines with timbers.

Early in May, the Wallace town council gave T. N. Barnard permission to place his photographic gallery in the alley, back of the Wallace Hotel. This was a temporary measure, while Barnard was putting up a building to house his studio. This pioneer photographer had been in the district for several years, and he had formerly operated in Murray and Wardner. He had acquired some of his training in this trade while working with L. A. Huffman, the photographer, in Miles City, Montana, and later at Buffalo, Wyoming.

In the Beaver Mining District, much work and interest were given to the following mining properties: the Virginia, Carlisle, Toughnut, Alpha, Tuscumbia, Sitting Bull, Silver Tip, Parrott, Colwyn, Sunset, Big Bug, President and the Mountain Goat.

Vedder and Company, who ran a general merchandise store, gave an assignment for the benefit of their creditors. This appeared to be the nearest thing to a business failure that the local newspaper publishers would admit to up until that time. Vedder attributed the difficulties to the inability to make local collections from their debtors. Vedder's problem may have been an indication of tougher times to come. The *Murray Record* quit publishing on June 2. O. H. Culver was its editor and manager, and it had been published tri-weekly for four years.

Tough times or not, the people loved to play for good stakes. The Wallace baseball team played the Burke team for a $500 purse. Cedar stumps provided too great a hindrance to the sport in Wallace, so the game was played in Osburn. Wallace won 17 to 8.

The end of June 1889 in the Wardner area brought with it the tragic news of an accident between two stagecoaches. These

stages hauled passengers from the railroad depot at Wardner
Junction over a mile or more up the hill to the town of Wardner.
It was quite customary for the two stages to engage in a race
from the depot to determine which was to have the lead on the
road to Wardner. The loser and its passengers had to eat dust
all the way. The stages wrecked going into the first turn and
seven people were injured. Two weeks later, Professor Clayton
died from injuries he had sustained in the wreck. He was a
geologist of prominence, well recognized throughout the West.

The *Wallace Free Press* changed hands at the end of June in
1889. The Dunn Brothers sold out; Frank Tibbals was listed as
the publisher, and Ed L. Tibbals was the new manager.

The district court sentenced J. C. Oland, a Negro, to hang for
the first degree murder of Charles Porter, committed in Mullan
during the prior January. The sentence was to be carried out
by the Shoshone County Sheriff on August 31, in the county jail
at Murray. Oland's lawyer, Judge Mayhew, immediately went to
Boise to see what could be done to lessen the sentence.

The business climate improved as the summer progressed.
Donations were taken to buy instruments for a band in Wallace.
The money was raised in three hours. Two stages left Wallace
every day for Murray, and the Granite Mine in Burke canyon
had increased its payroll to 52 men.

The Poorman was the largest shipping mine in the Coeur
d'Alenes at that time, with a 100-man payroll. It paid its first
dividend on July 15, of 3 cents per share on 500,000 shares. The
Poorman shares were then selling for 90 cents each. The Poorman was then sinking a shaft to the 300-foot level. The miners
had sunk to 25 feet below the 200-foot level by mid-July. They
were sinking at the rate of ½ foot every 24 hours. The Poorman
shaft sinkers were using compressed air as a power source for
their drills. This was an innovation to the men, who had been
drilling by hand. However, hand drilling was not then a thing
of the past. It continued into the twentieth century and caused
many miners to die prematurely from silicosis because of the
dry rock dust they breathed.

CHAPTER 15

AUGUST THROUGH DECEMBER — 1889

Immense forest fires raged throughout North Idaho early in August. The nearest big fire, between Delta and Murray, did considerable damage. The fires sent up so much smoke that the sun was nearly obscured. One fire, burning on a high peak southeast of Wallace, presented a grand sight at night to the townspeople. The forest fire problem plagued the district all through August. The fires started to die out, allowing the air to clear up, but suddenly they took off again. A rain storm ended the fire threat toward the end of August. The 1889 fire season had been the worst since the entire south fork area had been swept by fires in the 1860s.

However, the dry days of summer did explode in Spokane Falls, where the entire business district was destroyed by fire on August 4. Damages were estimated at $6,000,000, with insurance covering less than half the losses. The inferno caused many Spokane transients to hit the road. . . . No small part of them came to the Coeur d'Alenes.

Speculating that the rebuilding of Spokane Falls would soon take place, Holley, Mason, Marks and Company immediately placed a large order for hardware items in Chicago. Their order made up many carloads. Upon arrival, the hardware items were sold right from the box cars sitting in the Spokane railroad yards.

Charles Hussey, owner of the Morning Mine, announced that he had purchased the Evening Mine, and claimed that he owned

the largest ore body known in the Coeur d'Alenes at the time. . . .
The Morning Mine finished building a bucket tramway to transport ore from its mine to the mill. The tramway was 2¼ miles
long and had a capacity of 250 tons every 24 hours. The cost
of carrying a ton of ore was less than 12 cents. The steel cable
was one inch in diameter and carried a bucket every 90 feet.
Each bucket held 140 pounds of ore.

The local business outlook was improving all the time. Rumors
were afloat that Wallace would soon have electric power from
a light plant to be powered by water from Placer Creek. - - -
Carl Mallon of Murray, came to Wallace to look for a site upon
which to build a brewery. What surer sign of prosperity could
one ask for?

The Poorman declared its second dividend on August 15. Four
cents were paid on each of 500,000 shares, and the price of the
stock raised to $1 per share. - - - Other dividend payers in the
district were the Bunker Hill, Sierra Nevada, Tiger, Granite,
Custer, Occident, Golden Chest, Syd Mills, Baby Fraction, Gem,
Mother Lode, Treasure Box, Myrtle and Fay Templeton. Several of these were gold properties on the North Side of the
county.

In Wardner, the Bunker Hill, Sierra Nevada and Stemwinder
all had their own mills. In Canyon Creek, the Poorman, Tiger,
San Francisco, Gem and Granite mills were in operation. Mullan
then had the Gold Hunter and Morning mills. Three more mills
were being planned or erected in Canyon Creek at that time:
the Hidden Treasure, Badger and Black Bear.

*　　*　　*

After the rains had cooled the ashes of the forest fires, Harry
L. Day continued his search for mineral lands in the Burke area.
His prospecting took him to the Tiger Peak country, at the head
of Gorge Gulch above Burke, where he and his partner, Fred H.
Harper, located the Hercules and Firefly mining claims on Au-
gust 24, 1889. The fire had burned the brush from the Murray
Trail and exposed mineralization to their inquiring eyes. Al-

though Harry Day, with his two brothers Eugene and Jerome, worked constantly at the job, it was to take them more than a decade to put the Hercules on a profitable basis.

The Day brothers were assisted in the efforts to "bring in" the Hercules by such men as August Paulsen, a dairy employee, Levi W. "Al" Hutton, a railway engineer, C. H. "Dad" Reeves, a barber and father-in-law of Fred Harper, Dan Cardoner, a native of Spain who was a grocer in Burke, Frank M. Rothrock, a butcher and cattle buyer, and H. F. Samuels, a lawyer. Each of these men became wealthy from his share in the Hercules.

The father of the Day brothers, Henry Loren Day, left the woods of his native Maine in 1854, as lumbering was playing out, in search of a better life. In that year he traveled across the Isthmus of Panama and to the gold fields of California. Little more than a living was his reward in placer and lode mining, so he sold timbers and ran a freighting business. In 1860 he moved this business on to the Comstock area of Nevada. About 1870 he moved his growing family to Truckee, California, where he remained until 1886, when he was enticed to the Coeur d'Alenes because of the discovery of such claims as the Bunker Hill. Upon his arrival in Wardner, he opened a general store and dairy business under the name of H. L. Day & Son. Harry L. Day, his oldest son, worked in the store in the winters and prospected in the summers. Later Harry Day was a millman in the Murray district and also worked as a bookkeeper in Moore's furniture store in Wallace. All the Day brothers and sisters: Harry L., Eugene R., Jerome J., Eleanor and Blanche were to share in the profits of the Hercules mine for years to come.

❋   ❋   ❋

August 1889 closed with Colonel Wallace operating his little steamboat, the *Irene*, on the waters of Coeur d'Alene Lake. It was a place for recreation even then. Carl Mallon had found a site for his brewery, and he had three men clearing land at the west end of Bank Street, an area full of immense cedars. And

the Heller House's Bill of Fare and Wine List included such
things as:

Porterhouse steak	65 cents
Half a pheasant	65 cents
Russian caviar	20 cents
3-Star Hennessy cognac	$2.50 quart

A new town called Pottsville was started several miles east of
Mullan to serve the railroad crews working on the track from
Mullan to the Idaho-Montana Summit.

On September 16, the Poorman paid its third dividend, at the
rate of 4 cents per share. Over the summer it had paid out $55,-
000 in profits to its shareholders.

Toward the end of September, Adam Aulbach took over the
editorial and business end of the *Wallace Free Press,* and Ed
Tibbals was no longer connected with the paper.

After Mr. Adam Aulbach came to Wallace to print a paper,
the town was never the same. He was 43 years old at the time
and brought with him a background in journalism from throughout the West. He started in the printing trade in his native Illi-
nois, and then went on to St. Louis. In 1863, he and four others
left St. Joseph, Missouri, with ox teams bound for the West.
Aulbach arrived at East Bannock, in Montana Territory, during
the summer of that year. He mined and merchandised in that
area and at Virginia City. Aulbach claimed in later life that he
was drafted into the vigilance committee at Virginia City, where
he witnessed several of their early hangings.

From 1864 until 1866, Aulbach served in the First Nevada
Cavalry. After his discharge he worked on the *Salt Lake City
Vedette,* a strongly anti-Mormon paper. He proceeded on to a
newspaper at Corinne, Utah, and later worked on the *San Francisco Chronicle* and the *San Jose Herald.* In the fall of 1876, he
went to Eureka, Nevada, and edited the *Daily Republican.* The
year 1877 saw him back at work in San Francisco, where he
stayed for three years, before returning to Eureka, Nevada. Once

again, in 1883, he started traveling, and wound up working in Philadelphia and New York for a short time.

On April 9, 1884, Aulbach came to Belknap, Montana Territory, to lay the foundation for establishing a newspaper in the newly discovered gold fields of the Coeur d'Alenes. He soon brought his equipment over the mountains into Murray and printed his first newspaper on July 8, 1884, under the title of the *Idaho Sun.*

He had planned a very patriotic and impressive first issue for release on the Fourth of July, but just as he was about to print it, another Murray editor, Henry Bernard, shot and killed his printer. Adam Aulbach pulled his front page and waited developments on the killing so he could open with a slam-bang story on the subject. It seemed the victim, John Enright, lingered on for about a day before he died, and it then became a source of speculation as to whether he died of the gunshot wound or from medical treatment received.

＊　　＊　　＊

The case involving the Wallace Townsite was continued over the court term at Rathdrum, where it had been moved on a change of venue obtained by Colonel Wallace. The U. S. Land Commissioner had looked over the Colonel's petition for relief and denied the same. The Commissioner stated that duplicate scrip had been issued upon that held by Colonel Wallace, upon representation of a former owner that the original scrip had been lost.

The district court postponed the hanging of J. C. Oland at Murray, until the Negro's motion for a new trial could be heard and determined.

White & Bender, Murray grocers, bought out George and Human's grocery in Wallace, and Harry White took personal charge of the Wallace end of the business. - - - Jesse Tabor erected a 24 foot by 30 foot building on Sixth Street, between Cedar and Bank, which was to house a store and barber shop.

Others were planning the building of churches for the Catholics and Episcopalians.

The Wallace Manufacturing, Electric and Water Company was organized during mid-October. Plans were drawn up for a mile long flume which was to bring Placer Creek water to furnish power for 1,000 lights. Their entire plant would cost about $8,000.00.

The townsite trouble was still boiling in the background all the time. One man "located" the town baseball grounds, but a group of indignant Wallace citizens tore down his notice of location, and no further trouble was had—a town as progressive as Wallace had to have a baseball field. Its town team was to leave on October 25 to play the Spokane team for the championship of Washington and Idaho, and for a purse of $1,000. The magnitude of the occasion demanded that the Wallace team stop at Fort Sherman for a practice session on their way into Washington. A sad day fell on Wallace when its team lost to Spokane, 21 to 1 in seven innings.

Meanwhile, throughout the district, small items were making news. Lumber was selling for $12 to $14 a thousand, and some building was taking place in Osburn. Mrs. C. B. Taylor was Mullan's first school teacher. Al Dunn was appointed as the new postmaster for Wallace, replacing Mrs. Lucy Wallace. William Worstell provided the undertaking services, which Wallace was to find necessary now and again. In Mullan, J. D. Garvin's water plant was ready to serve all who desired to pay $2.50 per month for water.

On October 31, news reached Wallace that the Secretary of the Interior had decided against the "Jumpers" in Wallace, and that Colonel Wallace's claims prevailed. The report continued that duplicate scrip had been issued to the heirs of Bourke, the Indian to whom the scrip was originally issued, upon the representation of the heirs that Bourke was dead. It was reported that the Colonel had located Bourke and that he was alive. . . . Nothing was heard from other sources, including the attorneys working on the case in Washington, D.C. The only source for this news was the newspaper printed in Spokane, and the Wallace people were reluctant to believe the reports, perhaps out of fear for their land holdings. Within a week, it was determined that the Wallace townsite article, which appeared in the Spokane paper, was false. The citizens settled back to await further developments from the nation's capital.

Aulbach took a strong interest in the entire district. His newspaper was extremely outspoken on subjects attracting his interest. One of these was the attempt by W. B. Heyburn and Billy Osburn to move the county seat from Murray to Osburn, which Aulbach described as a town having less than 20 male residents. . . . Aulbach and his ever present derby hat had moved from Murray to Wallace and he felt the county seat should do likewise.

The town of Wallace was excited on November 14 by the finding of skeletons of three Chinamen under some logs near the Wallace Northern Pacific depot. The town had a mystery, but soon some of the oldtimers remembered that in 1873 a safe at Cedar Creek in Montana was robbed of three or four thousand dollars in gold dust. They remembered that three Chinamen were suspected, and that they were followed over the Mullan Road into Idaho, where the Chinamen were killed while trying to elude their pursuers.

At that time, the people in Wardner were incensed to hear that some parties contemplated bringing in Chinese labor, and they held a meeting, which "resolved to keep the heathen out of camp." Adam Aulbach was pleased with their decision, commenting that the issue of Chinese labor in the Coeur d'Alenes had been settled at a 4th of July meeting in Murray several years before. The threat to bring cheap labor had prompted the first meeting also.

Chinese labor was looked upon with great disfavor by most men in the mining camps at that time. Earlier rushes had included many Chinamen, who were exploited by mine owners for cheap labor. The same Chinese stayed around after the rushes subsided and made out an existence on claims that were unprofitable to white miners. In the early years, Idaho's mining camps had many Chinamen, but by the time the Coeur d'Alene mining district arrived, the decision was uniformly held that no Chinese were welcome in the district. Those sentiments were to apply over the years, until such time as a custom of "no Chinese allowed in the district" had grown up, and few of the citizens were to realize the reason behind the custom and practice.

The electric company paid $623 for its mile-long flume, which had been finished. The company was working on the Placer Creek dam, which was to provide water for the power plant under construction alongside Placer Creek, near the baseball grounds.

The Poorman paid its fourth dividend on November 26, in the amount of 3 cents per share. This one mine was the big producer at the east end of the county during 1889. The business houses of Wallace reflected every piece of good or bad news that came out of the Poorman.

The *Helena Journal* described the last mining season in the Coeur d'Alenes as being one of progress and advancements. Houses were being built on every side. There were no empty buildings in the business district, and Wallace had four or five hotels, which were full most of the time. The Helena paper reported that the saloons were well patronized, with very active faro games for the players. The saloon bands were playing such tunes as "Johnny Get Your Gun" and "Sherman's March Through Georgia." The news report continued by describing the girls, with abbreviated skirts, who solicited drinks in the showhouse, and who by their smiles and appeals drew the last quarter from their unsuspecting visitors. The reporter added that drinks were ordered fast and furious, and it was necessary to go outside to get a breath of fresh air.

It is always interesting to find out how an outsider looks at a place. Aulbach chose to copy reports on the district which he lifted out of Portland, Salt Lake, and other papers. The Helena paper described Wallace as having saloons without number, five or six big grocery and supply houses, a fine drug store, a bank, good hardware store, two or three doctors, three big livery stables, and a dozen restaurants.

At the depot one could see car after car load of ore, coming from Mullan, Burke, Gem and Nine Mile. Galena ore in sacks, concentrates in sacks, and everything in the shape of mineral had to be transported from Wallace in sacks until the through railroad lines were completed. At that time the ore and concentrates could go in loose form by the carload. The railroads could not furnish enough cars for the ore shipments, which amounted to about 3,775 tons per month.

Hotels charged $2.50 per day for board and room, and $1.00 per day for board alone. Mullan was described as having wide streets, good houses, and fine hotels. Burke had many large stores, hotels and saloons, with 600 men on the payrolls. Gem had 250 men on its payrolls, and it was full of miners' cabins, saloons and boarding houses. Nine Mile had 150 men employed, and Osburn was populated by about 60 people.

It is interesting to note that the Helena paper described Wardner as a dull town then, but it predicted that it would not be in a short time. About 1,000 persons lived at Wardner, Milo, and Wardner Junction. Kingston, Mud Prairie, and the Mission had about 700 people, mostly engaged in railroading or lumbering. Delta once had 3,000 people, but less than 300 called for their mail there in 1889. Murray was full of empty houses, and was described as wearing a dull and cheerless air. Up Pony Gulch a forty-ton mill crushed gold quartz on the Fay Templeton mine. Two arastras were also running for the purpose of crushing gold ore.

Perhaps it would be well to comment on the foregoing statements concerning the sacking of all ore shipments on the train. The narrow-gauge railroad was the only one operating to the "outside," and its cars held loads of 10 to 15 tons. These cars were transported to the Mission, where the loads were placed on the boats or barges and transported downriver and across the lake to Coeur d'Alene, where the shipments were once again placed on the rails. The train then took the ore to Hauser Junction (near Rathdrum), where the loads were transferred to trains operating on the main line of the Northern Pacific Railway. Later, when standard gauge trains were to serve the district, it was not necessary to sack the shipments because their loads were shipped in the same car all the way from the district to the smelters, thereby avoiding the intermixing of ores from different mines.

On December 9, amid a furious snow storm the Washington and Idaho Railroad, a branch line of the Union Pacific and Oregon Railway & Navigation systems, laid its broad-gauge track along the narrow gauge road, on the north side of the river. A celebration was held for the arrival of the crews. The Morning Mill in Mullan had about 200 tons of concentrates piled up awaiting the arrival of the broad-gauge train. It was expected that this train would take over most of the business and passenger travel going west.

The December 7 issue of the *Wallace Free Press* carried a headline: "One Dago Dead". . . . On the third, at the Italian railroad camp about a mile and a half up the South Fork from Wallace, an Italian shot two other Italians, killing one of them. Aulbach characterized the killing as "assassination," rather than murder, inasmuch as the victim had been shot through the back of the head. - - - "a table knife, something on the style of a Bowie, which were ordinarily used by Italians, was said to be either in the hands or belt of the dead man." . . . Perhaps this can account for the fact that the gunslinger was never prosecuted.

The year closed in a flurry of activity. The telegraph line was on its way to Wallace. The electric company ordered a lamp plant capable of lighting 650 lights from the Thomson-Houston Company, at a cost of $4,500.00. Toward the middle of December it was announced that the Episcopal Church in Wallace would be sufficiently finished to allow a Christmas program to be held there. The plans, which had been announced earlier, for a Catholic church did not materialize until years later.

Wallace had progressed from the community Christmas tree of '87 in the Heller House to the first religious service held in a church building. Previous religious gatherings in Wallace and the other towns were held in meeting halls and other buildings providing sufficient space.

On Christmas Eve of 1889, the Episcopal Church was not finished and it was barely enclosed, but two large stoves furnished vigorous heat. Owing to the great crowd on hand, an occasional blast of cold air through the improvised door was welcome.

> "Before the platform stood the Christmas tree, its branches bending with presents, while the strings of corn, colored glass globes and the little burning wax tapers gave to it an attraction that was as pleasing to the eyes as time allowed for the tree's preparation."

Presents were distributed to every child in town. The Reverend Mr. Gunn, present but ill, announced there would be no church on Christmas because of his enfeebled condition. The Wallace Silver Cornet Band furnished the music, and the children gave their recitations. A little girl named Hannah Worstell recited "Santa Claus and the Mouse." . . . Such was the first service of Holy Trinity Church.

One store, that of Follett & Harris, received a Christmas shipment from the Palouse country of 800 chickens, over 100 turkeys and geese; the rest of the box car shipment was made up of butter, eggs and oats. Aulbach cited this as the beginning of a wholesale trade between the Coeur d'Alenes and the Palouse.

The townsite trouble was still up in the air, and no news was forthcoming on that score. However, toward the end of December, Colonel Wallace was appointed Deputy Attorney by Captain John Mullan, the attorney for the Coeur d'Alene Indians. Wallace was to appear for the tribe in a meeting between Chief Seltice of the Coeur d'Alenes and the U. S. government, scheduled for January 3, for a final ratification of the treaty between them of

September 1889, which ceded to the United States, the northern and eastern portion of their reservation. Judge Willis Sweet was to be present for the federal government.

It was speculated that the Indians might refuse to sign the treaty because, by the terms of a former treaty, the one of March 26, 1878, the United States had purportedly promised to pay the tribe a large sum of money for some ceded lands, but the tribe had never received the money. If the treaty were signed by the Indians, the ceded land would be thrown open to public settlement sometime during the coming year. "Boomers" had been waiting on the northern line of the reservation for most of the winter for any word of "opening day."

The end of 1889 brought two stories of unusual interest to the townsmen; the first one reported the arrival of the first passenger service on the broad-gauge railroad from Spokane. The line bore the name of the Washington and Idaho Railroad Company. It scheduled a departure from Wallace at 6:15 a.m. and arrived at Spokane at 12:25 p.m. The fare was $6.50. The return train left Spokane at 4:00 p.m., and arrived in Wallace at 10:15 p.m., with a half-hour stop in Tekoa for dinner. It was reported that the dinner stop was the only unpleasant part of the trip.

> "The butter was vile, the coffee made from corn husks roastedly rank, the biscuits like cobblestones, and the cold meats tougher than kids who grow up without parental restraint."

The second story of interest concerned a woman named Ione Skeels. She had been tried before a jury in Spokane Falls for the shooting death of her husband, Charles W. Skeels, during March, 1889. Previous to the marriage she was well known in the district, having been a competitor of Molly b'Damn and Terrible Edith during the gold rush in Murray. She was known to most of the miners as "Broncho Liz." She had met Skeels in the Coeur d'Alenes, and they struck it off pretty good. Skeels was married and their relationship presented problems. He solved some of these by inducing Broncho Liz to cut her hair and dress like a man. She then went with him to his father's farm, where he introduced her to his folks. She worked as a hired man on the farm for several months without her sex being discovered by other than Skeels. This gave Skeels time to obtain a divorce from his wife.

On January 2, 1888, Liz married Skeels in Moscow. A short while later he sent her to Montana, where she remained until February 1889. By that time she started wondering what her wandering husband was up to. He was in Spokane "on business." After her arrival there, she found out he was paying attention to other women. On March 1, she learned that he was spending the night with Frankie Howard, a variety actress, in a building known as the "Actor's Flat." Liz enticed Skeels from the building by having a messenger tell him that he was needed at his business house. When Skeels saw Liz, he struck her, and she immediately evened the score by putting three bullets into him. . . . The verdict of acquittal was popular in the Coeur d'Alenes, as it "was fully justified by the evidence, which showed that the deceased was a bad and dangerous man in the community." One editor wrote that Skeels "lived by the smell of powder and died by the force of it."

CHAPTER 16

JANUARY THROUGH MARCH – 1890

Business was good in Wallace in January, 1890. The merchants announced they were no longer closing their stores on Sunday afternoon. Everything was going full blast seven days per week. Wallace's transient population was immense, considering the size of the town. The Northern Pacific Railroad was working on its line which was to bring trains into Mullan from Montana. In mid-January, six Italians were killed in a dynamite blast, while working on a rock cut for this Northern Pacific extension.

Shortly after midnight on January 4, a fire broke out in Page's Laundry in Wardner, and for a time it threatened the entire town. The left hand side of Main Street was a sea of fire and the buildings on the right hand side were charred. The fire burned for over four hours. The water was frozen, causing the fire fighters a very difficult time. They finally checked the flames by the use of "giant powder." It had been the biggest fire in the Coeur d'Alene Mining District until that time, and losses were estimated at $70,000.

The winter brought many problems for the district, including a flu epidemic. It was estimated that one out of every five people in Wallace was struck by the flu during January. The winter snows delayed the meeting between representatives of the federal government and the Coeur d'Alene Indian Chief, Seltice. After a postponement of several days, the meeting took place on the 7th of January and the treaty was signed by Seltice and eight members of his tribe without much parleying. If the United States Senate confirmed this treaty, the ceded land would be opened for settlement. The Coeur d'Alene Indians would be required to move to the more southern part of their reservation. The tribe in 1890 consisted of 208 men and 215 women. The size of the tribe had been numerically at a standstill for some time. They had 7,000 acres under cultivation and possessed 1,000 horses, 300 cattle, 400 hogs, 10 mules and 600 fowls.

On Prichard Creek, George Ives, a noted placer miner, panned out $90 in gold from a little crevice in the rock at the west end of Main Street in Murray. He had been working in that general area for the past six months. He panned out two nuggets, one weighed 4 ounces and the other 1 ounce.

Dutch Jake Goetz and Harry F. Baer, two noted miners who had made their fortune on the North Side and from the discovery of the Bunker Hill, had established a saloon business in Spokane. Word reached the district in January that Harry Baer shot a 240-pound thug in his Spokane saloon. The Spokane coroner's jury returned a verdict of justfiable homicide, which pleased his many local friends.

The whole district was suffering from the ice blockade on Coeur d'Alene Lake once again. Burke merchants complained of the lack of food and other goods caused both by the blockade and the local snow problems.

January brought much activity to the Poorman Mine. It had reached the 300-foot level in its shaft sinking operations, which made these the lowest workings of any mine in the district. The ore had improved at every level. It was rumored that an English syndicate was in the process of buying control of the Poorman. Toward the end of January, it was necessary to close down the mine because every available space and bin in the concentrator was of ore. This situation could not be remedied until the ice blockade opened up and the ore could be transported.

J. C. Oland, the Negro being held in the Murray jail under a death sentence, committed suicide in his cell on January 20. His case had been on appeal to the Idaho Supreme Court.

❖   ❖   ❖

In Justice of the Peace Angel's court in Wallace, on January 21, two local lawyers got into a fight. One was J. C. Harkness, who also served as the county probate judge, and the other was William Stoll from Burke. Both men were six feet tall, and Harkness weighed over 200 pounds. Stoll had the temerity to chuck Harkness familiarly under the chin while making an uncomplimentary remark to Harkness, who responded by delivering a very heavy blow to Stoll's right jaw. Before the fight was finished, Stoll suffered other abrasions about his face. Harkness was uninjured. They both had gone to the floor in a wrestling and slugging match.

❖   ❖   ❖

Late in January, Wardner had snow-slide problems. These had been an annual problem since 1887. . . . In Burke the post office and some stores temporarily changed location in fear of snow slides. It took three engines to buck their way to Burke on January 31, as snow was piled up 20 feet deep in places.

February brought serious snow-slide problems to the entire district. Temperatures fluctuated between 30 degrees below zero and chinook conditions. Such problems were present every winter, but not to the extent of the winter of 1890. A "chinook" on February 2 brought rain. By 10:00 A.M., the rain caused the first snow slide, a short distance below the Granite Mill, killing two men on the railroad track. At 2:00 P.M. on the same day, two more men were killed in a snow slide a mile below Burke in a narrow part of the canyon. Three hours later, six men were killed by a snow slide which struck the boarding house at the Custer Mine. The toll would have been much higher had not the snow problems caused the Custer management to "lay off" over half of its crew. These men had left the camp to go to Wallace for their wages, thereby missing the slide. . . . One more man was killed by a snow slide late in February in Butte Gulch, near Murray.

Deep snows and slides near Wardner seriously hindered mining operations; the Last Chance tramway was destroyed in part by slides and would not be repaired until spring. As a result, the Last Chance Mill was idle, and no ore was to be shipped until the snow melted off. The Last Chance was engaged in sinking a double compartment shaft at the end of its lowest tunnel, 900 feet from the opening at the surface. The Stemwinder Mine was forced to shut down for ten days because of damage to its rope tramway by slides. The Sierra Nevada Mine worked a light force in February because its ore bins were full and shipments could not be made.

The cold weather did benefit one man, however. Carl Mallon had harvested 520 tons of ice, which he placed in storage for Wallace's summertime needs.

*   *   *

The Poorman, which was almost exclusively owned by Butte investors, was the subject of rumored sales. B. C. Kingsbury admitted the property had been inspected, but denied that an English syndicate had purchased it. He stated that any sale to a foreign syndicate would have to be conditional until Idaho became a state so the provisions of the harsh alien property law could be avoided.

The operations at the Poorman were shut down most of February as the ice boat made only one trip a day, hauling 50 tons of concentrates. This amount was apportioned to the various companies and the Poorman foreman was allowed to ship only 15 tons per day. All its storage facilities were full.

Con Sullivan, one of the early owners of the Bunker Hill and Sullivan, was prospecting in the Butte area. Sullivan followed mining throughout the remainder of his life and went to the Alaska gold rush in the late 90's, where he met his death at the hands of a murderer.

Adam Aulbach threw another of his tantrums in the paper. He was enraged by the recent action of the Idaho Supreme Court which had scheduled settings of the District Court for Osburn during 1890. They had ignored Wallace's request for the Court. Aulbach charged that Clagett and Heyburn had misrepresented Wallace as an overflowed swamp and thereby gained the court for Osburn.

March approached, and spring was not far in the future. When the electric plant machinery arrived in Wallace, the company announced that it would charge for service on the basis of the number of lights used. The Miner's Union of Wardner announced that it would give a dance there on St. Patrick's Day. The railroad company announced that if sufficient interest was shown in the St. Patrick's dance, it would make up a special train to leave Wallace at 7:00 in the evening, and leave Wardner Junction returning to Wallace at 6:00 A.M. on the following day. Special trains for sport and holiday occasions were quite commonplace at this time.

At the California Mine, in Nine Mile, ore was being prepared for shipment to the Washington-Idaho depot in Wallace, where it was placed on trains bound for Omaha. Scott McDonald had three sleds to carry the ore; these sleds had a lower box bed, not over a foot deep, and were loaded at the mine from the ore bins. At the depot, the load was shoveled from the sleigh box onto the platform and then into the box car. No sacks were used, which amounted to a great savings to the company. As it was downhill from the mine to depot, only one pair of horses was needed to tow the sled. Each team drew from three to four tons to the load and made three trips a day when the road was in good condition. The owners tried to bring down thirty tons a day while the weather held out. This was the first ore to be shipped out of the Nine Mile camp in a crude state and was unsacked and unpicked. The owners stated that a railroad up Nine Mile would add about twenty tons of ore daily to the output of their mine.

During the prior year the North Fork Hydraulic Mining Company had built five miles of flume and ditches near the Big Jam, and in March they turned their pipeworks on some 200-foot gravel bars for the gold miners near the Big Jam. On Eagle

Creek, Syd Mills was getting his bedrock flume underway. On Fancy Gulch, work had started on Mill's Big Placer Claim; and at the head of this gulch Dan McGrath put in considerable iron pipe for hydraulic work. In Daisy Gulch, Frank Grove and others were in good shape for a bedrock flume. From this point for five miles on the northside of Prichard Creek there was much work dedicated to taking gold out during 1890. Other gulches then being worked were Missoula, Dry, Nugget, Alder, Gold Run, Cougar, and Wesp.

On March 16, a cleanup of 42 ounces of gold was made from the Billy Miller Claim. This cleanup included one 11-ounce nugget, the largest found in Trail Gulch in about a year. The Mother Lode arastra was grinding quartz ore, averaging about $20 per ton. The Occident Company next to the Mother Lode had a main tunnel in over 600 feet and its two arastras were to be started in the spring of 1890.

During mid-March, John Kessler, one of the district's old pioneers passed away. Better known as "Huckleberry John," he had led a pauper's life at Delta and earned his meager living by picking the wild berries.

> "The deceased was not much over 40 years of age, and a very bright fellow, but whiskey, to which he was inordinately addicted, burned the wick of life down to the socket."

In March, the Wallace School had 46 children enrolled, but only one teacher. There were other children in the town, but the accommodations for schooling were not sufficient, so some of them had to do without schooling. The school was in a log cabin toward the westerly end of Bank Street. It was suggested that a new school house be built near Second and Pine.

❈   ❈   ❈   ❈   ❈   ❈   ❈   ❈

It was at this time that a 16-year-old Italian boy by the name of Louis Sala passed the Statue of Liberty, on his way to Ellis Island. His father had traveled to the United States during the 1860's, and, after making a small stake working in the Montana mines, had returned to his native Province of Venezia. Like so many immigrants, Louis Sala did not come to this country in search of "riches," but left absolute poverty in search of "a living." Before this boy's journey would take him to the Coeur d'Alenes, he would follow the paths of employment across the nation; he would work in the mines at Ironwood, Michigan, and Hurley, Wisconsin, in order to secure funds to travel to his uncle, Sam Sala, a blacksmith at the Poorman mine.

Later in the year Louis Sala arrived in Burke, and slept in the Poorman blacksmith shop until he was employed in the mine and able to make better arrangements. He faced many struggles in future days to evolve from an immigrant into a "citizen" and he was connected with the Coeur d'Alenes until he passed away in 1954. His lot was not unlike that of many other men of his time. In the Coeur d'Alenes, he was to be confronted with persecution and prosecution; but he found peace and prosperity.

CHAPTER 17

APRIL THROUGH JUNE – 1890

April brought signs of spring to the gulches, and the oldtimers recalled that the last had been the toughest winter since the gold rush of '83. Both winters brought about the same snowfall, but the last one included much rainfall in the valleys. Although the railroad had cleaned up the creek bottom while building its line, the townspeople were warned of flood danger. Wallace's snowfall for the past winter totaled 17 feet 6 inches. Adam Aulbach took the winter in stride when he reported:

> "We have only one abominable mud hole - - - Sixth Street, from N. P. Depot to Bank Street."

J. F. Ingalls was hard at work on the Lucky Friday claim near Mullan with two men. They put up about three hundred sacks of free milling ore, which they mined while sinking a shaft. One of the owners, Bob Horn, of Milo, reported that they had from 8 to 18 inches of clean cut mineral. They were preparing to ship a number of cars of ore.

At the Empire State Mine at the head of Nine Mile creek, J. F. Callahan and J. Wemes were injured in a blast, and it was thought that Callahan would lose his hearing as a result.

In April, the Morning Mine sent 20 tons of concentrates to Denver daily, and the Poorman mine had declared Dividend #5 in the amount of 4 cents per share. It was at this time that the *Spokane Review* stated editorially:

"The prospects in the Coeur d'Alene mountains do not pay for their development."

Perhaps such comments by others prompted formation of the Wallace Rod and Gun Club. The group ordered 1,000 blackbirds from Spokane for a shoot to be held in April.

Time was taking its toll. X. S. Burke, an early pioneer, died in Wallace. He came with the "Black Hills Crowd" and did much work as a civil and mining engineer. - - - The Cataldo Mission was aging very rapidly and its hilltop site gave the elements an opportunity to hit it from all sides. Efforts had been made to preserve the building by boarding it, but they were only partially successful. On its door in April 1890, was a sign:

"Contributions received to keep the Church in repair."

Even the pioneers recognized the great historic value of the Mission.

The electric company announced its rate schedule for lights in Wallace. Residences with 3 or more lights would be charged $1 per light per month; two lights at $1.25 each per month; and one light cost $1.50 per month. An intermediate rate was charged stores and shops, with the highest rate of all to be paid by the Wallace saloons. It was estimated that electricity would cost about one half as much as coal oil for lighting.

Signs of discontent arose from the southern part of Shoshone County. The Chinese in the Pierce City area had all their claims jumped by white men. The Chinamen had been working claims abandoned a long time before by white men. Judge Willis Sweet ruled a short time later that all aliens were barred from holding mining claims—in a case involving Chinese claiming placer land. . . . At Lolo, an organization of "regulators" had been formed, and they were dissatisfied with the powerful minority which seemingly had been in charge of the county government in their part of the county.

Meanwhile, E. D. Carter arrived back in Wallace. He was the owner of the Carter House and several other interests, but his home was at Humbird, Wisconsin. He, like many others, only lived in this district during the good weather, and wintered elsewhere.

The Wallace and Sunset Railroad incorporated during mid-April, with plans to go from Wallace to the Sunset mines area. In Osburn, lumber for their new courthouse was arriving daily and work on the building had commenced. It was to be finished in time for the court to sit in late May. All the activity in Osburn occasioned the establishment of another newspaper, the *Coeur d'Alene Statesman,* which printed its first issue toward the end of April.

There did not seem to be much lawlessness in the area at that time, but the newspapers did mention, on more than one occasion, the practice of pistol whipping by the police while making arrests.

April went out like a torrent. On the 30th, flood waters threatened the Sixth Street railroad bridge, and the citizens had to band together and collect funds, with which to pay for the raising of the bridge two feet at one end to allow the raging waters to pass. Their efforts took them four hours, but the bridge was saved. Some joker at Mullan telephoned a Wallace man and informed him that he had ordered 500 life preservers for the people at Wallace. Aulbach did not think the call was funny, and he suggested that these items could better serve the people at Osburn. He was still angry about the court sitting in Osburn, instead of at Wallace.

Billy Osburn built a hotel in Osburn to accommodate the visitors to the coming term of the District Court. His new establishment had 20 rooms and housed about 100 guests.

Wallace once again was undergoing its annual building program. Work started on the Holland Memorial Hospital at the west end of Cedar Street. Archdeacon Gunn of the Epriscopal Church was in charge of the building and it was to be operated by James Holbrook and his wife. By paying $1 per month a person could insure hospital care, medicine and medical attendance. It was the first hospital built in the South Fork drainage; but, plans were being drawn up for a second hospital even before the first was finished. It was to be built on East Bank Street by Dr. W. S. Sims, an ex-army surgeon and Dr. L. S. Watkins, from Louisville, Kentucky.

Wallace had then attained a population of 1,000 persons, and Cedar Street sported 10-foot plank sidewalks on both sides of the street for its entire length. Bank Street was soon to receive the same treatment.

The night shift at the Tiger Mine complained about the boarding house food, and they were promptly laid off. The next morning, on the sixth of May, the day shift refused to go to work until the other shift was rehired. The outcome of this labor trouble was never reported, but it is known that this first strike in the district lasted for more than five days. One way or another the matter was settled as the Tiger Mine was soon back working.

James Trembath, a Cornish miner, walked into the wood chute at the Poorman Mine and fell a distance of 200 feet; he was killed instantly. The mouth of the chute was level with the railroad tracks, and was used for the purpose of lowering timbers and laggings down to the lower levels. Trembath was said to have been under the influence of liquor.

Near Murray, George Ives cleaned up 8 ounces of gold or $128 from his hill claim overlooking that town. That cleanup was the result of two men's work for six days.

Upstream from Murray, near Sullivan on the Thompson Road, a discovery of galena ore was made. On May 10, news of this discovery leaked out and there was much excitement. The ledge had been stripped and shown for a distance of 2,000 feet, displaying three separate veins. The first locations were made by Cater and Darling. Others soon moved into that area. . . . It was noted that carbonate ore had been found in that area in 1884, but that everybody wanted gold in those days.

May came to an end with Mullan announcing that it was

building a race track on four acres of Web Leasure's ranch. It was to provide an area for recreation. Plans for a baseball diamond were included.

In the fall of 1889 there were only 4 phone subscribers in Wallace, and by June, 1890, there were 16. Phone rental was $6 per month, plus 25c per call.

June was a month of much activity. Six railroad lines were being built or planned in the district. The Northern Pacific was working on a line over the divide above Mullan; the Union Pacific was working in Canyon Creek and also up Nine Mile. The Wardner Line, the North Fork Line, and the Wallace-Sunset Line comprised the railroad projects. This was thirsty work, and Denver Shorty, also known as R. H. Bromley, provided the biggest beer hall in the Coeur d'Alenes. It was 25 by 70 and had a piano; before the end of June it was to have 16 light globes dangling from the ceiling.

Early in June, Charles Keikeritz was shot and killed at Kingston by Ed Harrington. The parties met in a saloon in Kingston and the deceased called Harrington a s - - o - b - - - -. Harrington said his mother was on her deathbed and he would not submit to the epithet. The deceased repeated the vile language and struck Harrington, who quickly drew his pistol and fired. The ball struck the deceased in the forehead, killing him almost instantly. Harrington proceeded to Wardner and gave himself up to the authorities and was later charged with murder. . . . The victim was well known in the district inasmuch as he had a short time before caused quite a stir by eloping with his bride on a handcar.

The electric lights were finally lit in Wallace on June 25. The power was obtained from a Humphry turbine water wheel.

The Custer, in its lower workings, hit a vein after drifting a little over 500 feet. The showing was about four feet of good ore. This was at a depth of about 600 feet from the surface, and was the deepest work thus far in the district. It prompted Aulbach to state:

"It proves that our ore veins go down and gives them an undefinable value."

Carl Mallon had the Coeur d'Alene soda and mineral water works going full blast. He had a large ice house with about 300 tons of ice, together with a fine bottling works. His cellar was dug into the mountainside.

The Wallace *Free Press* reported:

"A Swede named Mattson died in a fit at Kingston on June 10."

The newspapers did not pay the Swedes much respect, but at least it gave them a last name.

McMahon's New United Shows came to Wallace on June 18, and its chief attraction was Queen Jumbo, "the largest animal known to history"—$1 for adults and 50 cents for kids under 12. Eight hundred attended the matinee of the circus and 1,200 went to the evening show.

"The circus lived up to expectations, and the shell game did quite well."

The Poorman paid its 6th dividend in June. It was then selling for $1.05 per share in Butte. . . . the cable on the Morning tramway had broken again and no further attempt was made to repair it. A new cable was ordered from England and it would arrive sometime in July.

Reports were heard from the Nellie and Knickerbocker mines, just below Osburn, on the south side, to the effect that prospects looked good. The owners felt there was a good chance of the development of an extensive dry-ore belt from Big Creek to Placer Creek at Wallace. (Dry-ore is an argentiferous ore [containing silver] that does not contain enough lead within itself for smelting purposes.)

Tilley and Clough made a preliminary run from Wallace to Murray carrying a large load of passengers on their stagecoach. Joe Tilley of Wardner handled the lines. The firm had a contract for carrying the mail six times a week to Carbon, Delta and

Murray. They purchased a light thorough-braced coach, and stocked the line with the best horses available. The teams were changed at the station in Carbon. The road was very bad in spots, and the county commissioners stated the county had no funds available for the repair of the road.

From the nation's capital came the repoort that the House Committee on Indian Affairs had reported favorably on the bill to confirm the Coeur d'Alene Indian treaty, which ceded a part of the reservation to the government. It was expected that summer would pass before the anxious settlers could swarm into the lake region and make themselves comfortable for the winter. A week or so later some opposition to ratifying the treaty was heard. Some New England religious groups opposed the treaty on the ground that it was forced on the Indians to deprive them of their land. Some opposition was coming out of Spokane land speculators, who objected to the agreement because it provided 50 acres about Post Falls to a man named Post, who had lived on the ground for years with the consent of the Indians. The tribe desired that Post be given title to his land. A large number of settlers were still waiting on the borders of the reservation, and they were growing more disappointed by the day.

Very little prospecting had been done in the Placer Creek area before 1890, but at that time Corbin and McCormick were running a tunnel 2½ miles south of Wallace on the mountain east of Placer Creek. They called their claims the Spring Mountain, Iron Duke and Sarsfield. The tunnel went in 300 feet toward the ledge, when a cross drift started. They found high grade galena and some gray copper. J. Clayton Miller was hired to survey a road and to run a line for a water ditch. These properties were incorporated by D. C. Corbin, McCormick and others under the name of the North Idaho Mining Company. Aulbach stated that their locations were in line with the "dry ore" zone running from Big Creek to the Idaho-Montana divide. The Argentine mine, 3 miles west of Wallace, was located on this zone.

Aulbach also complained that large amounts of trout were

coming to the Wallace meat market, and he felt that they were being killed by giant powder or clubs. The latter method he attributed as a favorite one with the Italians on Prichard Creek. He called for more law enforcement in this regard.

In the June 28 edition of the *Wallace Free Press*, Aulbach announced that a complete newspaper plant was for sale for $400 cash, by the publisher of the paper. The article did not hint that it was the printing plant used for printing the *Wallace Free Press*. In any event, it seems that this issue was the last ever printed under that name. The next time Aulbach's name is found, he was editing a paper called the *Wallace Press*, in November, 1890.

Earlier, on the 14th of June, the Dunn Brothers, with W. H. Fortier, once again appeared on the Wallace scene as publishers of a paper. Their new product was called the *Coeur d'Alene Miner*. Perhaps the advent of this paper spelled the demise of Adam Aulbach for a short while. The Wallace citizens were not going to wait long to witness hard and bitter competition between Aulbach and the Dunn Brothers. Alfred J. Dunn was 28 years old, and his brother, J. L. Dunn, was 30 years old. Both had many business interests besides printing a newspaper.

The old Mullan wagon road was opened in June for travel to Missoula. Prospectors with their outfits were daily seen going through Wallace to the St. Regis country. It was predicted that much mineral would be found in that area.

The *Coeur d'Alene Miner* presented a rundown of all the business houses in Wallace in June, 1890. Among other things, the town could afford: 1 brewery, 28 saloons, 1 theater, 1 teacher, 1 preacher, 5 doctors and 10 lawyers, 1 bank, 1 drugstore, 8 restaurants, 2 lunch counters, 6 hotels and 3 lodging houses.

CHAPTER 18

JULY AND AUGUST — 1890

Late in the afternoon of July 1, the *Coeur d'Alene Miner* received a telegram from the *Spokane Review* advising that Idaho was going to become a state. Immediate arrangements were made for a big celebration. Forty-four shots of "giant powder" made up a salute from the hill overlooking the town. It was thought by the townspeople that Wyoming had been admitted as the 43rd state and Idaho the 44th. On the 3rd day of July, Idaho was officially admitted to the union as the 43rd state and a great celebration was held. The next day over 3,000 people celebrated the 4th of July in Wallace.

Without doubt, the crowd of over 3,000 that gathered at Wallace to celebrate statehood was the largest crowd thus far brought together in Idaho's Panhandle. The Northern Pacific ran excursion trains from Mullan, Burke, Gem and all the points east. Five carloads of people came out of Canyon Creek on the morning train, besides those traveling in other conveyances. A considerable number of citizens came over from the North Side.

The crowd gathered at the pavilion at about 10:00 a.m. The band played several selections and Judge A. E. Angel read, in clear and distinct tones, the Declaration of Independence.

The featured speaker of the day was Judge William H. Clagget, who recommended the local citizens learn the words of the Star Spangled Banner so they could do a better job in joining the ceremonies the next time. His speech was followed by that of Willis Sweet who thought it would be an equally good and appropriate idea

> "That we also learn the Lord's prayer, that we may join with the parson here."

The ceremonies at the pavilion were followed by various races and other sporting events. . . . At about 12:30 p.m., the crowd commenced to make its way to the river bank to witness the tub race. The next sporting event of the day was a scrub horse race, followed by foot racing for boys and men. Others participated in sack races, horse races, and shooting contests.

The most interesting event of the day was the blooded horse race, and three entries participated: Steamboat Charlie, Johnny Smoker, and Mullan Chief. The winner turned out to be Steamboat Charlie, who was awarded the race after being constantly crowded by Johnny Smoker.

A Grand Ball ended the day, and 300 people danced until the early hours of the morning. The events of the day were considered quite successful, and all the visitors to Wallace were satisfied with their trip. The amount of money collected from all sources totaled about $1,250, which did not quite meet the expenses of the day. . . . But all was not a total loss. The strawberry and ice cream stand, conducted by the ladies, netted nearly $100 for the new school house.

The mines were taking all of the attention of the people during this summer. Production was greater than ever. The Poorman Mill was using 15 or 16 cords of wood a day for power purposes, and part of its power was furnished by water. In the wintertime, when little water could be had at the Poorman, 25 cords of wood were used daily.

Bob Horn came to Wallace on the 10th of the month to complete arrangements which gave him sole control of the Lucky Friday Mine. He was going to continue work upon that property. Horn, a 40-year-old native of Maine, came to the district in September, 1883, and assisted Samuel Hayes in laying out "Hayes

City" in the gold fields. Soon a crowd of men came from the Black Hills country and insisted on changing the name to Eagle City, and their demand was met. Horn and his partner, Alf Brile of Spokane, sold the Golden Chest Claim in the Murray district very early during the rush, and Bob Horn moved to the south side of the district in 1885, where he helped lay out the area first to be known as "Jackass," then as "Milo," and lastly as Kellogg.

A. J. Prichard was active in the Nesmith Consolidated Mining Company, which handled his Evolution Lode Claim. Prichard himself was doing the greater part of the work and then had some 15 tons of galena ore on the dump. He claimed to have had two feet of concentrating ore in his workings. Mrs. A. J. Prichard was running a boarding house at the time at Gray's Landing on Pend Oreille Lake.

On July 24, the temperature climbed to 101° in Wallace, making it the hottest day in the history of the town until that time. It was more than the heat which caused Colonel Wallace to advertise his willingness to settle his claims on the townsite property with any property owners on an individual basis. He reported that he was leaving the town of Wallace permanently that summer. . . . Not much news had been heard on the townsite legal cases, but the remote rumblings out of Washington, D.C., indicated that a ruling adverse to Colonel Wallace was forthcoming.

The town of Wallace had come a long way since the Colonel had built his cabin there in 1884. A large portion of the land at the bottom of the gulch which was to be Wallace, was covered by a cedar swamp. Six years of hard work had gone into draining the swamp and cutting down large cedar trees. One by one the gigantic cedar stumps had to be removed so that the land could be cleared for building sites. Pioneers had come and risked all of their capital and effort to set up homes and business houses. Six years had brought the town from the swamp to a small metropolis of wooden frame buildings. The town had passed the log cabin stage and some of these buildings were three stories

high, and considering they were made out of wood, quite large.
. . . In the mineral field, six years had brought the people from
the crudest of mineral prospecting into the most modern methods
of mineral production. Governmentally, the Territory of Idaho
had grown into official statehood. . . . An axe was soon to fall.

On Sunday evening, at about 5:30, on July 27, a defective flue
in the Central Hotel, owned by O. E. Mattson, on North Sixth
Street, caught on fire. The flames were difficult to control in the
summer heat, and they traveled from that hotel in a northeast-
erly direction. A short time later, winds from Nine Mile Canyon
changed the fire's direction to southeasterly. The flames progressed in that direction until the entire business portion of Wallace had been destroyed. The loss was placed at half a million
dollars. Everything from the depot, near Sixth Street, and across
the town's business district and past the Carter House had
burned. A good portion of the residential area on the west end
of town escaped, however. In the newspaper's list of losses,
"20 dives" were set forth as having had a value of $8,000. No
further explanation was offered defining that term.

As the fire raced across the town, attempts were made to stop
its progress by dynamiting buildings. These efforts were unsuccessful, and later were to cause hard feelings between some of
the citizens involved.

Almost all towns in the American West have had major fires
as a part of their background. Wooden frame buildings and
poor fire protection made for such tragedies. The one striking
feature of Wallace's destruction by fire in 1890 was the attitude
of the town merchants. Before the flames were put out and before some of them had lost their buildings, the merchants were
running for the railroad yards to get to the boxcar that held the
telegraph key. There they wired for goods and items needed for
rebuilding a town not quite yet destroyed. No greater optimism
could be expressed under the circumstances.

The first issue of the *Coeur d'Alene Miner* after the fire consisted of a one-page edition printed on scorched paper. It re-

ported that many businesses were being conducted in tents while plans for rebuilding were made. Already it had been announced that the Carter House would be rebuilt. The Bank of Wallace re-opened in a tent, next to the vault which remained in the ruins of its former building.

Money, aid, and food were sent from Mullan and other neighboring towns into Wallace. Stacks of lumber were piled in the streets for building purposes even before all of the smoke had died down from the fire. Building material was not yet available to satisfy the town's demands. Many businesses were to occupy tents long into the coming winter for this reason. Meanwhile, the town council of Wallace met and passed a set of fire ordinances, attempting to prevent a future holocaust by requiring better building practices. With the rebuilding program, real estate values throughout the district jumped substantially. W. C. Human sold a 25-foot lot adjoining the Bank of Wallace for $2,200 cash. The fire had destroyed almost all of the downtown wiring from the electric plant, and it was announced that electric service would be restored by September 1.

The *Spokane Spokesman* carried a report that Wallace citizens completely lost their heads, and that whiskey barrels were rolled out into the street and 600 crazy men and women indulged recklessly in the liquor, until beastly drunk. The Dunn Brothers were incensed by this report and stated the actual facts were as follows:

"One party of about eight or ten men and one woman did secure a barrel of whiskey and roll it up the valley beyond the city limits, where they made a night of it. It is also true that some fifty men were drunk in the vicinity of the Northern Pacific Depot, but everything was orderly in the city proper, the *Spokesman* to the contrary. Our citizens are justly incensed at such exaggerated, not to say malicious statements, and the *Spokesman* has not advanced its interest in publishing them."

Most of August had been dedicated to the rebuilding program. Toward the end of the month, news arrived that Colonel Wallace had been beaten in his townsite case. The ruling cited the fact that he had received legal notice of the government's decision of January 24, 1887, declaring his holdings invalid and that he did not appeal within the statutory period. John Mullan served as one of his attorneys in this case.

CHAPTER 19

SEPTEMBER AND OCTOBER — 1890

The County Commissioners had failed to render any assistance toward building a new jail at Wallace. There were many disreputable characters about Wallace who would have been more at home behind bars, but Marshal Short said the only thing he could do was to give them a start down the track with the toe of his boot. He had been doing this almost daily. Sometimes the men returned and sometimes they did not. The newspaper reflected that if Wallace had a jail, these persons could be locked up at night and made to work on the street during the day time.

The Sheriff of Missoula County had recently raided and locked up nearly every saloon along the line of the Northern Pacific Railroad from the end of the track to the Idaho border. The saloons were located on railroad ground and harbored some of the hardest characters known in the west.

Along the Northern Pacific tracks above Mullan, at Pottsville, Andy Galbreth was killed in a knife fight. He had been known as Big Andy and his killer was known as Slim.

> "The effects of railroad pay day will be remembered in Mullan. Sunday was not the calm quiet day of rest it should have been. There were numerous fights with serious results, some shooting, and the life of one man was ended by a knife in the hands of another."

On that same day, in a row at Mullan, a man by the name of

Casey, who was an ex-sheriff in Colorado, was shot at two or three times, but not injured. . . . There were several hundred railroad laborers in the vicinity of Mullan employed by the Northern Pacific. Nearly all of them were transients and lived at the settlement known as Pottsville.

An Irishman by the name of Patrick Sullivan was killed when he fell 130 feet down a shaft in the Poorman Mine on September 3rd. It is interesting to note that the newspapers usually wrote up persons of the Irish origin in very respectful terms, and sometimes with a touch of humor or sentiment.

The rebuilding of Wallace in September was proceeding rapidly. The town had more business houses than ever before and the population was still increasing. The new buildings were superior to the old ones and no less than nine buildings were then under construction. The Carter House was being rebuilt on the same site as before, and it was a wooden frame building. The advent of colder weather encouraged many who were using tents to board and frame them up into comfortable quarters for the coming winter.

Just over the divide, at the head of Gorge Gulch above Burke, T. H. Harper made a discovery within a stone's throw of the trail leading from Burke to Murray. He found an outcrop of about 12 feet of white quartz and carbonized iron, with galena mixed all through it. He immediately located the Happy Day Mining claim. It was situated directly across the old trail, which had been traveled for years without anyone noticing a sign of mineral. An extension was also located called the Gray Eagle. The owners of the claims were T. H. Harper, Henry Day, and C. H. Reeves. Men and supplies were sent up early in September to start work on the claims. The mountain was extremely steep at the discovery point and depth would be gained very fast.

The Missoula County Sheriff was still having a tough time with bootleggers along the line of the Northern Pacific Railroad near the Idaho border. He had arrested many of them, but it did not stop the sale of liquor. One individual had been arrested three times and given bond each time, but kept on running a saloon at the same old stand. There was no law limiting the sale of whiskey on the Idaho side of the line. Just on the Idaho side of the border, on the top of the summit, was a saloon. This must have been one of Idaho's earliest efforts to attract tourists from outside of state.

The *Coeur d'Alene Miner* charged in a Republican editorial that there was no conflict between labor and capital in the Coeur d'Alenes, but that Democratic orators were trying to make the public believe so. It reported that miners were being paid $3.50 a day whether the mine was making a thousand dollars a day or was one hundred thousand dollars in the red. This newspaper was starting to declare its views on the subject of labor questions.

At the Morning Mine in Mullan, the new cable for the tramway had arrived. It was working well and brought a bucket of ore to the new mill every 35 seconds. In Kellogg, at the Bunker Hill, 275 men were working in mid-September, and it was announced that the payroll would grow to 400 men before the end of the month.

Meanwhile back in Wallace, the town needed a new graveyard. About 20 persons had been buried in the original one on Buena Vista Heights and it was getting full. Most of them had been killed either in mine accidents or snowslides.

Above Mullan, the railroad town of Pottsville had grown to sixteen or eighteen tents, shacks and cabins, which were occupied as saloons, gambling houses and dance houses, "with the usual run of women that frequent such places." Of the 30 or 35 thousand dollars paid each pay day, very little of it was left in the pockets of men who earned it. Fights were frequent and one man had been murdered on their last pay day and another had been injured.

Simon Healey reported that ore was exposed at a new low depth of 500 feet in the Poorman Mine. He declared:

"'That settles the future of the Coeur d'Alenes."

Miscellaneous news tidbits late in September included the announcement that the Holland Hospital was scheduled to open the first of October. The name of the Heller House was changed to Frankfurt House. The largest brick building in town, which was being erected by White and Bender, was to be finished by October 1. . . . Possibly the most important news of all was that 5 cent beer had come to Wallace. It was regretted that only one saloon was selling for that price so far.

One evening, late in September, James Brady and Patrick Driver were hired by the Democrats to go up on a hill north of Wallace and shoot "giant powder" in honor of Martin Maginnis, a prominent Montana Democrat, who was visiting the town. The two men had fired only a few shots, when moans of pain were heard. A railroad worker scurried up the mountain to investigate the sounds and found the two men covered with blood and their clothing hanging in shreds upon them. The cause of the explosion was unexplained and Driver was very seriously injured. However, both recovered and probably resolved never again to get so noisy in their politics.

The Wallace voting register books were closed on September 26 and showed a registration of 597 men who were American citizens; the oldest registered was 66 years and the youngest 21. The average age was about 36 years. Judge Angel took the trouble to analyze the register list. It showed 1 Austrian, 1 Bavarian, 27 Canadians, 3 Danes, 11 Englishmen, 1 Frenchman, 24 Germans, 2 Italians, 54 Irishmen, 5 Norwegians, 4 Nova Scotians, 4 from New Brunswick, 1 Prussian, 1 from Poland, 2 Russians, 6 Swedes, 4 Scots, 4 Swiss, and 2 Welsh as nationalities. Another table he prepared showed that the registrants represented 36 of the then existing 44 states in the Union. There was not a native son of Idaho recorded on the list.

In a registration list prepared at Eagle City for the 1884 election, it was interesting to note that one native son of Idaho was listed. His name was Courtney Meek, born in Idaho in 1838, the son of Joe Meek, the famous Mountain Man. The registration list also included the name of Wyatt Earp.

The citizens took their politics seriously. Of the 597 men registered at Wallace, 594 subsequently cast their votes. More than two thousand votes were cast throughout all of Shoshone County. The Wallace vote of 594 was the largest, and the next largest precinct was that in Wardner which cast 292 votes.

Among the subjects voted upon at the election was a proposal to move the county seat from Murray. Most of the interest shown was by the towns of Murray and Osburn. In the final returns for the county seat election, Wallace had received 711 votes, Murray 362, Gem 1 and Osburn had garnered 997. No city having received a majority vote, the courthouse remained at Murray.

In the last election, Shoshone County cast about one-eighth of the total vote of the state. Its vote was the largest, and Ada County was second, with Latah County third. Of the cities, Boise cast the most votes; Pocatello was second and Wallace third.

October saw the town of Coeur d'Alene suffering a big loss by fire. Nine business houses there were totally destroyed.

The *Coeur d'Alene Miner* announced that with the election over it would revert from a daily to a weekly paper. It was quite commonplace for small-town newspapers at that time to print daily shortly before elections so that they could offer their candidates greater support.

On October 4, the Union Pacific Railroad laid track down Hotel Street to a point near Sixth Street. The citizens in that area were quite angry and called a meeting for that evening. Nothing much was accomplished at their gathering, but afterwards a dozen of the most hostile left together. By midnight, they had torn the railroad track up. Nothing was done about it by the Union Pacific, which made no further attempts to put track into that area.

Wallace was growing to be a good sized town, but it still had some of the small-town problems. In the letters to the newspaper, a party complained that Pete Bernier's chickens were in the habit of drinking the water from the tank on the hill, which supplied the town with water for household use. It asked that this practice be stopped.

Colonel Wallace was denied the right to appeal to the Secretary of Interior on his townsite case. The case seemed hopeless for him. Late in October, Ediam's Mountain View Addition to Wallace was opened up for sale. This area did not base its title on any claim derived from Colonel Wallace.

Robert Short, the Wallace City Marshal, with the aid of several citizens, escorted 13 undesirables out of town in a group. These were not the first to leave, nor would they be the last. The *Spokane Review* stated that a year before, after the Spokane fire Spokane Police had evicted their bums toward Wallace, and now Wallace was returning the courtesy.

CHAPTER 20

NOVEMBER AND DECEMBER — 1890

Adam Aulbach was back in business again. The *Wallace Press* was his publication and it probably grew out of the *Wallace Free Press*. This gave Wallace two newspapers and time was to find them editorially opposed on both politics and their outlook on the labor-management questions.

The Morning Concentrator was to be enlarged from a capacity of 100 tons to 175 tons daily. This was at the same time that a union was being formed by the miners in Gem. Holly, Mason, Marks & Company finished their new building, which was 80 by 50 feet and two stories high. It had the only elevator in town and the building was purported to be absolutely fire proof. The walls on the first story were 22 inches thick and were built to be a part of a six story building if the need ever required it.

At this time Wallace had two theaters. One was the Gold Mine Theater, owned by B. H. Trout with H. W. Weaver as manager. The other theater was on Bank Street under the management of Tilton and Wilson, and bore the name of the Theater Comique.

By mid-November, the big news in Burke was the re-organization of the Miner's Union there. Thomas Doyle had been elected President with Hugh McGee as vice-president. It already had a membership of 130, which was entirely confined to Burke. It

109

was interesting to note that being an Irishman was a necessity for election in this union.

Eight to ten horses had been used in packing ore from the Mammoth Mine to a point on the railroad a mile below Burke. During November they shipped one carload from that mine which was expected to realize $2,000 above expenses. All their ore had to be sacked for shipment.

The *Coeur d'Alene Miner* included an ad for the Crazy Horse Hotel: "The only second class hotel in Wallace." . . . Meals were 25 cents and board and room for a week was $6.50. Beds per night went for 35 cents but one could rent a cot for 25 cents.

On November 16, in the presence of invited guests, O. B. Hardy, the principal owner of the Black Bear Mine on Canyon Creek, turned the water on the five-foot Pelton wheel, which powered the machinery of the Black Bear Concentrator. This was the sixth mill built on Canyon Creek. Manager G. B. Perelli watched, while his wife broke a bottle of wine that mingled with the water as it passed through the jigs. It was an unqualified success. The mill was to have a capacity of 150 tons of ore daily. An enormous sum for developing this mine had already been spent, but there was more than enough ore piled up on the dump to repay the investors.

In mid-November, the Miners' Union at Gem organized with a large membership. It was the third union in the district.

❈   ❈   ❈

On November 17, between four and five in the afternoon, six County prisoners made a dash for liberty from the county jail at Murray. They attacked Jailor Ives, bound and gagged him, and the escapees left him locked in one of the metal cells. They took two revolvers and $70 in money before leaving the jail. They stayed in jail until nearly dark and then went on the hillside back of the courthouse in Murray. This was too steep a hill for them and they came down and followed Main Street to the bridge, which they crossed and took the road to Delta, stopping to cut the telephone wire as they left. It took Ives about two hours after their escape to chew through his binding ropes and attract the attention of Murray citizens. A posse was quickly formed. William Tinker, Will Hooper, O. D. Jones and George W. Chapman offered their services.

The posse did not know which way the prisoners had gone, so the first two took off and followed the Thompson road while Jones and Chapman followed the road to Delta. When Chapman and Jones reached Delta they were informed that several men had passed there about thirty minutes before. After telephoning ahead to Beaver, Jones and Chapman kept on their way. When about 100 yards from Beaver, they saw some men in a field on their right, but they showed no signs of what they had seen and said nothing and rode onto the station. There they put their horses in stable and came back to the house where they notified the inmates to follow them. They went on to the foot of the grade leading to Osburn (via Two Mile gulch). There, Jones, Chapman and the people from the house hid themselves by the roadside.

In about five minutes, the six fugitives proceeded up the road to where the group was hidden. Three of the escapees were a little in advance of the others. When the first three were abreast of Jones and Chapman, they arose and covered them with the revolvers. By this time Mr. Clough and the Wallace stage driver had come up in the rear and brought the other three men under control. The prisoners were then marched back to the Beaver Hotel in columns of two's, where they were searched and put under strong guard.

During their flight they had thrown the stolen money away, but it was later recovered. Mr. Clough then went on to Murray and notified Sheriff Cunningham of the capture and the Sheriff went with two teams and brought the prisoners back to jail the next day. At the time of their capture, the prisoners were armed with two .44-caliber revolvers and a double barreled shotgun. The prisoners who had escaped were Nicholas Tulley, who was being held on a charge of Assault with Intent to Kill a woman in Wallace; Edward Smith, a highway robber; Thomas Ryan and John McEvoy, for grand larceny; Henry Goodman for highway robbery and Peter Snowball, who was being held for the murder of John Galbreth at Pottsville. It was necessary to file the bars on the cell at Murray in order to release Jailor Ives.

* * *

At the grand opening of the Theater Comique on Bank Street, on November 17, Doctor E. O. Smith was badly injured:

> "The Doctor was in the main auditorium admiring the beautiful legs on the stage. His attention was so riveted on the nimble performers with laughing eyes and heaving bosoms that he did not notice an aerial performer in the rafters ahead, who was trying to 'skin the cat' and do other tricks. Suddenly the elevated spectator who was giving a free exhibition, dropped. It didn't kill him. He escaped injury, but the doctor was taken home badly bruised. He didn't know what had struck him—whether it was a Democratic cyclone or the sandbag of a 'hobo' in the 'badlands.' The 'Doc' is recovering."

There was hardly standing room in the main floor and boxes. The main room had boards laid across the ceiling joists, from which the feet of many spectators intent on seeing the show dangled.

The Union Pacific track had been laid through the streets of Burke to the Poorman Concentrator. There had been much opposition to using a street, but after it had been done and the tracks were planked, the people seemed to be reconciled. About all the available room in the street was taken up by the two railroad companies. The Union Pacific track deprived the merchants of room for their woodpiles. This was a serious matter, but it was generally conceded that the track improved the appearance of the street. The Union Pacific started negotiating for a building site for its depot.

Colonel Fuller finished his three-story brick hotel on the north-west corner of Cedar and Sixth Streets in Wallace, and the building was wired throughout for electric lights.

The Coeur d'Alene National Bank building was finished at the end of November. It was a two-story brick building fronting 50 feet on Sixth Street and 75 feet on Bank Street. This building was later to serve as the Shoshone County Courthouse. The adjoining part of the building facing Sixth Street would be occupied by McNab and Livers Drugstore.

The first dance in Nine Mile was held at the Gibbons' Hotel on November 27. The town was then called Monarch (now Black Cloud). Not much time had passed since Nine Mile could boast of only two ladies, and those only at certain times of the year. In 1890, a dance would attract any number of men and more than a dozen ladies within a day's time. From a few log cabins, Monarch had grown to a thriving little town. When sleighing was good, the people of Monarch and Nine Mile could be sure that Wallace people would be there.

The Helena and Frisco Mining Company's concentrator had been enlarged to give the mill a daily capacity of two hundred tons. This was the largest capacity of any mill in the district and the mill was lighted by electricity.

Aulbach was soon to comment:

> "The mass of venison brought to this market during the past month seems to indicate that the royal bucks are still numerous in the mountains. But the way they are slaughtered for a few paltry dollars will soon thin them out. Some of the carcasses shipped here from Coeur d'Alene City have been enormous size."

By mid-December, the Bank of Wallace fell victim to the first run on a local bank. The bank, after having paid out some

$13,000.00 in currency and having failed to receive expected funds from Spokane, found it necessary to close the door. Charles Hussey was the principal owner of the bank. Peter Porter had been appointed receiver and took charge of the remaining resources of the bank. The run started after news of a difficulty of the Spokane National Bank came to Wallace. The Wallace Bank predicted it would probably reopen within a week in charge of a receiver. It was hoped and anticipated that no one would lose money in the transaction.

In December, some more townsite troubles occurred in Wallace. The Committee of Seven met at Jones and Harkness' law office on December 2, in the evening, to settle the trouble over four lots on East High Street claimed by Mrs. McFadden, a good looking young widow, and which were jumped by A. C. Crawford, a young man of pleasant appearance. The case had been heard three months before and the Committee decided in favor of Mrs. McFadden. However, Crawford refused to abide by the Committee's ruling, alleging that the members' minds were swayed by a chivalrous feeling and that the testimony was made secondary to the appealing eyes that looked longingly for a pleasant home and lovingly on the four lots on the hillside. Jack Dunn denied the soft impeachment, while a blush suffused his cheeks, even to the bare spot on the top of his head. After hearing testimony, the Committee declined to reverse its decision, and once again awarded the lots to the lady.

Early in December, a promising ore strike was made while assessment work was being done on the Hecla claim in Burke. That claim lay between the Oreornogo and the Poorman and was owned by Simon Healey, George W. Hardesty and others. Assays revealed $20 in silver and only a small amount in lead per ton.

"The Hecla at Burke . . . is a full-fledged lead prospect, with high grade silver ore tendencies. The vein is reported to be so well defined that hopes are entertained that a mine will be developed."

Aulbach's fight with the Dunn Brothers reached a white-hot stage. He wrote a front-page editorial, "The Lying Dunns," in which he stated that the Dunn Brothers had accused Adam Aulbach of selling himself and the editorial policy of his paper out to the Democratic Party for the sum of $300. The Dunns went on to say that the Democratic Party got the worst of the bargain. Aulbach denied this accusation and contended that instead he had been treated shamefully by the Democratic Central Committee of this county since his voluntary return to the "party of the people." Aulbach stated that his bill of two years ago for tickets, advertising, job work and hall rental against the committee amounted to $149.50. Not a cent of this was paid until the prior August when he received $75 on account, leaving a balance of $74.50 still due. Aulbach added that the "libelous Dunns" were too ignorant to discuss the issues of the campaign.

*   *   *

During mid-December a fire alarm was given at the Crazy Horse Hotel, and Henry Howes was among the first to leave the hose house for the purpose of towing the cart to the scene of the fire. When halfway to the fire, he fell by the wayside, and the cart passed over his legs, rendering him unfit for further active duty that day.

Henry E. Howes was a pioneer merchant in Wallace. Born on the Isle of Man in 1848, he was brought to the United States in 1849 after the death of his father. Howes was raised by Richard King in Ohio and grew up in the lumbering business. He and his partner, H. G. King, made their way westward in 1886. They made their home with Colonel Wallace, and their first venture was in a sawmill in Wallace. In June of 1886, Howes and King bought a stock of groceries and set up a grocery store in a log cabin. Howes later became a stockholder in the First National Bank. He married Elizabeth King, a sister of his partner.

In Burke, on December 12, S. S. Glidden closed the Tiger Mine and Mill because of trouble with the Miners' Union. He discharged his total payroll of about 75 men. One man, Robert

Jones, had refused to join the union, so the union asked the mine foreman, Parker Woodman, to fire Jones, and their request was refused. The union met on the 11th in the evening and resolved to give the foreman until the first train to get out of town. Woodman informed Glidden, who then ordered the mine closed, and ordered the pumps on the lower levels pulled. Woodman took the first train to Wallace. The president and secretary of the union were also on the train. . . . At the Poorman Mine, Simon Healey, the foreman, fired a miner who refused to join the union.

The labor trouble at the Tiger was brought to an end on the 13th. District Attorney O'Neill, informed the Burke Union President that the union did not have the power to exile anyone. Consequently, the union invited Woodman, the foreman, back to Burke and stated that he would be protected. The miner involved, Robert Jones, who had refused to join the union, left the district.

In Mullan, a miners' union was organized early in December. This was the fourth union in the district. The Mullan Union had 54 members with J. J. O'Brien, President and Frank Guthrie, Secretary.

During mid-December, plates in the crusher at the Poorman Mill cracked, causing a breakdown. This made it necessary to shut down the Poorman operations, putting nearly 150 men out of work. The shutdown lasted three or four weeks until new parts arrived and were installed. They could not be duplicated nearer than Chicago.

In December, the Gem Miners' Union announced they had purchased a building for $475 and they would convert it into their union hall. The Gem Union solicited Gem and Wallace merchants for funds with which to build their hall. They raised $200 at Wallace. The Gem Union met every Wednesday night and almost every miner in that area as well as in Nine Mile was a member.

The end of the year was to close with many activities and occurrences. Among these happenings was the reopening of the

Carter House on December 23. The lights were once again turned on in Wallace after great difficulty with the plant equipment. The lighting was superior to that in Spokane. There were between four and five hundred globes burning in Wallace, nearly all sixteen candle power. The lights were turned on at about 4:00 in the afternoon and they burned until 7:00 A.M. the next morning. None of the lights had their own switches, but instead, were all switched on and off at the electric plant.

On the 23rd, a celebration was held in Wallace's pavilion to mark the connection of Wallace and Missoula by the Northern Pacific Railroad. The last spike in the track was driven, and Miss Garrett Glidden, the ten-year-old daughter of S. S. Glidden, broke a bottle of champagne to commemorate the event, at a point about one mile west of the Montana line. This track put the Coeur d'Alenes 200 miles nearer the East, but the line would not be operated regularly until the following spring. J. R. Stephens, the Division Manager in charge of construction for the Northern Pacific Railroad in this area, was presented with a $450 watch by his crew.

A curious announcement appeared in the *Wallace Press:*

> "A grand opening ball will be given by Gracie Edwards at the Star, Corner Fifth & Pine Streets, Wallace, Tuesday evening, December 23, supper at 1:00 o'clock a.m. All are respectfully invited."

The end of the year had arrived, and Wallace was still in the throes of rebuilding after their tremendous fire of July. Some indications of labor difficulties had been seen throughout the year, but no real harm was felt as yet. The mines in the Coeur d'Alene district had an avenue to ship their ore to the East in a more direct manner. The year had brought failure to some of the Wallace banks and merchants, but in all it was one of progress. The town had its first brick building and was certainly rebuilding with an air of permanency.

CHAPTER 21

JANUARY AND FEBRUARY — 1891

The new year brought the opening of two new banks. The Miners' Exchange Bank of Wardner opened on the 2nd of January, and a week later the Coeur d'Alene Bank opened in Wallace, with its owners including Patrick Clark of Burke, and Finch and Campbell, of Wallace.

There was a strong move to make all the miners join the unions and some men did not desire this. The agitation became so marked at one of the mines in the district that quite a number of men were let off.

By this time, Pottsville, a village of 15 or 20 huts, the very active settlement of the prior fall, was nearly deserted, the railroad line had been finished and the construction crews had departed the area. It was said that the Coroner made frequent visits to Pottsville because of its "reckless diversions."

The Coeur d'Alene Railway Navigation Company launched a new steamer early in January. It was the fastest and largest on Coeur d'Alene Lake and Captain I. B. Sanburn broke a bottle of champagne in its honor. The new boat, named the *Coeur d'Alene*, was 140 feet long with a 26 foot beam, and six feet four inches deep. The steamer cost $30,000. It was built from Oregon fir and cedar and Idaho pine, and traveled between sixteen and eighteen miles per hour.

The Frisco property at Gem was under the management of A. M. Esler, a very outspoken gentleman from Montana. Aulbach chastised Esler for stating that he would shut down his Frisco Mine before he would pay shovelers and car men $3.50 per day as was being urged by the Gem Miners' Union.

By the end of 1890 the various miners' unions throughout the district had united in a Central Miners' Union, with headquarters in Wallace. Its first act as a Central Union was to look into the establishment of another hospital in Wallace. John Clark was the Secretary of the Central Union, and he was in communication with Mother Superior at the Spokane Hospital and Bishop Glorieux at Boise.

New buildings built since the fire in Wallace totaled in value about a quarter of a million dollars. Wallace was growing from a town into a city. Elsewhere the United States Postal Department announced that it was dropping "Falls" from the name of Spokane Falls.

The Poorman Mine received seven carloads of electrical equipment. It was the first shipment of electric works of its kind to the Northwest and probably the largest shipment of its type west of the Mississippi River. It was expected to save the company $30,000 a year in fuel and would be in all respects superior to the old methods of power. As the newspaper put it, the Poorman was to be "run by lightning."

The Committee of Seven was still active during January on questions growing out of the townsite trouble. They took under consideration the problem of a lot in the business district belonging to W. S. Haskins which was jumped during mid-January. The decisions of this Committee of Seven were well abided by and no record can be found of any appeals to the Courts of Idaho from the decisions made by the Committee of Seven.

* * *

During mid-January, two men were killed by gas at the Custer Mine. They were John Tackett and Jake Gordon, both under 30 years of age. On January 21, they were buried at Evergreen Cemetery (Buena Vista Heights). About the time the procession left Worstell's undertaking parlor, the Episcopal Church bell sent out its solemn toll.

Just as the mourners left the foot of the knoll, upon which the cemetery is located, J. M. Harris and O. J. Cooke shot Zacheus Lewis. Their fight took place on the bench on the opposite side of the canyon, within view of all the persons in the funeral procession.

Lewis wound up with four bullet holes in him. He was described as being no saint and had a reputation as an Indian fighter in the mountains. The dispute took place over who had prior claim to land. Harris had claimed the acre involved several years before and had built a fence around it. No house was ever built. Lewis contended that this made it locatable for actual residence and started to build a small frame house there. Harris was a young real estate dealer in Wallace.

In Wardner, Frank Hyatt killed Ed Harroun, known as "Arkansas" in a gunfight over a faro game, at Josh Collins' saloon. The coroner's jury returned a verdict of justifiable homicide, inasmuch as Harroun fired the first shot.

On the 19th, J. H. Smith, the Union Pacific contractor, came to Wallace with a grip full of money and paid out $13,000 to the Union Pacific laborers, most of whom were Italians. There had been joy in the Italian quarters all week.

Another lot in Wallace was jumped, and the prior occupant, Lee Ware, complained to the Committee of Seven. He said that he had not been able to rebuild a frame home since the fire. After deliberations the Committee of Seven announced its decision: at 10:00 A.M. on January 24, a group of citizens would place Lee Ware in possession of his property.

When the appointed time came for Ware to regain his land, over 100 citizens gathered and marched to the premises. There they put off the occupants who had refused to move earlier. . . . It was now the understanding that there were no vacant lots left in town for jumping, and that in the next case of lot jumping, the jumper would be asked to leave town permanently.

Colonel Stewart Fuller, who came to Murray in 1884, sold the Monarch Mine for $30,000 late in January. As a result most of his attention could be given to operation of the Fuller House. Freight rates on ore leaving the district were raised $2 per ton. The mine owners were not at all pleased as it meant up to $40 a car load more for freight and in some cases $100 a day to some of the mines, over and above what it cost them before.

February started with the town trustees taking steps to secure a patent for the Wallace Townsite. It was estimated that the cost would amount to about $3,000. $2,000 of this amount would go to their Washington attorney, Mr. Mathews, and the land would cost $2.50 an acre. The remainder of the costs were for incidental purposes. . . . Colonel Wallace's petition for certiorari on the townsite case was denied by the Secretary of Interior on January 31.

There had been a renewal of hostilities between A. M. Esler and the Miners' Union. Mr. Esler wanted to make a slight cut in wages, but the union objected. He then threatened to go to Western Montana and import miners, and attempted to do so. The Montana miners were informed of his purposes and would not cooperate with him. They told him that they were in sympathy with the Coeur d'Alene Miners and gave him some sage advice and advised him to move on further.

*　　*　　*

In February, 1891, Wallace had thirty places licensed for the sale of liquor and two gambling licenses were issued (P. J. Holohan and Northcutt & Co.). Wardner had 19 saloons, Murray, 5; Mullan, 15; Burke, 6; Gem, 5; Osburn, 3; McAulay, 4; Kellogg, 2; Eagle, 2; Delta, 1; and four more scheduled elsewhere in the county. Three of the liquor licenses in Wallace were sold to women who ran "saloons." They were Lottie Wilmington, Lizzie Williams and Grace Edwards. All five merchandise licenses which were sold in the Pierce City area were purchased by Chinamen.

The miners at the Morning Mine had been forced to wait some time for their money after the recent bank failure in Wallace, but they finally received their pay in mid-February.

It was the practice that if a union miner was killed or died, the union handled the funeral and the burial, but if a union man was also a member of a fraternal organization in the area, the union would step aside and allow his brethren to handle the arrangements.

❊   ❊   ❊

In its February 21 issue, the *Coeur d'Alene Miner* set forth an innocuous announcement which was to have great ramifications in the next few years:

"A meeting of the mine owners and mine managers of the Coeur d'Alene mining district was held at the town of Wallace, Idaho, February 16, at which every mine in the district was represented, and a Miner's Protective Association was organized for the purpose of mutual protection and taking such action jointly as may be for the best interest of all concerned."

No further comment was made in the paper.

It had been a fairly mild winter and while spring had not yet arrived, quite a number of miners were making plans to leave for the Seven Devil's Country in Southern Idaho soon. C. C. Eckert, Jim Wardner's ex-partner, left for North Carolina where he planned to engage in gold mining. Toward the end of February the icemen in the district were getting a little nervous. The winter had been too mild, and Carl Mallon reported the ice crop was a failure. He stated that he would buy an ice making machine for the coming season.

Until 1890 all milk for Wallace had to be imported from out of the district. Robert Neil established the Coeur d'Alene Dairy, two miles west of Wallace, during February, and he had 50 cows on his ranch.

❊   ❊   ❊

Colonel F. J. Heller made an emotional plea to the court in asking to be excused from jury duty. He was excused on the grounds that he had served in the same capacity every term of the Court since 1884. He stated that he would continue serving, but it caused him to leave his business from four to twelve weeks each time, and he could not afford it.

It was difficult to obtain jurymen for duty in Murray, because of the travel and prolonged stay that was necessary. On February 22, a number of the jury failed to respond and they were without valid excuses. Judge Holleman promptly fined each of them $40. It was a common practice to plead sickness at home or other excuse to avoid jury duty. Earlier in the month, while trying to secure a jury in the Snowball murder case, all the available jurors had been questioned and the deputy sheriff was ordered to get six more jurors. - - - The next morning the Judge was more than a little upset when he found that one of the six summoned was a boy under 21, two could not understand the English language, one was not a citizen, and one was "just a remove from the jim jams."

Another man, James Andrews, was killed at the Custer Mine in a blast. - - - The bill providing for a mine inspector passed by both houses of the legislature, but the bill was vetoed by the Governor.

The great mill for the Bunker Hill and Sullivan was to be ready to run late in March. The tramway was just about completed in February.

CHAPTER 22

MARCH — 1891

March opened with the Central Miners' Union advocating the building of a hospital in Wallace. The site had not yet been selected. On the 4th, William Ferriand was killed in a blast at the Custer Mine. He was the eleventh man killed in the past year at the Custer: six in snowslides, two gassed, one lacerated in the compressor room, one in a blast and this man.

The bill opening Indian land of the Coeur d'Alene tribe for settlement had passed both houses, and it was thought the President would have to issue a proclamation declaring this land open before settlers could take up homesteads. The "Boomers" were at hand, ready to take up the land as soon as word came from Washington. Beginning at the mouth of the St. Joe River and extending all the way to the Mission, men camped along the Union Pacific tracks, and there would be a lively scramble for land. It was anticipated that some trouble might arise over land disputes. The expected passage of the Indian Appropriation Bill would distribute more than $500,000 to the Coeur d'Alene Indians. This money and the opening of the Reservation were looked upon as the first blessings of statehood.

The town fathers were notified that the township in which Wallace was located must be surveyed before the General Land Office would act upon the application for a townsite patent.

A new boat was being built by the Northern Pacific on Coeur

d'Alene Lake. It was 162 feet long, 26 foot beam, and a depth
of hold of six feet. For want of a better name, she was tenta-
tively called "*Queen of the Lake.*" She would make the trip
from Coeur d'Alene to the Mission in six hours instead of the
prior time of ten hours. She had a gentleman's waiting room,
dining room, 16 state rooms, ladies' cabin, 24 by 30 feet and
even had an upright piano. The engine had 800 horsepower.

White and Bender were sending 100,000 pounds of goods to
the Murray Store by way of the Two Mile road from Osburn.
There was a clamor in Wallace for the building of a road over
Dobson Pass to Carbon and Murray. Such a road would make
Wallace the center for the Northside traffic, instead of Osburn.

The miners had a rule that no one, except those in charge of
the tramways, could ride in the buckets. On one of the coldest
days of the March cold snap, one of the miners at the Custer
wished to come to Wallace. By wagon road this was eight miles
of hard walking. The tramway took the straight route over the
mountain and gulch from the mine to the mill (2 miles) and
from the mill to Wallace the distance was four miles of easy
walking. The miner doubled himself up in one of the buckets
and took a firm grip on the iron rod and started the journey.
Sometimes the bucket was so near the ground it almost scraped
the surface of the deep snow. And again in crossing a draw it
would look down 150 feet.

Everything went well for fully two-thirds of the distance and
then the buckets began to go slower, and probably at the highest
elevation of the line, his particular bucket, with its load of human freight, came to a standstill. It stood midway between the
tall towers which supported it, 150 feet from the ground, for
more than four dreadful hours. The weather was cold and the
wind blew through his whiskers, but he was in it and all he could
do was keep his grip on the bucket. This he did and finally landed
at the mill a very cold man but not seriously injured. His name
was withheld to protect his job.

Some of the "Boomers" had entered the reservation land, but it was determined that they would have to leave and wait for the proclamation of the President. Some thought that six months might pass before the settlers could go upon the land. Troops from Fort Sherman were patrolling the area to make certain that no one made a premature entry.

The electric lights were finally turned on in Mullan, but Wardner still was without electricity. It was claimed that Wardner lacked an available water supply for that purpose.

On March 9th a snowslide took place at the Last Chance Mine in Wardner causing several thousand dollars damage. No one was killed, but the night shift had a narrow escape. The slide started several hundred feet above the mine, ore bins were swept away and the tramway damaged. At the same time a snowslide occurred on Canyon Creek. No one was hurt. The "up-train" on the narrow gauge had just passed.

At Murray, Snowball had been acquitted of murder as the state did not have much evidence against him. The charges of robbery and jailbreaking against him were dismissed before his trial.

In another case, Adolph Fisher, while being sentenced for grand larceny, asked the Judge to make his lawyer give him the $55 fee back. "I paid him to defend me and he ain't done it."

On March 17, 1891, St. Patrick's Day was observed throughout the district. In Wallace, Professor Bair and his band played Irish and American songs in the streets. In the evening, the Central Miners' Union gave a ball at Utley's Hall for the benefit of the proposed hospital. Two carloads of miners came down from Gem and Burke and the day was unmarked by a single unpleasant event, which spoke well of the Irish.

The Miners' Union claimed it would have 1,500 members by the first of June.

There was still some question as to whether a presidential proclamation was necessary to open the ceded lands of the Coeur d'Alene Indian Reservation, or whether the reservation was open to homesteaders from the moment the treaty was ratified by the President's signature on March 3. The "Boomers" kept waiting for their opportunity to claim land.

The building of the Bunker Hill tramway was finished during early March. It was known as a Bleichart tramway, of a German patent, manufactured by the Trenton Iron Company, of Trenton, New Jersey. E. W. Benner, of Oakland, California, was the builder of the tramway at Wardner. The tramway operated well, was extremely solid and traveled with scarcely a tremor or jar. It operated without loud or oppressive noises. By mid-March the tramway was daily transporting ore from the mine to the concentrator, and would continue to do so until the five thousand-ton ore bin was filled. The concentrator would be completed and put into operation about April 15.

The tramway was held aloft by 52 supports, the highest one being seated on a corner lot in the heart of Wardner, and was 89 feet, 6 inches high. Each support consisted of square sawed timbers, jointed and securely bolted, which rested upon a foundation of well framed heavy square timbers, which were also jointed and bolted. The tramway was 8,907 feet long. There were two cables, one called the standing and the other called the traction. The breaking strain of the traction cable was 21,000 pounds.

The cable contained 133 buckets which were placed at intervals of 135 feet. Each bucket had a carrying capacity of five cubic feet or 700 pounds. Timbers twelve feet long could be hauled in these buckets. The speed of the tramway was controlled by the brakeman at the brake station, and at the greatest speed the buckets went past that point every 35 to 40 seconds. At that rate, the tramway could transport 400 tons in ten hours, an amount sufficient to keep the concentrator running for 24 hours.

There were two prominent peaks over which the tramway was constructed, necessitating the building of "rail stations" to prevent the cable from cutting. These stations were 210 and 196 feet long. When the buckets reached the rail station, they ran off the standing cable and onto rails.

The company had timber hangers that could be run onto the line in case timbers longer than 12 feet were to be transported.

The brake station building was located in Wardner and was 35 feet high, 24 feet wide and 80 feet long. At each end and at the brake station, the main sheaves were eight feet in diameter, and the grooves were filled with rubber and leather packing to prevent wearing of the traction cable which revolved around the sheaves. In front of each main sheave stood a single sheave six feet in diameter, having a groove filled similarly. The cable played around these sheaves in the same manner as a chain on a chain block.

At both terminal points and brake station, the buckets left both cables and ran upon a track which was elevated about eight feet from the floor; and at any of these points, buckets could be taken off or on in a few seconds. If, for any reason, the attendants could not get them into position in time to catch the lug, the lug passed on without a bucket. The waiting bucket could then be placed on the next lug. The bins at both ends of the tramway had a capacity of five thousand tons each.

The new steamer being built on the Coeur d'Alene Lake for the Northern Pacific Railroad, was to be called the *Georgie Oakes*, after the daughter of President Oakes of the Northern Pacific Railroad. The steamer would be ready about May 1, and was scheduled to take the place of the *Coeur d'Alene*.

Mullan, Idaho, about 1890.

Wallace, Idaho, after the great fire of July 27, 1890.

First workings of the Bunker Hill Mine, showing original
outcrop and tramway.

Wardner Junction, about 1889, with its narrow-gauge railroad tracks in the foreground;
Kellogg in the center, and Wardner up Milo Gulch.

CHAPTER 23

APRIL — 1891

April started with the Central Miners' Union having received propositions for a hospital site from both the people of Wallace and Osburn. On the 8th of the month, an agreement was signed between the Union and the citizens of Wallace regarding the site for the Miners' Union hospital. Wallace agreed to donate the Union a tract of land near Canyon Creek. In addition, Wallace was to bring water for power purposes to the hospital site, and the townsmen were to furnish a temporary hospital building while the other one was being erected. The Union agreed to make permanent hospital headquarters in Wallace and to erect a suitable hospital building within the year. All agreed that the site was a beautiful one, being a bench with a perfectly smooth surface of several acres, with a gradual and increasing slope up the mountains.

Silver was priced at 98 cents per ounce and lead at $4.32 per hundred.

The Poorman property was being converted to electrical power. During April, it was being worked by steam power and the set up would allow for either steam or electrical power. Pat Clark, the manager, had been investigating electricity for more than a year. As wood was expensive, the cost of fuel for operating their machinery had been nearly one hundred dollars per day and sometimes the mill was forced to shut down because there was not sufficient wood at any price. This wood problem was aggravated by the snow blockades.

The Tiger Mine had been the first in Burke to ship ore. In 1887, the Tiger Company built a wagon road from Burke to Thompson Falls and ore was hauled out over this road. . . . In 1891 all ore was being lifted from the Tiger three hundred foot level by a small water wheel. F. R. Culbertson, the superintendent, stated that the ore was getting better at depth in his mine. The Tiger was prepared to hoist by steam power in case of a break down of the water wheel. They planned to install a new hoisting plant during the coming summer which would be capable of doing work until a depth of one thousand feet had been reached.

Secretary of the Interior Noble finally advised the local area that no proclamation would be necessary before entry could be made on the ceded Coeur d'Alene Indian lands. The northern section of the former reservation, which was opened to settlement, contained 300,000 acres, which could be entered into under the homestead act upon payment of $1.50 per acre, the first half of which must be paid within two years.

W. A. Dunn located 160 acres of land in Lane and he stated that nearly all of the land he located bordered on the Coeur d'Alene River. He added that in his opinion no more than 3 out of every 10 of the settlers then on the land would remain to prove up and obtain title to it. He felt that most were just squatting on the land so they could sell their claim to it.

The Indians endeavored to make some trouble with the new settlers, but no serious difficulties were anticipated. In various places, the Indians had made claims for their stock and for the considerable wire fence near the Mission. These improvements were not mentioned in the treaty because they were not considered to be of any value. But afterward the red men viewed them with big eyes. During early April, four Indians came up to the Mission bearing a letter from an Indian farmer named Gildy. Addressed to the settlers, it advised them to pay the Indians what they demanded for all the improvements on the occupied land. The settlers refused to pay anything saying the improvements had no value. But finally the settlers offered to pay $40. The Indians insisted $60 was a fair price for the wire fence, and the white men agreed to pay them that sum. But then another Indian demanded pay for his labor in building the fence, the settlers refused and all dealings ended.

The Indians were very angry and set fire to the grass along the river. Some of the settlers barely saved their tents and camp outfits. The Indians said that they would return to compel the settlers to pay or vacate. Mr. Dunn said that he was confident that someone was furnishing the Indians with whiskey and that was the real cause of the problem. He also reported quite a number of prospectors were on the ceded ground. Most of them were camped near Black Lake below Medicine Mountain. Reports were heard of good mineral discoveries being made, but they lacked confirmation.

The work at the Morning Mine and Mill ceased, pending a proposed sale to a syndicate headed by James Wardner. The Hunter Mine was not operating because of internal dissension.

*   *   *

A meeting was held in Murray protesting the bringing of Chinese miners into the north side. Apparently some mine owners on Prichard and Trail Gulches wanted to do so. Aulbach stated that there was no change in the district's sentiment toward the Chinese from that brought out at the 4th of July, 1886 meeting at Murray. It was then resolved that no Chinaman should be allowed to come to the north side. The same resolution to keep the Chinese out of the camp prevailed in 1891:

"No Chinamen are wanted in the Coeur d'Alene."

"There is not a placer mining camp on the Pacific Coast which has not been ruined on the advent of Chinamen. The white miners have got to emigrate when the pigtails put in their appearance. The leprous sons of the flowery kingdom are a blight in a mining camp."

The well attended meeting was short and to the point. Doctor J. A. Campbell, a resident since '83, called the meeting to order and made a strong speech in opposition to the importation of the "long-tail orangutans," as he called them. He related his experience with the Chinese in California. This was the third time the Chinese question had been protested by the miners of Murray and they were determined to protect themselves and their families against the "slave labor of the thieving Chinese."

❋   ❋   ❋

Early in April Union membership throughout the district was estimated at 600. It was agreed to assess each member $2.50 to create a fund for the purpose of setting up the hospital. This would be added to the $1,500.00 in the union treasury which also could be used for that purpose.

On the east side of Canyon Creek, almost in the town of Burke, was the Hecla property, owned by Patrick Clark, Simon Healey and George Hardesty. They drove a tunnel up the hill several months before and opened a body of ore. They then came down almost to the foot of the hill and started another tunnel to tap the ledge. They were in about 110 feet in April, 1891. In a short distance further they expected to find ore. The Hecla claim was adjacent to the Oreornogo. It was correctly predicted that these men were opening up a big property.

The Helena and Frisco Mining Company paid their dividend number 12 of $10,000.00 on April 5, making a total of $120,000 paid by them in the previous twelve months. The mine was developed by two tunnels; the lower one reached the vein at a depth of five hundred feet. A third tunnel was being driven and was in 608 feet. When it reached 1,000 feet, it would tap the vein at a depth of 800 feet. The mine and the 100-ton mill were owned by Helena people, and the principal owners were S. T. Hauser, A. M. Holter and John T. Murphy.

During the week preceding April 11th, the Morning miners received 10% of the back wages due them from the time of the Hussey bank closure. The entire amount of back wages due at the time of the bank failure was about $15,000. One hundred and fifty men were employed at the Bunker Hill, and this was to double before the end of the month.

The Hunter Mining Company at Mullan contracted with the Northern Pacific for four cars a day, which meant a shipment of at least 40 tons of concentrates of first-class ore each day. This would be a big addition to the ore output of the district. Billy Daxon and Will Harris were building in Gem; when finished they would start a saloon in the premises.

Thomas Doyle, President of the Burke Union, escaped injury in a cave-in at the Poorman on April 20. Charles Wright was killed a short time after the cave-in by a fall down the Poorman shaft.

The American House had been remodeled for use as the temporary Miners' Union hospital. It needed only papering to make it ready for occupancy and the furniture had been ordered. The Helena and Frisco Mining Company paid dividend number 14 on April 23. This was their third dividend in April and amounted to $30,000 in all, making $140,000 paid to date.

Rumors of mineral strikes had come from the Coeur d'Alene Indian reservation for several weeks. Several men were placer mining with some success in the mountains near Wolf Lodge.

The Odd Fellows Lodge and the Knights of Pythias purchased two acres of ground from John Clark in Nine Mile, about one mile north of Wallace, for burial purposes. They paid $20 an acre. It was expected that other groups would make arrangements for more land in the area.

Two years before, when the town was jumped, Henry Howes located two lots on Bank Street and sold them to J. M. Harris for 25 cents each. Harris held them for a few months and then sold them to John Cromie for $25. On April 23, Cromie sold the two lots, exclusive of improvements, for $1,800. This sale was made to John A. Finch, who planned a brick building having a 50-foot frontage on Bank Street between Fifth and Sixth Streets.

The April 25 issue of a Wallace paper carried the obituary

of William H. Otto, the first man to be buried in the Nine Mile cemetery. He was 28 years old at the time and died as a result of being kicked in the stomach by a horse.

The County Hospital with its ten patients was located in Osburn. Dr. I. H. Kelly invited the newspaper to inspect his facilities. The newspaper was not satisfied with its visit, but did not criticize the doctor. It said that he was doing the best job possible with his facilities and pay. The hospital consisted of seven tents. The first was his office, the next two were wards, then the cooking and dining room. Beyond this was a store room and then the doctor's home. Lastly, there was an operating room. The beds did not have the appearance of being changed and aired as frequently as necessary, but in all other respects the quarters seemed clean, comfortable and healthy as the circumstances permitted. The newspaper praised Doctor Kelly, who had been the county doctor for a year, and during that time he had only lost one county patient . . . "and that one was practically dead when brought to him."

A visitor coming up the Coeur d'Alene River late in April noticed over 47 new frame buildings completed or underway on the reservation land. They varied from shacks to fairly good buildings. Many more probably could not be seen from the boat, and the visitor stated that it appeared every foot of the ground had been located.

There were 475 lights burning in Wallace, and 156 more were ready to be lighted. Another 100 lights were in buildings wired for lighting.

On April 21, two petitions were submitted to the Wallace Board of Trustees. One dealt with the various hurdy gurdy houses and houses of ill fame which were being maintained on Cedar Street, the principal street in town. The other petition cited the Miner's Resort, or Milwaukee Beer Hall, as being a disorderly and disreputable house, stating that it should not be allowed to do business. Both of these petitions were tabled by the city fathers.

CHAPTER 24

MAY — 1891

Civilization was slowly creeping into the Coeur d'Alenes, whether it was desired or not. The Catholic Church in Mullan was completed except for the door and the windows, and it was being painted. In Wallace, J. M. Harris was selling pianos for 15% down and the balance in easy equal installments over a 24-month period.

The Dunn Brothers, in an editorial in their paper, took a strong stand on an old problem:

> "A boisterous dance hall in the business center of Wallace, with the rooms above occupied by women whose characters are too plainly apparent by every act and feature, and who frequently appear before the windows in indecent exhibits, to the disgust of respectable people in the community, is not conducive to a high moral standard."

Times were good. . . . Bunker Hill's new concentrator made its first shipment of seven carloads (140 tons). The Poorman had paid $275,000 in dividends to date, making it the biggest dividend payer in the district.

At a meeting of the Burke Union, a majority decided to pay $1 per month for the benefit of the Miners' Union Hospital in Wallace.

The Black Bear mine had a gushing stream of water running from its No. 2 tunnel during all seasons. Some ingenious fellow worked out a system whereby the stream was piped through a winze to tunnel No. 3, where the stream of water was directed to strike a small water wheel attached to a fan. The force was sufficient to send a needed blast of air through the air pipes to all parts of the mine.

The same mine was the scene of a new experiment with an electric drill. It was named after its inventor, M. H. Marvin, and did not strike as hard as an air drill, but struck much faster. The rate of striking for the electric drill was 600 times per minute, twice as fast as an air drill. The first experiment underground with an electric drill was conducted on May 1, and T. N. Barnard covered the event with his camera. The electric drill made 3 inches per minute in hard rock, and its inventor felt this could be improved to 4 or 5 inches.

The new Bunker Hill Concentrator was the largest in the world and was located 2 miles from Wardner. The building was 447 feet long, and 72 feet wide, with a height of about 5 stories. One hundred feet of space of the southern end was devoted to ore bins, and the remainder was the machinery department. The machinery was placed along the full length of the floor and arranged in two sets, so that by shutting down one set, the other was in effect. There were 28 jigs in the mill; 4 massive roller ore breakers, 14 by 36 inches; 6 round tables; 6 Frue Vanners; and 6 stalls for the concentrator, with a storage capacity of 800 tons. In the center of the spacious room, against the west wall, was a platform, from which 2 perpendicular shafts extended to the basement below, where two Leffel water wheels were located. Those wheels drove all the machinery in the mill.

From the platform, the power was turned off or on at will. It was almost entirely automatic and had a capacity for reducing 400 tons of crude ore every 24 hours. Running at its full capacity, it produced 80 tons of concentrates every day, or 2,400 tons per month. At the prices then prevailing, this production would yield about $200,000 per month.

The ore bins in the mill had a capacity of about 4,000 tons.

They were so arranged that the ore emptied itself into an endless row of sheet iron buckets and was carried to the crushers without any handling. The ore was not handled by hand after it left the mine.

The Union Pacific had a side track at the mill, and the cars were loaded in bulk direct from the platform. The water power system was one of the best on the Pacific Coast. The flume was about 2 miles long, and at the mill the flume was 8 feet wide and 7 feet high for 500 feet, making a giant reservoir. The water had a fall of 68 feet through a 4-foot pipe, which gradually tapered.

The mill superintendent was Robert Cheyne, the pioneer millman of the district. He was in charge of building the first mill for the Bunker Hill, and had reduced the first ore in this district. He came from Helena to Wardner. Cheyne stated that the cost of reducing silver-lead ore at the Bunker Hill had dropped in the past seven years from $2.00 per ton to 30 cents per ton. He was still a young man, but had followed mining in Africa, Russia, Germany, Australia, Asia and South America.

John Hayes Hammond (later the president of Bunker Hill) made a trip through the district in May, 1891. He was the mining inspector for the State of California. D. O. Mills, Silas McCormick and the Crockers had just bought large interests in the Bunker Hill. Hammond said Californians were just beginning to take an interest in the mines of the Coeur d'Alenes.

Silver was priced at 97 cents per ounce, and lead at $4.22 per hundred.

Aulbach reviewed the mid-May performance of a traveling troupe thusly:

"Trice's Louisiana Minstrels . . . gave a performance at Utley's Hall on Monday evening to a crowded house. Were we to be severe on the company, we would say the entertainment was rotten. There was scarcely a redeeming feature in the program, except to those who had never seen a minstrel performance. The kid was really the entire show, and without him the troupe would be like the play of Hamlet with Hamlet left out. . . . The gags were musty with age, and the singing, with the exception of the tenor, between a buzz saw and a steamboat caliope. Our people are liberal patrons of the stage, but they do not like to be imposed upon, and it would be well for the next bum company to provide themselves with heavy clothing and stand prepared to take a midnight walk down or up the track. Good companies are advised to come; others are invited to stay away."

On May 12, a strike started at the Black Bear mine. O. B. Hardy, the manager, had posted notices a few weeks before that all employees would be expected to board at the company's boarding house. The miners rebelled and a strike started. A number of mines had this requirement.

On May 9, the Miners' Union Hospital was temporarily set up in the American House building on east Bank Street. It consisted of one ward with 6 beds, and by mid-May had two patients. . . . The Holland Memorial Hospital charged $15 per week for board, nursing, medical attention and medicine. Miners insuring with this hospital could get all of these items for $1.00 per month.

There was a need for hospital services as well as for Wallace's two undertakers. Michael Cantry and Patrick Stack were killed in a blast in the Tiger on May 12. Two days earlier, John Gleason, an owner of the Formosa, was killed by rolling timbers near Gem, Patrick Kane died in a blast at the Granite Mine in Nine Mile.

The unions were solvent, and all members of the Mine Owners' Association agreed to protect the new union hospital by honoring wage deductions for the purposes of the hospital. All the major mines belonged to the Mine Owners' Association by that time, except for the Bunker Hill, which was opposed to the hospital being built in Wallace. The Wardner Union joined the hospital federation, and a proposition was made to the Central Miners' Union Trustees by which the hospital would pass into the hands of the Sisters of Charity. Sister Superior of the Spokane

Hospital was in the district on May 19, 1891, with a sister from Montreal to look over the proposed site of the permanent hospital.

On May 21, the *Georgie Oakes* made its first trip from Coeur d'Alene to the Mission. Stage fare between Wallace and Murray was reduced from $3.50 to $2.50.

The end of May saw the miners back at work at the Black Bear mine after their strike; however, the boarding house matter was not fully settled.

CHAPTER 25

JUNE, JULY AND AUGUST – 1891

Seven Italians had been hired at the Black Bear Mine, located a half mile above Gem. On June 4, a meeting was held of the Gem Miners' Union and immediately thereafter 400 union miners marched from Gem to the mine and called the Superintendent and the seven Italians out from underground. They all marched back to Gem to talk things over at the Miners' Union hall. All the union miners' demands were acceded to. The Miners' Union had no objection to Italians working in the mine provided they received miner's pay and joined the union. The company's policy that every employee board at the company boarding house was waived at this meeting. Some of the miners had gone on strike over the company's boarding house policy.

Late one evening in June, a Union Pacific car got away from the yards at Mullan. The track was in fine condition with a descending grade, and the car gained speed. It passed through Wallace about 10:00 p.m. and Captain Horton said it was going so fast that it took two men to see it—one to say, "Here she comes," and the other to say, "There she goes." The car came to a standstill near Kingston where the track was almost level for a considerable distance. The distance traveled was about 24 miles, and the car must have made the trip in less than 20 minutes.

Work began on a 200-ton concentrator for the Coeur d'Alene Mining and Concentrating Company which owned the Union Mine at Burke. It was located on a western extension of the

Tiger lead. The mill was located on the east side of Canyon Creek just above its mouth, and it would be the seventh concentrator in Canyon Creek. Finch and Campbell owned one-half of the Union Mine. They also were part owners in the Galena, Gem and Banner Mines.

The June 5 train brought two Catholic Sisters to Wallace, Sister Joseph and Sister Madelaine. Men representing the Miners' Union and the citizens group met with the two sisters at the Carter House to discuss the new hospital. Plans called for a three-story brick building to cost about $30,000.

Sister Joseph, formerly of the Sacred Heart Hospital of Spokane, was to have charge of the Miners' Union Hospital after the 1st of July, when it was to pass from the Unions' hands into those of the Sisters of Charity. Four Sisters were expected to arrive late in June to constitute the working corps. At that time the contractor would also arrive and start work on a temporary hospital on a portion of the new site. The wooden temporary facilities would be ready in about three months. After the completion of the main hospital, these temporary quarters were to be used as the laundry and a storeroom.

Elsewhere, the county hospital was moved from Osburn to Wardner by county physician I. H. Kelly.

The Killbuck Claim was the scene of a new mineral strike. W. P. George and Lee George, the owners, and H. Herrington were engaged in running a ditch to bring water for sluicing away the loose earth in order to find the ledge 200 or more feet below the prior discovery. When this was done, they began the summer work.

The Killbuck was located six years before in 1885 by accident, when Lee George was prospecting and sat down on an uprooted tree to rest. He picked up a piece of rock, broke it and found shiny galena. Wardner and Blossom took a lease on it and did considerable work, but apparently not in the proper place. About three years later, E. O. Cox leased the property and worked a number of men all winter. He made several shipments, with good returns, but failed to take out sufficient ore to pay for the entire work he had done. There was ore on every level, but it, was irregular. Since then nothing but the annual assessment work had been done.

The George boys went back to work upon the Killbuck, where the underbrush was dense, and hunting for the ledge was difficult. Less than 100 feet south of their original discovery, they found indications and a small amount of shoveling proved that they had struck the right place. By June 4, a tunnel was started and three sets of timber had been placed. The ledge was remarkably well defined. Between the walls the distance appeared about seven feet and the footwall was smooth and solid. The hanging wall was not so good as the other, but was coming in good shape. Near the center of the ledge, probably a little nearer the hanging wall, was a body of carbonate nearly two feet in thickness. No powder had been used thus far, as everything between the walls was decomposed lead matter, easily handled with picks.

They were just beginning to dump, and a fair proportion of this was marketable ore. The tunnel was near the top of the hill and this did not permit much depth. The George boys had turned down one opportunity to sell. The Pioneer Sampling Works was just a mile down the canyon from the mine, and located at the mouth of Lake Gulch. A good wagon road had been built to the mouth of Lake Gulch and connected with both the Union Pacific and Northern Pacific Railroads. This ledge appeared to be the same one that ran through the Maloney and Argentine Mines. The ore in the latter, however, was of a different character. (The Killbuck claim is a part of the modern day Galena Mine property.)

In June, at the Last Chance, the electric plant was completed and electric power was used for drilling. The drills struck from 400 to 1,000 strokes per minute and bore 18 inches into a quartzite formation in four minutes' time. They were mining in a body of ore containing wire silver and lead.

J. K. Clarke of Butte was President of the Poorman Mine, and he scheduled regular monthly dividends. Clarke described the Poorman workings:

> "We are now running the mill from the 400 level, producing about 200 tons of crude ore per day, which makes from 40 to 42 tons of concentrates per day, from which we get over $40 per ton at the present prices. Judging from its past record, we have from 15 to 18 months ore in sight, without doing any sinking or development work. We have all virgin ground from the 500 to the 400, and about two-thirds of the ground from the 400 to the 300 is still virgin. The 300 level is a short level, only 83 feet long, but it will take about five months to work it out. Besides this we have a good block of ground on 100 that we cannot take out at present on account of the water in the bed of the creek. There is a great deal of ore in the old level that will pay to work out in the future. We are running at a great disadvantage now on power. We are burning about 1,000 cords of wood per month, costing $4.50 per cord. We expect to do away with this as soon as we can get our electric plant completed."

June, 1891, saw the towns of Harrison and Medimont laid out on the land which was formerly a part of the Indian Reservation. Noah Kellogg was employed as a road overseer for the county. . . . A cleanup from the Mother Lode's five-stamp mill netted 51 pounds of gold, valued at about $13,000.

* * *

July came to the district and the people were engaged in their summertime occupations. Wardner boasted a fine baseball field on the bench overlooking the Union Pacific tracks. . . . Its only fault was that it was built on a slope.

At Burke, S. S. Glidden purchased a hoisting plant for his Tiger Mine which would work to a depth of 1,200 feet. It was so arranged that it could be operated by either steam or water. It could hoist 6,500 pounds at a speed of 500 feet per minute. The plant included a three-nozzle reversible Pelton wheel.

At Wardner, after the resumption of operations by the Bunker Hill, mines in that area were progressing faster. For about three miles in length upon the vein, at intervals of every fifty feet to one hundred feet, active operations were being pursued. There were 12 to 15 mines in various stages of development upon this vein.

At the Last Chance, a drift was extended into the hill and across ore-bearing ground, from what was considered the vein proper. The mineralization extended in all directions, and in places there were great caverns taken out of the earth 100 feet in extent. This was very rich ore, much of it so pure that it was sacked in the mine. Ore was said to be almost pure if it gave assays of 80% to 85% lead and the remaining 15% to 20% was sulphur and silver. The portion that was run through the mill made one ton of concentrates from every two or three tons of crude ore. The production at the Last Chance mine was limited by the capacity of its 60-ton mill.

The Stemwinder and Tyler mines were having equally good fortune on their properties. The Bunker Hill was nearly doubling the capacity of its mill.

The 4th of July was celebrated in grand style. A parade was held, which included three platoons of Union War veterans; thirteen guns were fired at sunrise and forty-four at sunset in Wallace to mark the great day. Speeches were made and many races were run.

One of the most interesting contests was the drilling match. Four teams were entered. It was held at the intersection of Cedar and Sixth Street in the broiling sun. A rope was stretched around the square to keep the crowd back from the two huge granite boulders. All of the contestants drilled in the same rock for a 15-minute period. Florence McCarty and Bill Ford were referees; A. B. Campbell was the Judge, with Alliene Case and Simon Healey as timekeepers.

Mike O'Neill and Tom Gaffney of the Tiger were the first drillers. They carefully arranged their drills and their start looked promising, but the drill stuck fast after 8 minutes of fine work. Another hole was started and all went well until time was called. Their first hole was 9½ inches, the second 9⅜, making a total of 18⅜ inches drilled.

John Riley and John Kempsey, of the Monarch, were the next to go. They drilled a single hole of 18 inches. They had bad luck with their drills. Tom Gaffney and Mike O'Neill again went to work as a third team but their positions were reversed. Gaffney was then the striker and O'Neill the drill turner. This time their drill got stuck and they made only 17¾ inches.

The last team was John Eston and Eban Corkish of the Granite Mine. They made favorable progress, but had started so close to another hole that they were forced to start again. They made 17⅜ inches.

O'Neill and Tom Gaffney were the winners. The granite was too hard for most of the drills which had been furnished to the contestants and some of them flattened out or broke in two. The prize was a $100 gold watch and $50 in cash. The contest showed that the turner of the drill had about as difficult a task as the wielder of the six-pound sledge.

Good sportsmanship at these 4th of July celebrations always predominated, or almost always. A fight did develop over a horse race which was to be run that day. Angus Sutherland tried to run in a "ringer" under the name of Potlatch, but the horse's real name was Smoothwire. Smoothwire had a fine record on all of the Northwest tracks, where he had been beaten only once. The other favorite in the race was a horse named Antelope. In any event, the race was never run. But the argument did not end as quickly. Follett and Harris sued Adam Aulbach and others for the $200 purse of the horse race which was never run. They claimed their horse, Antelope, was there and ready and willing to run. Apparently Aulbach's position was that of purseholder.

People from the surrounding towns came into Wallace for the celebration. Over a thousand dollars had been awarded in prizes. There were foot races for the children and men, and a dry hose race for the two hose companies in Wallace. Hose Company No. 1 got a stream of water running through their hose in 32 seconds.

At the celebration in Wardner, James Callahan, who had a contract on the Last Chance Mine, won the prize in the drilling contest by drilling a hole in solid granite of 20¼ inches in 15 minutes.

The Mammoth Mine, located on the divide between Canyon creek and Nine Mile, on the Canyon Creek side, was about 6 miles from Wallace. During July, 1891, twenty-five men were on the payroll and 2,000 sacks of ore were waiting to be loaded on the train. . . . The silver price was $1.01 per ounce, and lead was $4.45 per hundred.

*   *   *

If a woman wanted ice, she simply pinned a piece of white paper to her front door and the ice man would stop by. If a businessman wanted to send a box to any one of the various depots, he simply hung out a red, white or blue flag. Each color represented a different company and the appropriate express man would stop by and pick up the package.

On July 14, the County Commissioners honored the petition of Gem Citizens by appointing George A. Pettibone as Justice of the Peace. One year later he would be a fugitive from justice. Business was so good in Wallace that the Crazy Horse Hotel was once again enlarged, to a 100-foot front, three stories high. It had 52 rooms for guests besides cots for 30 in the attic.

The Swing Door Cabin no longer stood two miles west of Wallace. It was destroyed before 1891. It had been a landmark for the early pioneers in the area and more than one mineral location notice cited it as a monument. The Notice of Location for the Killbuck claim was one of those using the Swing Door Cabin as a point of reference. . . . The cabin got its name because its door was suspended from leather hinges attached to the top of the door, rather than on the side. When one went through the door he had to jump aside so as to prevent getting hit by it on a return swing.

In July, 1891, the mining companies at Wardner paid out a total of $125,000. Late in July, the temperature rose to 101 in the shade, making the 25th the hottest day of the year.

The Poorman shaft was down 500 feet and the ledge had been followed from it for a distance of 40 feet in each direction. Mr. Healey stated that the ore was better at that depth than above. The Poorman had 200 men on the payroll.

On the 21st of July, the miners at the Granite and Custer Mines in Nine Mile gulch struck to get $3.50 per day for the shovelers and car men. Two hundred men were out on strike and most of them were members of the Miners' Union at Gem or Burke. It was their desire that all men employed underground be paid $3.50 per day, which was the miner's wage at the time and consequently it effected only the carmen and shovelers, who were getting 50 cents less per day. Nearly all of the men were in Wallace on July 22 and the strike was the principal subject of conversation. It was feared that the strike would soon extend to the other mines. Everything was orderly thus far.

The Gem and Burke unions had given George B. McAulay, the manager of the Granite, and C. E. Porter, the manager of the Custer, nine days' notice of their intention to strike if the wages were not raised. The managers had ignored their ultimatum. Not a single man was left working underground in either mine.

During the prior winter the mines in Canyon Creek raised carmen and shovelers to $3.50 per shift, which was the wage paid by the Tiger from its start.

In Wardner, there was no indication of a strike. The $3.00 rate prevailed there and it was believed that that rate was fixed by the Wardner Union.

Mullan, Burke and Gem Unions worked strictly on the rules of the Butte Union, where the $3.50 rate prevailed.

The strike of the miners lasted one week. The Union had won. . . . The Mine Owners Association agreed on the 28th to pay all underground workers $3.50 per day. . . . The Granite reopened with a limited force and the Custer made arrangements to reopen within a short time.

The narrow-gauge between Wallace and Mullan would be eliminated by the advent of Northern Pacific's broad gauge. Regular trains started running August 1 between Wallace and Missoula. No narrow gauge ("chippy") trains ran to Mullan after July 23.

A Court case regarding land in the Wardner area was decided favorably in August for the Bunker Hill interests. John Hayes Hammond, President of the Bunker Hill, stated that they were concentrating 480 tons daily, with plans to raise that figure to 750 tons daily. They had plenty of water power flumed a distance of three miles from the South Fork of the Coeur d'Alene River.

"It is our intention to use a part of this power for electric drilling, as the experiment proves its success in other mines."

The Northern Pacific announced its freight rates from Wallace to eastern points, and they were from forty cents to sixty cents per hundred lower than rates from Spokane to the east. The narrow gauge from Wallace to Burke was to be widened immediately for wide gauge track.

It was predicted that these freight rates would have effect on future purchases from this area.

The Frisco paid two dividends during July, each amounting to $10,000.

The Shoshone County assessed valuation had grown from $32,000 in 1884 to an estimated two million dollars in 1891. The 1891 tax levy for state and county purposes was $3.55 per hundred dollars assessed valuation.

Two Union Pacific boxcars, loaded with 20 tons of concentrates each, from the Gem Mine, got away while being switched at Gem on the 2nd of August. Michael Mullan, brakeman, was on top of the rear car. He tried to put on the brakes but they did not hold. He then laid down flat on the top of the car. The two cars ran away and left the curve immediately east of Wallace. Mullan was thrown 75 feet through the air and died of his injuries three days later.

*   *   *

Two months before, during the middle of June, the Union at Wardner petitioned V. M. Clement, the manager of the Bunker Hill, that the arrangement for paying $1 per month for medical treatment without hospital facilities should stop and that the same money should be deducted from each man and paid toward sustaining the Miners' Union Hospital in Wallace. There were about 125 names on this petition. Clement's only answer was his offer that the Bunker Hill would donate land and lumber for a hospital in Kellogg to be open to all who paid $1 per month toward its upkeep. The rest of the expense would be borne by the other mines and merchants in the Kellogg area. Clement obviously did not want his money going to the Union Hospital in Wallace.

On August 4, notices were posted at the Bunker Hill to the effect that an election was to be held on the 6th by Bunker Hill and three choices were given:

1. To continue the present arrangement;
2. To build a hospital on company ground in Milo (Kellogg) and the company was to furnish lumber and ground and the union was to solicit funds for the expenses;
3. Exemption for hospital deduction upon signing contract with Bunker Hill releasing them from all liabilities for sickness or injury while on the payroll.

The election was held and the miners as a body refrained from voting. One hundred twenty-three other employees voted and 108 of them voted for the foregoing choice number two. As a result of this election, the following notice was posted by Bunker Hill:

"NOTICE TO EMPLOYEES . . . By the vote taken this day, the ticket headed 'Wardner Hospital' was carried by a majority of 93. Accordingly $1 per month will be retained from each employee's pay for the benefit of the Wardner Hospital. As previously notified, any and all employees who do not wish $1 per month retained for this purpose are not only at liberty, BUT ARE REQUESTED to call at the company's office for their time. . . V. M. Clement, Manager"

About an hour after this notice was posted at the entrance of the mine, the night shift quit in a body with the exception of four or five men, who were afterward brought out. This closed the mine in which about 300 men had been employed. The mill soon closed down and 65 more men were idle. Superintendent Jenkins said trouble could be foreseen for a long time.

The miners declared the Bunker Hill action was solely to break up their Central Union, and then be in a position to handle the local unions at their leisure. A Committee from the Central Union called upon Superintendent Jenkins and notified him that the men were striking for $3.50 per day for all underground employees. These men carried the title of candle bearers. Further, the men demanded the privilege of protecting the Miners' Union Hospital. The committee also stated that none of the company's departments could work until the union's demands were complied with. Manager Clement said nothing, but went to the Okanogan country for a week. Wardner was lively; yet quiet and orderly.

A week later the Bunker Hill strike continued, and no men were working at the mine. The Bunker Hill sent circulars all over the country asking for men to come there to work.

*   *   *

The Miner's Union Hospital had moved into its temporary quarters on the bench near the mouth of Canyon Creek. The newspaper carried a quarterly report of the Miners' Union Hospital which listed all the patients for the past three months, and their *ills* were set out in the article. The patients were treated for injuries suffered in the mines, "lead poisoning," "chills," "neu-

ralgia of the stomach," "congestion of the liver," and other disorders.

On the 13th of August, the Wardner Knights of Labor com-
mended the Miners' Union stand against the Bunker Hill and
offered their support. On the 18th, the Wardner Miners' Union
held an informal meeting and conducted two non-union men out
of Wardner canyon and across to Wardner Junction. The two
men had offered to work for $2 per day and they were taken
down Main Street on a rail.

On August 20, a notice stating that all underground men were
to be paid $3.50, and that the hospital deductions were to be
paid in accordance with each employee's desires, was posted at
the Emma and Last Chance Mine. The notices stated that these
terms would be guaranteed by the company. The strike had not
extended to that company, and this notice was considered to be
indicative of forthcoming action by the Bunker Hill.

The 21st brought the end to the strike at the Bunker Hill. It
had lasted two weeks. The terms of settlement were that all
candle bearers were to be paid $3.50 and that the hospital deduc-
tions were to be paid in accordance with each employee's desires.
No gum clothes (for wet work) were to be furnished by the company. Clement agreed in writing to rehire all old employees,
and that they would be given preference over any new men. By
the terms of the agreement no collection for medical insurance
was made if the miner gave a release to the company for injury
or illness while on the payroll.

*   *   *

Down at the reservation, each of the 426 members of the
Coeur d'Alene Indian Tribe was to receive about $1,100 as his
share of the money that the United States Government was to
pay for their lands near Coeur d'Alene Lake.

On August 19, four men were killed in a blast at the Black
Bear Mine. The mouth of the tunnel was blocked for twenty or
twenty-five feet. The men were not hurt in the blast, but died
of gas during the five hours it took to dig to them. Two hundred

and twenty-five pounds of "giant powder" had exploded underground, causing the tunnel to cave in and imprison these men.

The Mammoth Mine shipped $10,000 worth of ore realizing $90 per ton, and $5,000 was paid out by them on the 10th in dividends. District Attorney O'Neill got the bulk of this, being the principal owner of the mine. The last cleanup of the Spokane Hydraulic Mining Company, of which Jesse Coulter was the manager, amounted to $11,000 for a 40-day run.

Seven tons of Jo Dandy quartz were run through the Treasure Box arastra a few days before and netted $8 per ton. The quartz was free milling, the purest on the northside. Thirty tons were to be run through the Mother Lode Mill in a crude state. Twenty-two men were employed at the Golden Chest Mine and Mill. At the Golden King Mill, below Murray, eight men were employed by the Ward Brothers. The Mother Lode then employed fifteen men at the mine and mill. The Mother Lode property turned out a bar of gold as a result of seven days' work, having a value of $1,800. . . . The gold properties on the north side were operating on a small scale, and all of them seemed to be doing well. Grinding of the ore by arastras was very common.

By August of 1891 there were 91 miles of railroad tracks, exclusive of side tracks, situated in the county. Forty miles of these tracks were operated by the Union Pacific and the remainder by the Northern Pacific. In addition, the Northern Pacific had graded five miles up Nine Mile and planned to lay tracks there. The first freight came over the Northern Pacific line from Missoula to Wallace.

Three hundred and seventy businessmen from Helena and Missoula visited Wallace on a Northern Pacific excursion during the middle of July. When they visited the mines they saw A. M. Esler's big canvas sign on the Frisco Mill:

"Under Cleveland	Silver	$ .92
	Lead	$3.60
Under Harrison	Silver	$1.19
	Lead	$5.10"

The Montana men were fascinated by crap shooting which was not done in their state. It was "all the go" in the Coeur d'Alenes, and puzzled some of the visitors very much. Apparently, the trip by the Montanans into the district was too much for the county government. The commissioners demanded that the sheriff either collect a license for the crap games or close them up.

Late in August, it was estimated that 330 tons of concentrates were shipped daily from the mines in the Coeur d'Alenes. The Bunker Hill was shipping 75 tons; the Poorman, 40 tons; Helena and Frisco, 30 tons; and they were the largest shippers. It added up to yearly production of $10,000,000.

Some of the merchants built an Ore Pyramid at the corner of Bank and Sixth Streets. The ore came from the various mines in the district. The best sample in the pile was from the Black Cloud Mine and it contained 60 ounces of silver per ton and 70% lead.

About August 20, Edward Young was shot and killed by his ex-partner in the saloon business, William Doherty. The shooting occurred in Burke. Both Doherty and his victim were brought to Wallace by train and Doherty was taken by a deputy sheriff to the Hanley House for a drink before going to Justice of the Peace Angel and then to jail. Aulbach said all prisoners in the Coeur d'Alenes were allowed to brace up with whiskey before facing a judge. Rumor said that Young was Doherty's fifth victim. Doherty was later sentenced to 12 years in the state prison for second degree murder.

During a one month period, $13,776 in gold was mined at the Mother Lode Mine at Murray. This meant a dividend of about $8,000 to the owners as the expenses of this company were less than $5,000 per month.

In August, Campbell and Finch paid the last $23,000 on the purchase price of the Standard and Banner Mines and for two-thirds interest of the Sullivan Fraction in Canyon Creek.

The Central Union made a demand on the Custer Mine during the last week in August, to retain $5 from each underground non-union employee as an initiation fee into the union. The company agreed to do so with the consent of the men. It appeared that another strike was averted.

CHAPTER 26

SEPTEMBER — 1891

Fall came to the district and found the Bunker Hill shut down again and 400 men were out of work. The reason was that it had water trouble with the Emma and Last Chance companies. This caused Aulbach to comment:

> "There seems to be a weakness now on the part of Bunker Hill and Sullivan Company to shut down at the slightest provocation, and the company's movements are puzzling the oldest inhabitants. The Bunker Hill and Sullivan is such a big company that little things ought not to trouble it."

The mines in Canyon Creek were putting out a payroll of about $60,000 per month, and the Wardner area was paying the same. The Mullan mines paid out about $10,000 monthly. The Union mill, with a 250-ton capacity, was scheduled to start up on October 15. Another miner, Martin Quinn, was killed in a fall at the Union Mine.

The White and Bender Company incorporated. Harry White was the general manager; John A. Finch, president; Patrick Clarke, vice-president; Charles E. Bender, secretary-treasurer. They proposed to carry a general merchandise stock to the value of $100,000, and would maintain stores in Wallace, Gem and Burke. They had closed their Murray store. In Wallace and Burke they had brick buildings, and in Gem they had a stone building. Amasa Campbell, George W. Hardesty, and Simon Healey were also financially interested in this firm.

Enthusiasm was slowly growing for the prospects of the Hecla claim near Burke. It was reported to have a strong 6 or 7-foot vein of good ore in the prospecting tunnel. Work there was continuing. In Wardner, the Bunker Hill resumed work in the middle of September. The Stemwinder mine had its new tramway working and was expected to resume work shortly.

On the 18th, two locomotives and six coaches and a baggage car pulled out of Wallace, bearing 350 local citizens bound for an excursion to Helena. The town band made the trip, which was primarily a businessman's excursion. The railroad and the great state of Montana were trying to tempt business in their direction. The Northern Pacific did not charge the local men any fares for this trip. The railroad also sold excursion tickets at very reduced prices for a trip to Spokane, at any time between the 22nd and 27th. The main attraction there would be Sarah Bernhardt, who was to perform on the 23rd and 24th.

Trowbridge and Nelson, the local brickmakers, had already sold every brick they had made during the summer of 1891 at $7 per thousand. Their production totaled about 400,000 bricks. Aulbach bought 75,000 of these bricks for his building, and the White and Bender building took about 150,000. The Providence Hospital took the remainder of the brickyard's supply. . . . A two-story brick building cost about $4,000 to $4,500 to construct in 1891. - - - Carl Trowbridge said he could have sold another 200,000 bricks if he had them.

The original townsite cases were 13 legal actions in which the Wallace Townsite Company had sued 13 Wallace citizens $1,000 each for "jumping" land which the company claimed it owned. These cases were started 2½ years before. They came up for trial at Rathdrum in September '91, and there was no appearance by Colonel Wallace or any other representatives of the townsite company. The cases were then dismissed. . . . These dismissals ended the Wallace townsite litigation in the state courts.

Work on the Miner's Union Hospital had been delayed for lack of building materials. The newspaper referred to it for the first time as the "Sisters' Hospital."

Late in September, the Wardner Union and the Bunker Hill signed an agreement in settlement of a labor dispute there. It provided $1 per month was to be collected for the union hospital fund. The Union agreed to furnish a resident physician. The Central Union "hereby guarantees to protect all the company's property, its agents and officers from any acts or demonstrations of violence, or threats from individuals or bodies of its members." The need for this last provision was not clearly spelled out in the newspaper reports, but it certainly must have been drawn up to meet a demand by the company.

The agreement further provided:

> "The company is not opposed to the Miners' Union nor to union men, but distinctly reserves the right to employ or discharge whomsoever it pleases. It will accept orders given in favor of the Miners' Union for initiation fee, providing the person giving the order has that much to his credit, but the company is not to be made a party to forcing the men to join the union. The company will neither discharge nor protect men for refusing to join the union, this being a matter that does not concern it in any way, and in which it will take no action whatever."

CHAPTER 27

OCTOBER, NOVEMBER AND DECEMBER
1891

The month of October started off in a violent manner. On the first day, Dave Grant, a shiftboss at the Gem Mine, fired Charles H. Stowe. On the next day, Stowe showed up to go to work and an argument soon followed between he and Grant. It ended in a quick manner. . . . Stowe stabbed Grant to death with a miner's candletstick, after Grant refused to give him a candle so Stowe could go on shift. Jobs must have been pretty hard to get. . . . A jury acquitted Stowe a month later.

In Wardner, B. Presley purchased a hearse for $700. It was the first such vehicle in the district. Up until this time a spring wagon had been adequate.

Ed Perraton, manager of the Crazy Horse Hotel in Wallace, created a free employment office in his hotel. He invited employers throughout the district to submit their labor needs to him, and there would be no charge for his services.

The Dunn Brothers complained that Wallace was becoming a regular dumping ground for everybody within two or three hundred miles, who lived on public charities. Half a dozen of these cases had been conspicuous during October. Among the latest was an insane woman shipped into Wallace from the Palouse area. A subscription was raised, and she was shipped back to Tekoa.

J. S. Dodson advertised that he would collect horses from all over the Coeur d'Alene district for the purpose of taking them to winter quarters about 15 miles south of Cheney. He had used that place for the prior three years, and the stock always returned in good shape in the spring. He charged $12 per horse for his service. Advertisements on this subject had been published during the prior few years. Sutherland and White also provided a similar service. . . . It is pretty tough country when they have to take the horses out during the winter. The reader might reflect on the thought that no Indian had ever found it to his choosing to live in the district now occupied by the mines of the Coeur d'Alene.

*   *   *

On the 3rd of October, Lulu Dumont drove a stiletto into Frankie Dunbar seven times. Frankie was a girl of eighteen years. Both women were of the "fallen sisterhood" located on Pine Street, and they had been fighting over money. The wounds were not fatal, and Lulu was not to be found. It was rumored that a fireman had stowed Lulu away on his tender and had taken her to Montana. Aulbach was to say: "Lulu Dumont is still missing, and the chances of her capture are slim."

*   *   *

The town fathers of Wallace levied a one per-cent tax for the year. It was to provide ample funds for the governing body and to pay the town's debts. More than half of the debts were for the fire hose purchased shortly after the fire.

The *Spokane Chronicle* published a story on the history of the district. It stated John Carten located the Tiger claim and sold it to John M. Burke for $35,000 before $100 worth of work had been done on it. It was the first sale of mineral land in the South Fork area.

The town of Moscow had a system of fines which had assumed the shape of licenses. They were being imposed in Moscow on houses of ill fame. Unless a fine of $10 per month was paid, the gals were to be arrested and processed accordingly. The first collection by the town marshal netted $130 and one refusal.

In Burke, Johnny Burns bit off the nose of a man named Lafferty during a misunderstanding. Burns had been with the Poorman for the prior two years, and it was said that his friends were hiding him out from the law. No record of his subsequent arrest can be found.

At the Poorman, Patrick Foley had been blinded in a blast several months before. His friends deemed it best that he be with his own people, so they gathered a fund of several hundred dollars for his travel. Foley left for Mohill, Ireland, on the 14th of the month.

* * *

"Old Baldy," a pioneer pack horse for Howes and King, met his demise at the Sixth Street crossing in Wallace. His successor, the Iron Horse of the Union Pacific, was unable to stop to allow the horse to cross the tracks. "Old Baldy" had been used four years and averaged a trip a day, carrying about 250 pounds per trip. He carried ore cars, stoves, turn sheet, track iron, giant powder and other supplies to the miners. It was calculated that he had carried 365,000 pounds over those rough mountain trails. "Old Baldy" could never be replaced and his loss was to be keenly felt by his owners.

The Crown Point-Eureka Mine on Government Gulch was optioned to Clarence Cunningham for a period of twelve months for $30,000, on condition that he do the development work. The property had a tragic history. After the original location of the Crown Point by Larry O'Neill in '86, it was relocated by John Caldwell on the basis that no discovery had been made earlier. In an attempt to regain possession, the O'Neill party lost one man, Jack McAuley, who was shot in a pitched battle. A. B. Campbell was also shot through the shoulder, and lingered several days on the verge of death. He finally recovered and went to live in Oregon. An armistice was agreed to after that affair. But the next summer, Lew Robertson, one of the Caldwell party, was shot and killed in Wardner. In order to obtain this option, it was necessary to settle with all these conflicting interests.

Left: Hand tramming in a small mine. Note the candles held by the miners and the 4-way turn sheet in the foreground. *Right:* Hydraulic operations at the Arizona Placer Mine in Dream Gulch, near Murray, Idaho.

Very early scene of a miner in the "cage," preparing to go down the shaft. Note the miners' candlesticks.

Left: Frisco Mill in Gem, Idaho, before the explosion on July 11, 1892.
Right: Frisco Mill after the explosion.

Soldiers camped near Carter Hotel in Wallace in July, 1892.

By October, 1891, the channel of the South Fork was cleared and lowered four feet from the Sixth Street bridge to below the railroad yards. This gave Wallace better drainage and reduced the high water danger. The town was not to be a swamp forever.

The Gem Miners' Union had grown from fourteen members to 580 in one year. It owned its own union hall and did not owe any money.

One of its newest members was a man called C. Leon Allison, who arrived in the district about September 5. He was employed at the Gem Mine and had joined the Union two weeks after his arrival. Time was to prove that his real name was Charles Siringo, but that is getting ahead of the story.

In Moscow, the people were building the State University Building and a building to be known as the Moscow Hotel. The *Moscow Star* reported that school children of that town were increasing at an "alarming rate." Culture was hitting the Palouse, and Moscow took the opportunity to drive out its hobos and "nocturnal ladies."

Aulbach's *Wallace Press* moved into its new building on Bank Street late in October. It was the first building west of the White and Bender building, and had two rooms on the first floor. The front room was occupied by Charles F. Easton's jewelry store, and the rear room was the quarters for the *Wallace Press*. Its presses could turn out ten to fifteen thousand impressions daily and were run by water power furnished from the mountain stream in back of the building (thereby giving the name of Printer's Creek to the stream flowing down the mountain south of Wallace).

The second floor was to be a Masonic Hall and included one big room and several smaller ones. Adam Aulbach could not resist the temptation to call attention to the fact that not only did his building have electric lights, but each and every light had its own switch. This made it unnecessary to wait for the operator at the electric plant to turn off the lights all over town.

Two types of electric service were then available: the first was for all night lighting, and the other provided lighting only until eleven p.m.

The Masons had had a charter for quite some time, but they were not active until their hall was ready. Their paraphernalia was at the Northern Pacific Depot, and they were going to move into the new hall early in November.

* * *

At about this time Colonel W. R. Wallace severed his connections with the town he had founded. He had lost his townsite battle. . . . A decade later, in November, 1901, a Whittier, California, newspaper carried the Colonel's obituary. The report stated that Colonel Wallace and his wife lived at Preston, Arizona, and had only recently arrived in Whittier. He was survived by his wife and three adult children. There was no mention of his founding the Town of Wallace in his obituary; instead he was referred to as a prominent mining man and as a cousin of General Lew Wallace, the author of *Ben Hur*.

November, 1891, started off with bloodshed . . . R. A. Cunningham shot Gus Adams in a drunken gunfight at Burke on the 2nd. They were partners in a Burke eatery, and the reason for their fight was not known. . . . The citizens chased Cunningham and finally shot him before they were able to capture him. Both men were taken to the hospital.

At the Last Chance Mine, three men were badly mangled in a blast. Dan McLane died of his injuries. The blast had been set off by one of the men who had been making a hole in the caps for the fuse, with his candlestick. . . . Elsewhere in the district, two more men were killed in mining accidents during the prior 30 days.

At the Hunter Mine near Mullan, the miners went on strike on the 2nd. They were dissatisfied with the bill of fare at the company boarding house. They marched down to Mullan, and as the group started their march, one man intended to hold out from joining the crowd. He was ridiculed and jeered at by one of the miners, until he became angry and pulled a large knife with which to defend himself in case of trouble. This came near provoking a general row, and several knives were drawn, but conservative men interfered and prevented bloodshed. . . . The strike was settled the next day and everyone returned to work.

At the Mother Lode, Mr. Wilsey pounded up a powder box full of quartz specimens taken from his property. He ran the results into a bar of gold which weighed 11¼ ounces, or about $184 in coin.

Work was resumed at the Polaris mine below Osburn. This mine had produced some of the richest ore ever taken out of the district, but unfortunate partnership trouble caused a stoppage of work in 1889. W. B. Heyburn had obtained an option and commenced pumping the water from the shaft. A good wagon road led to the mine from the railroad. About 25 tons of ore were on the dump which would net $250 per ton. . . . Weldon B. Heyburn, a 39-year-old native of Pennsylvania, had been admitted to the practice of law in 1876. He was one of the earliest to arrive in the Coeur d'Alenes in 1883 and was very active in politics. He served as a delegate to four national Republican conventions and later was elected to two terms in the United States Senate from Idaho.

A grave of an unidentified man was found near the railroad yards west of Wallace, and a mystery enveloped the town. It was soon learned the body was that of a pauper who died in August at the hospital. Ward, the undertaker, was refused admittance to the graveyard for the purpose of burying this man, in the absence of authority from one of the societies which owned the cemetery land. Thereupon Ward resorted to "self help" to get rid of the body.

The big news in the saloon circuit involved a $3,000 pot in a draw poker game at the Shoshone Saloon in Wallace. The pot was opened by three nines, and the next hand held four clubs; the third player called with two pairs, and the last caller held only one ace. . . . They all drew cards, and the hand with the three nines did not improve. The "four flush" hand drew another club, and the two pair filled into a full house by drawing a king. The four-card draw to an ace hit three more aces. The betting continued until all the loose money on lower Sixth Street was on the table.

The Catholic Bishop of Idaho assigned Rev. R. Keyzer, a young Hollander to Wallace. He was to give Catholic services on alternate Sundays at Wardner, Wallace, Mullan, Burke and Murray. Father Keyzer immediately secured the American Hotel building in Wallace for temporary use and held the first service there on Sunday, November 22.

The mining district was getting old, and more time was elapsing between the various "firsts" for this thing or that. The first weddings, births, deaths, etc., were now history. But the district was yet to have its first train robbery. . . . On the 19th, the Northern Pacific train coming from Missoula was held up at the safety switch, on the west side of the Idaho-Montana border, about half way down the hill. The holdup was done by two men, in mid-afternoon.

The safety switch was so called because it was intended to catch all wild cars that might get started down the grade. Every train had to stop at this switch in order to change it so they could proceed on their way.

When the train came to a standstill near the switch, Robert Case, the expressman, was attracted by a noise at the side door of the express car. He opened it to see what was going on. He soon found out. . . . He was looking down the muzzles of two guns, and he threw up his hands. One of the robbers kept Case covered, while the other came into the car. Case was told to open the safe, and after a little persuasion did so. The robber cut into the various packages, and threw back those not containing money.

Two packages, one consigned to Mullan and the other to Wallace contained $2,000 together, and these were taken.

Case was told that if he attempted to leave the car and give alarm they would kill him. He obeyed and it was not until Mullan was reached (4 or 5 miles later) that he sounded the alarm. It was believed that the two robbers stood on the forward platform of the express car until the train arrived at Mullan and then quietly skipped off and disappeared. The robbers were never captured.

At the Custer Mine, ore was struck in a drift between the lower tunnel and tunnel No. 2, which averaged $500 per ton in silver. It was sacked for shipment.

Mike Lennon was looked upon as probably the best single miner in the district. Others won drilling contests, but Lennon was a one-man crew. During the prior year, he had tunneled 375 feet single handed. He did the timbering, sharpened his tools, and did his own cooking, at his workings in Nine Mile.

*   *

November started with violence and was to end the same way. On the 21st, a bucketful of ore dropped 70 feet from the Bunker Hill tramway onto the home of Mrs. Hood in Wardner. Two buckets had collided on the cable and the one dropped off. Mrs. Hood was killed, but it was said she moved into the house with knowledge of the danger involved. The Bunker Hill had bought all the available property under its tramway.

Up along Canyon Creek, Amos Weaver, who ran a sawmill, was shot to death by an unknown assailant on the 26th. The evil doer set fire to Weaver's body and home in order to destroy the evidence. No arrest was ever made for this crime.

The last news for November was the succinct report:

"Two weeks ago a boy was born to the wife of L. B. Lichenstein, and last Sunday the little one was circumcised according to the Orthodox Ancient Jewish Custom, a Rabbi from Spokane performing the ceremony in the presence of a number of invited guests. Refreshments were served after the ceremony."

In December the Tiger Mine installed a new double drum hoist. The drums were 6 feet in diameter and 3½ feet across.

The hoist was designed to raise ore from a depth of 1600 feet. It operated primarily on water power, until the creek became too low, and then they could change over to steam. The gallows frame was 50 feet high.

By December, the Poorman had the largest mining electrical plant in the world. The new addition to the Frisco Mill was completed. Electric drills were used and termed a complete success at the Last Chance Mine in Wardner. A new type had come on the market and was known as the Edison Drill. The Poorman was using one of these drills.

The union at Burke purchased a building for $600, which they were soon to enlarge. They then would have a hall 26 by 70 feet. It was felt that even this hall would not be large enough for the union in view of its present growth. The Bunker Hill started shipping its ore to Wallace on the narrow-gauge trains, and then transferred the loads to the Northern Pacific broad gauge for shipment to the Helena smelter.

When the reservation opened several months earlier, at least 1,000 men rushed in to Idaho from Washington and Oregon. Not all of them secured land, but not one in ten of them departed the state.

The Poorman declared dividend No. 18, for 2 cents per share. It amounted to $10,000, totaling $310,000 paid until that time. The latest quote of the stock was $1.15 per share. The main shaft was down 40 feet below the 600-foot level.

The year 1891 was gradually coming to an end. The unions were growing right along with the production from the mines. For example, the Gem Union grew from a membership of 24 to one of 525 men, during the prior 18-month period.

The Union concentrator was busy during December. The Union Pacific hauled about 7 carloads of ore daily from the Union Mine. . . . Near Osburn, a carload of ore from the Nellie claim returned $181 per ton.

The Union Pacific and the Northern Pacific were having difficulties between themselves over the tracks. They finally com-

pleted a traffic arrangement of considerable importance. . . .
The Union Pacific had been kept out of Burke by an injunction,
and the Northern Pacific could not get at the Bunker Hill ore,
which had to be shipped over Northern Pacific lines. The Northern Pacific agreed to pull Union Pacific cars to and from the
Poorman Mill, in Burke, and the Union Pacific agreed to pull
Northern Pacific cars to and from the Bunker Hill Mill. The
transfers of the cars were to be made at Wallace, where there
was a connecting switch. . . . Prior to this time the Poorman ore
had to be hauled down to the train in wagons because of the injunction. . . . But theirs were not the only railroad difficulties.

During the middle of December, D. K. Butler, a farmer who
lived near the Mission, found one of his cows dead. He concluded that it had been run over by the railroad, and immediately accused Horace Smith, the engineer on the freight. Smith
demanded an investigation. They cut open the cow and found
the stomach to be completely green. With a little further exploration, they struck ore. There was no question about the assay.
It was galena, already concentrated. In transferring ore to the
boats, there was some spillage. In all probability, a little salt got
mixed in with the concentrates and the cow ate the same. Mr.
Butler moved his cows from that pasture.

Once again, the Morning Mine was reported sold to a syndicate from Milwaukee. Any sale would be subject to confirmation by the court in charge of the Hussey receivership case. Reports of the sale of the Morning during Hussey's financial troubles occurred almost monthly.

Night engineer McMacklin was killed when caught in a fly
wheel attached to the compressor in the Hunter Mill on De-
ember 20. The next day, Jacob Quackenbush and Patrick Quinn
were killed in a blast at the Last Chance Mine.

The local unions were concerned with a new proposal regarding miners' wages at Candelaria, Nevada. At a meeting of miners
there, the companies submitted a new wage scale which tied
wages to the price of silver. When silver was quoted at less than

$1.07 per ounce, the wages would be $3.00. Between a price of $1.07 and $1.29 the wages would be $3.50. If silver went past $1.29, the companies offered $4.00 per shift. It was felt the Nevada miners would not accept this offer and that they would form a Miners' Union instead.

The Mine Owners' Association announced late in December that their member mines would stop shipping ore unless better freight rates were given to them. Rates had been raised about $2 per ton a year before. Carloads of ore averaged about 25 tons at that time, and the raise meant about $50 per carload. Charles Sweeney made the first announcement of this threat on behalf of the Mine Owners.

The year 1891 was cited as quiet and peaceful, but filled with progress. Two new large mills were added; there were then three in Wardner, seven in Canyon Creek, one in Nine Mile and two mills in Mullan. Nine million dollars in ore and concentrates were shipped from the Coeur d'Alenes in 1891, plus $250,000 in gold bullion.

The newspapers cited the prospects for 1892. There was concern over the threatened shutdown of the mines which would be caused by the battle over freight rates on ores. At a December 29 meeting in Spokane all producing and shipping mines agreed to extend the time for closing until January 15. All of them had agreed earlier to join in a general suspension of operations until the rates were reduced. The Bunker Hill was the last company to enter into this agreement. The Poorman Mine had already closed down and laid off its crew.

Hints and rumors were everywhere in the district. It was said that some of the mine owners were going to use the freight rate battle as an excuse to reduce miners' wages to $3.00 per shift.

The year 1891 may have been a peaceful year, but the coming year of 1892 was doomed before it had a chance to start. Time was to knit a story so complex that it was never to be completely unraveled.

CHAPTER 28

JANUARY AND FEBRUARY — 1892

The year 1892 was ushered in early by the prolonged whistling of locomotives in the vicinity of the "Y" above Wallace at 11:15 p.m. They announced the arrival of the rotary snowplow on the Northern Pacific tracks, which had just opened the road over the Montana Divide. To add to the noise, someone rang the fire bell, and many thought it was a fire alarm and got out of bed. They hurriedly dressed to protect their property. At midnight the firing of guns and another ringing of the fire bell officially ushered in the new year.

Aulbach took this opportunity to suggest that the Northern Pacific should lose no time in tunneling the Mullan Pass to avoid snow problems. Syd Mills closed down his placer operation for the season due to cold weather. Mr. Mills worked about ten months every year on his claims, and said that in all his experiences in placer mining this was the only area he had found where work could be carried on for a full ten months of the year.

There was a move afoot in Congress to change the date before which assessment work on mining claims had to be performed. It was January 1 in 1892, and this caused quite a hardship. There was a big demand for snowshoes to get to claims where assessment work had not been done, so they could be relocated.

Ingersoll drills were making the news. By using a power drill, tunneling cost $2.30 per foot, as against hand drilling, which cost $17.50 per foot. While these statistics were not from the Coeur d'Alene mining district, it still was a fact that the power drills greatly reduced costs and were to change many things in the mining world.

The Carpenters' and Joiners' Union was having internal trouble. It was formed by eight members to maintain wages of $5 per day. S. D. Amott, its president, got a contract to build a slaughterhouse for W. E. Harris, and he promptly hired his union men to work for him at 35 cents per hour. Ed Carruthers, a member of the union, became angry and started off on his own to be a contractor.

Over at Murray, the Golden Chest mill turned out gold brick worth about $1,800 in a week. John Coumerilh, the manager, had about twenty men working early in 1892.

There were 3,000 miners employed in the district, plus about 500 common laborers. The Granite and Custer did not close down late in December, but only reduced their forces. It was claimed that the Tiger would close down about the 15th. The Poorman was still shut down.

At the end of 1891, the Bunker Hill was producing 110 tons daily; the Poorman 40; Badger 35; Last Chance 35; Tiger 25; Sierra Nevada 25; Gem 20; Union 30; Custer, Stemwinder, and Grouse, 15 tons each; and there were eight smaller producing mines. The Morning Mine produced 40 tons per day when it was working. The 1891 capacity for production of concentrates in the district was about $13,000,000 annually, or $35,000 daily.

The miners came to the conclusion that the Bunker Hill must sooner or later abandon their tramway system and go to tunneling. It was clear that a tunnel of between three and four thousand feet could be used to transport the ore from the Bunker Hill and neighboring mines directly into the Bunker Hill concentrator on the South Fork, on a natural grade. This would also drain all the mines about Wardner from 500 feet to 1,000 feet in depth.

Both the Union Pacific and the Northern Pacific railroads informed the Mine Owners' Association that they would submit to a shutdown of the mines rather than cut their rates. After receiving the notices from the railroads, John Finch of the Mine Owners' Association announced that all mines having mills would close down. It was expected that Esler, Clark, McAulay and Glidden would go to Omaha and St. Paul to talk with the head men of the railroads. Finch had no idea how long the mines would remain closed.

By January 15, nearly all the men in Burke were laid off their jobs. Eighty men got the bad news at the Frisco on the 13th, and the Gem Mine laid off most of its crews on the 15th. Wardner pretty well shut down its production crews. Development and maintenance crews were still working. The Hunter Mine in Mullan did not cease work at that time.

Times were bad—and they were going to get worse. The *Coeur d'Alene Miner* carried an advertisement on the 16th stating that a handsome military sword and belt, held at the Crazy Horse Hotel as security for board and lodging, would be sold in front of the hotel in one week unless redeemed by the owner in the meantime. It belonged to Captain Linn, the company commander of the state militia unit located at Wallace.

Although this mining district produced about 25% of the U.S. lead in 1891, the miners here were going to feel the pangs of poverty in 1892. There were 122 miners at the Bunker Hill who had their wages "tied up" by court orders when the Bunker Hill Mine closed down.

Mullan was thus far not affected by the closing down of the mines. The Hunter was the only company running a mill. All the development work on Chloride hill and at other points about Mullan continued.

Large numbers of miners left the area for Butte during the last half of January.

On January 20, the Mine Owners' Association again met in Wallace on the freight-rate question. They agreed to close their producing mines to production for at least four months to fight for freight rate reductions, unless satisfactory arrangements were set up by the railroads earlier. The mine owners agreed that development work could go on, with the thought of employing as many married men as possible. About 200 married men were still on mine payrolls, but about 1,500 men had been discharged from the producing mines. The Argentine, Hunter, Sierra Nevada and the Mammoth mines were the only producing mines in the district being worked at that time. Apparently they were not members of the Mine Owners' Association. The railroads were losing $5,400 per day in ore freight revenues during the shutdown.

Another legal battle was underway. The Attorney General for Idaho telegraphed the District Attorney on the 26th. He asked him to recover Captain Linn's sword before it was sold for a board bill at the Crazy Horse Hotel.

The Bunker Hill had trouble with its aerial tramway in January. It had been guaranteed to haul 400 tons of ore from the mine to the mill, and 100 tons of materials in the reverse direction daily. Its performance was claimed to be about 50% of the guarantee. The tramway had started "bucking." The Bunker Hill took the buckets off the tramway and stowed them away from snow and rain, thereby relieving the cable of a lot of weight.

The beginning of February brought news of another sale of the Morning Mine, and this time it was official. The property was sold to a Milwaukee group for $200,000 down and $200,000 on credit. When little more than a prospect in 1887, the Morning Mine was purchased by Charles L. Dahler of Helena and Charles Hussey. They were offered $70,000 for it within a year. Hussey did not want to accept this offer, but Dahler wanted out. Hussey paid for the other share and later bought the Evening claim, after a Helena company had abandoned it. An 80-ton mill was built early in 1890. Then a bank failure put Hussey's property into receivership. Just before the bank failure, negotiations were under way for a sale to a French syndicate for $900,000, but Hussey would not agree because the middle men in the sale wanted one-third for their services. After the bank failure the squeeze was on Hussey, and the buyers were not so generous with their offers.

The bad times were caused by the mine closures, and the departure of so many people had reduced the number of gambling games in Wallace. Craps was holding its own and appeared to flourish where other games died.

It should be remembered that Wallace had two weekly newspapers in early 1892. The *Coeur d'Alene Miner* was run by the Dunn Brothers, and it obviously sided with the Mine Owners Association. The *Wallace Press* was printed by Adam Aulbach, who championed the cause of the miners. Thus far into 1892, neither paper suggested difficulties between the Mine Owners and the miners' union. The big trouble, at least on the surface, was between the Mine Owners and the railroad companies.

Although not a member of the Mine Owners' Association, the Hunter laid off 60 men on the 7th and stopped shipping. It was the last producing mine in the district to stop shipping ore. The cause of the Hunter's action was not known, but it was presumed to be in harmony with the other mines. There were no more than 350 or 400 miners at work in the area by the middle of February. These were doing contract and development work.

A committee of Mine Owners planned to go East to talk to the railroad management about freight rates toward the end of February.

A rumbling was heard in the distance. The Anaconda newspaper said the shutdown in the Coeur d'Alenes was based on a labor and management problem, rather than on freight rates. A Mullan report to the *Anaconda Standard* indicated that miners' wages in this district would be cut from $3.50 and $4.00 to $3.00, and shovelers and carmen would be cut back to $2.00 or $2.50 when work was resumed in the spring.

Pat Clark of the Poorman came back from meeting with the railroad people and reported that no progress was made. Another meeting was scheduled for about ten days later, which Clark would also attend. He said either the railroads would come to the mine owners' terms or the mines would remain idle in the Coeur d'Alenes. Clark denied that the question of miners' wages played any part in the shutdown, and stated that he believed that a good miner should be paid $3.50 a day. Clark was well-liked and respected by the miners and probably meant what he said regarding wages. His views on that subject were not shared by other mine owners, however.

The Mine Owners' Association held another meeting on the 15th for four hours. They would meet every two weeks until they reached a final decision. Their demand was for a $2 per ton reduction in freight rates; in other words, they wanted the rates of 1890 to be reinstated. In view of the amount of lead produced in the district in 1891, it was anticipated that the price of lead would rise if the shutdown continued. The Mine Owners' Association would not issue a statement on the labor problems being discussed locally.

The *Osburn Statesman* described Wallace as a town "manufactured out of debris and rubbish by the hands of men very low in the scale of humanity."

Coasting had been a popular sport at Wardner all winter. Heavy bobsleds started at the Bunker Hill mine and ran almost to Wardner Junction, more than a mile away.

Dancing was a popular entertainment throughout the district. Each town held dancing parties and invited people from the other towns. Special trains were sometimes made up and would leave for a dance as early as three in the afternoon and not return until daylight.

On the 25th a nugget was taken out just below Myrtle on Trail Creek, the largest ever found on the northside. It weighed 33¼ ounces, giving it a value of $532. The largest prior to that time was found by Jesse Coulter and weighed 33 ounces.

Articles of incorporation were filed for the Coeur d'Alene Hardware Company. John Finch was president and E. H. Moffit was secretary-treasurer. It took over the four outlets of Holley, Mason, Marks and Co., situated in the Coeur d'Alenes.

The Mine Owners' Association never released lists of its membership. Attempts were made to keep it a secret. However, the association sent a committee to St. Paul to meet with the railroads. Clement represented the Bunker Hill; Esler of the Helena and Frisco; Sweeney for the Last Chance; Clark for Poorman, Glidden for Tiger; Finch and Campbell for the Gem and Union; C. D. Porter for the Custer; and McAulay for Stemwinder, Sierra Nevada, Inez and Granite Mines. The Wardner Miners' Union announced that it would nominate a full ticket for county offices for the next election.

Adam Aulbach took issue with the Osburn editor for making the scurrilous remark about Wallace a week earlier, and for some reason the Osburn editor offered an apology. It prompted Aulbach to write:

> "The Ass is a long-lived and tenacious animal, but on being severely frightened he brays himself to death."

CHAPTER 29

MARCH AND APRIL — 1892

On the first day of March, petitions were put into circulation asking the District Judge to order an election for the removal of the county seat from Murray to some point agreed upon by a majority of the voters. Citizens of Wallace and Osburn showed the greatest interest in securing the county seat. A Burke citizen became incensed at the overtures being made in order to get Burke signatures on the petitions by backers of both Wallace and Osburn. He strongly resented the remark that "a jug of whiskey could carry a majority in Burke."

Thirty-five Wallace businessmen offered to provide a two-story building of better quality than the present courthouse and the land for the same, if the county seat was moved to Wallace in November. To show their good faith, they bonded themselves to the county commissioners in the sum of $20,000.

The Mine Owners' Association representatives returned from the trip to St. Paul, but they made no announcements regarding freight rates. There were rumors that a compromise was forthcoming, but they may have only represented wishful thinking.

With the miners still unemployed, a number of them left for the Slocan District of Canada, where there was a great deal of mining activity. The Slocan District was always a popular place for local miners to go when times were tough in the Coeur d'Alenes, or when miners had to leave because of labor trouble.

176

Nothing was heard from the Mine Owners' Association by the tenth of the month. They had not been meeting because a quorum was not present. Some of the members were still in the East. A meeting was scheduled for about the 15th in Spokane.

Just before the shutdown, the Gem union had 500 members, the Burke union had 600, Wardner union had 800 and Mullan had 300 members. The shutdown affected Wallace mostly because the transient population left the district. Most businesses were hurt. About eighty men were working in the woods and a few were doing construction work.

*   *   *

In March the County Commissioners were urged to build a wagon road between Wallace and Mullan. The former road had been closed for months, and it was impossible for even a horseman to get through. An unusual situation existed, in that horsedrawn wagons could not get from Wallace to either Mullan or Burke. Yet the modern Iron Horses made the trips with no difficulty.

A deaf and dumb young man by the name of Burton, son of a laundry woman in Murray, made a gold find about one-half mile above the Murray graveyard, on the road to Wallace. He ran a tunnel in about 20 feet from the road and found rich gold quartz. Some specimens resembled gold nuggets. One was brought to Wallace and three ounces of gold were obtained from a five-ounce quartz sample.

Aulbach recalled that probably more prospecting had been done on that particular ledge than any other on the Northside. Every miner who worked in the placers below there in '84 believed a rich ledge existed on the hill above the Gillette, O. K., Wooden and Last Chance claims. Thousands of dollars worth of gold was taken out of the lower end of the Last Chance and Wooden claims in such a rough state that most miners felt a rich ledge could not be a quarter of a mile distant; the gold was sharp and jagged, and much of it was "quartz gold." In '86 and '87, a tunnel was driven into the hill some distance above the latest discovery, but the job was given up after getting in 600 feet without finding any gold.

Father Keyzer started holding services in Worstell's new building on east Bank Street.

Adam Aulbach launched a tirade concerning William E. Borah: ". . . the newly imported Chairman of Republican Idaho State Central Committee, is chuck full of Kansas tornado eloquence."

Times were not good, but the citizens of Wallace voted on a bond proposition for the Wallace School, in the sum of $12,000 for the purpose of building and furnishing a brick schoolhouse. The school bond issue passed with only three votes cast against it.

In the middle of March, the Mine Owners' Association informed its former employees that the freight rate question had been settled and that the mines would reopen about the first of April. The railroads had made the demanded concessions. About 2,000 miners would be needed to reopen the mines, and former employees would be given preference.

The Mine Owners' Association took the opportunity to add one hour to the prior shifts of nine hours and to announce a new pay schedule:

> Miners, $3.50 per day for 10 hours work. Carmen and shovellers, $3.00 per 10-hour shift, except in shaft mines where they would be paid $3.50.

If the men desired, they would be granted a part of Sunday or the entire day off, except in pumping mines. Where miners or carmen were put on special 8-hour shifts, they were to be paid the same as for 10 hours. It gave the miners something to start from: a 70-hour week in a pumping mine.

Slogans appeared on the wall of the Wardner union hall:

> "The Union Forever"
> "In Union There Is Strength"

Friction was rapidly increasing throughout the district. In Wallace, Lt. W. E. Hood denounced Captain Thomas A. Linn, of Company A, 2nd Regiment of the Idaho National Guard, by labeling Linn as an incompetent and a drunk. Hood said:

"His (Linn's) drunken, disorderly behavior, his incapacity and utter worthlessness as a man and as a soldier, added to the fact that he now attempts to play the traitor by involving the militia in a controversy with the miners and also messing them up in an unfavorable light in the county seat contest, causes me to unite with many others to denounce him."

Linn answered that the Wallace company of the national guard was organized for the purpose of advertising Wallace, and denied that it was for the purpose of opposing unions in this area.

The soldiers were giving Adam Aulbach a field day. He hinted that the militia was "mine owner inspired" and labelled them as almost anything but soldiers. The Dunn Brothers paper would defend the militia from time to time, but the military unit was unpopular and quite difficult to defend.

Wallace's winter came to an end. The season's snowfall was 9 feet 7 inches, making it the lightest in the then recorded history of the area. The heaviest was 21 feet 8 inches in 1886-7. The town trustees received their patent on the townsite land and notified all claimants to lots in the 80-acre tract to describe their property and show why deeds should be issued to them.

The saloon keepers of Wallace organized to test the constitutionality of the high-priced liquor license law. Their attorney, Walter A. Jones, was in Lewiston arguing the case on appeal to the Supreme Court. Charles W. O'Neill, the District Attorney, appeared for the State. Aulbach predicted that if Mr. Jones could knock out the liquor license law, his chances for the Republican nomination for Attorney General for Idaho, would be much improved. . . . Luck was not with Jones, the Court upheld the liquor license law.

In the previous year, silver dropped in price from $1.19 per ounce to $.89. Lead dropped in the same period from $5.10 per hundred pounds to $4.10. The economic picture was looking darker all the time, but the county government had enough money to redeem all the county scrip which had been issued, with enough money left in the treasury to place the County on a cash basis.

It was rumored that 20 representatives of Montana labor societies arrived in Wallace during the third week in March.

The development work at the Granite Mine was progressing. The lower tunnel was in 800 feet, with 400 more feet to be made before ore was expected. The work was difficult as the formation was solid granite, and 15 feet a week was considered good progress with a powerful air compressor and Rand drills. It was predicted that when they struck the ore body, they would be 400 feet below the present workings, and they then would drive a raise at once connecting the two workings.

The Central Miners' Union answered the Mine Owners' new pay scale announcement by stating that they would not work under the new terms, but would work only under the old rates. The Central Union requested miners and working men to stay away from the Coeur d'Alene District until the difficulties between labor and management were settled. The Central Union contended that the Mine Owners broke an existing contract regarding pay rates without any notice to the union and without asking for a conference or arbitration.

The Dunn Brothers' newspaper reported that all this controversy was taking place in the newspapers. It intimated that the problem was not very big, and that it might be wiped out entirely by a conference between the two parties.

A number of mine owners stated that they would only resume under the scale of wages offered in their last announcement. They were prepared to remain closed for the rest of the year. An officer of the union stated:

"We are forced to resist the reduction. The Coeur d'Alene mines are practically machine mines. Few expert miners will in time be employed. The ore bodies are very large and regular, and the bulk of the work must be done by shovel-

lers and carmen. This work is hard. Although it can be
done by any man, a miner will do twice the amount of labor
of a cheap man. The miners don't want to air any griev-
ances, but they propose to earn decent wages. . . ."

The Mine Owners' Association announced that it would meet
again at the end of the month.

A. M. Esler, the manager of the Helena and Frisco mine, was
interviewed by the Helena (Montana) newspaper on the 22nd.
Esler said the Mine Owners' Association turned down further
wage decrease measures. He said an employment agency offered
to furnish them, for a reasonable fee, any number of skilled
miners at $3.00 per day and unskilled laborers at $2.50, which
labor they agreed to introduce and maintain, at their own risk,
within a reasonable time.

Esler said:

> "Their proposition was rejected, but if the union is going to
> make a silly fight against just demands, I think it will be
> forced by some bad counsellors in their organization, and
> there will result a contest which will cause a still greater
> cut. We can get more unskilled men than are required to
> work for $3 per day. There is room and demand there for
> 1,500 men at once, for men who are willing to work for the
> highest wages on earth in mines so near the surface, who
> will be satisfied with well enough and who are willing to
> attend to their own affairs and not attempt to run the busi-
> ness of their employers, without solicitation and extra com-
> pensation. . . ."

The meeting of the Mine Owners' Association was held on the
first of April, and no change in the situation came of it. The
Association stated its case at length through Spokane newspapers,
and accused the union of being agitator-controlled. A propa-
ganda war between the management group and the unions was
reaching full steam and was to continue for months to come.

The Mine Owners' Association released a statement to the Spokane paper in which they stated that the Sisters' Hospital was the only good thing done by the Union so far. They hinted that the Union was not controlled by the real miners. They said they lowered wages because shovellers and carmen were not as skilled as miners and they did not handle powder. The report continued that the unions had threatened to run the mine owners out of the country, burn their mills, blow up their flumes and murder the owners. The owners cited the low prices of lead and silver as reasons for their actions. The Mine Owners said they wanted no repetition of the affair, which occurred during the strike in Wardner in 1891, when it said 100 armed men waited at midnight on one lone man, who had a wife and family, and told him to leave the country at once or they would kill him. Their statement concluded by saying the mine owners would wait until April 1 for their men to make up their minds and return to work. If they would not work, the Association would claim its right to work the mines outside of any unions, and added that 2,000 miners were idle at Butte and many more elsewhere were looking for jobs. This became known as the Mine Owners' Association "Ultimatum."

In reply, the Union apologized that its literary ability was not as gifted as that of the hired attorneys of the Mine Owners. The reply chastised some of the mine owners (Bunker Hill) for their original stand against the Sisters' Hospital and for having called it "a foreign and unAmerican corporation," but who later chose to call it a "noble institution." It added that their stand against the hospital caused much of the existing friction. The union denied having any part in outrages in Wardner of a year before. It charged the Association with being more interested in crushing the Union than it was in the subject of wages. It further stated that its constitution was open for public inspection and that the Union did not use half the force to compel men to join, as was used by the Mine Owners' Association on the outside mines to compel them to fall in line. The Union accused the

Association of "blacklisting" men who were officers in either a local or the central union.

A local editorial accused the Spokane paper of publishing incendiary articles and falsehoods, and said:

> "If riots do not prevail in the Coeur d'Alenes, it will not be the fault of the *Spokane Spokesman.*"

The Dunn Brothers called for the mine owners and the unions to settle down to a conference table within the district and argue the subject. They ridiculed both sides for traveling to Spokane to publish their statements of the case.

John W. Sweeney, president of the Wardner Miners' Union, replied to the mine owners' statement and blamed the first pay cut in the district on Victor M. Clement, in 1887, when he assumed management of the Bunker Hill. Immediately after the 1887 reduction of wages, the miners organized the first union in Wardner on November 3, 1887. The situation in the mines was unchanged. No miners went to work in the Canyon Creek area under the new rate scale.

Resolutions of sympathy with the cause and position of the Union men were passed in public meetings of businessmen and non-miners in Wallace, Burke, Wardner and Mullan.

On the 5th, the Mine Owners' Association agreed to let their mines remain idle until June 1, and it withdrew the prior offer to hire at their pay scale. On the 7th representatives of the local unions in the district met with the Association at Wallace for 2½ hours. No agreement was reached, and it was felt that the last chance for settlement disappeared at this meeting.

Adam Aulbach reached new heights in his anger toward the Mine Owners' Association, which he described as the first combination of mine owners in history. He labeled it: "Organized capital against muscle and endurance."

Aulbach was dissatisfied with the last edict which closed the mines until June 1:

"The Mine Owners' Association has sentenced Miss Coeur d'Alene to 60 days imprisonment for alleged perverseness, but the young lady will come out of the bastille smiling."

"Our sympathies, first, last and all the time are with labor, and we would rather feed on the vapors of the dungeon with a toad than raise our voice or use our pen in support of an unjust effort to drive organized labor to the wars so long as that organized labor maintains a dignified and lawful attitude."

Truthfully, Adam Aulbach was just getting warmed up on the subject.

John A. Finch, secretary of the Association, said that he received a letter stating the unions were too slow and that 17 miners had met and condemned him to death unless the mines were started up immediately.

As if the Coeur d'Alenes did not have trouble enough, C. A. Salyer, the national organizer of the Prohibition Party, was to come to Wallace to lecture on April 20 and 21. Aulbach said:

". . . Heretofore prohibition had given us the cold shoulder, and we have drank up a million dollars worth of beer and whiskey in a year. It was a good time for him (Salyer) to come in here while the mines are closed, as the boys are on their good behavior."

Wallace elections on April 4 elected T. A. Helm, J. L. Dunn, John B. Cameron, George P. White, and Henry E. Howes as trustees. The 56 votes which were cast in the Wardner election put Harry L. Day, C. K. Poteet, John Pelkes and W. D. Shepherd into office as trustees for that town.

The Dunn Brothers wrote that they were being pressured to come out either for the Union or the Association in the present battle. They stated that they did not fully endorse the position taken by either party. Usually their editorials favored the mine owners, but every once in a while they would truly take a mighty crack at the Association.

Lead was priced at $4.25 per hundred and silver at 86 cents per ounce during the middle of April.

The Dunn Brothers editorialized that the Union and the Mine Owners' Association had widened the gap between them by arguing in the newspapers. The Association held another meeting on the 11th, and the members were quoted as saying that they would not hire any union miners until they severed their connection with the Miners' Union and would work at the Association pay rates.

Rumors were now about that miners were being imported from Michigan and California, and that the mines would start up on May 1; also that the mills in Canyon Creek were guarded by new faces.

There were people in the community with the audacity to think that the advance guard of the Pinkerton Detective Agency had arrived in the district. The record of the Pinkerton Agency in labor management problems was well known throughout the country.

The third week in April found the labor situation getting worse. The mine owners were discharging the few union men still in their employ. The Mine Owners' Association met in Wallace, but in secret, and with no announcements afterward. On the 21st, six men at the Standard Mine near Burke were given 24 hours to withdraw from the union in order to save their jobs. They quit work instead. The rumor was around that the Hunter Mine would withdraw from the Mine Owners' Association because it was a wet mine and had no objection to paying $3.50 to all underground employees.

The Central Miners' Union committee met with the Trades and Labor Assembly in Butte during April, and the Montana group pledged moral and financial aid to the Coeur d'Alene Miners Union, and instructed all miners and workingmen to keep clear of the Coeur d'Alenes while the trouble continued.

G. M. Dallas, secretary, and J. J. Barry, of the Montana Miners' unions, arrived in Wallace on the 21st with good cheer and strength for the local miners.

Friends of the mine owners said that they would hold out for 50 years. Aulbach's answer was—

> "Well, there is one consolation. All the mine owners are getting along in years, and at the end of the half century we'll all be in the land where the mine owner will be no better off than the humblest miner."

The newspaper in Wardner attacked Adam Aulbach, stating that while Aulbach sounded off on union principles, etc.; he employed no union men in putting out the *Wallace Press*. Instead he hired only two children to assist him; and the Wardner paper proceeded to describe the boys as bleary eyed, hump-backed and decrepit. They said Aulbach was too cheap to hire union labor. . . . These were pretty severe charges and would be hard to answer by anyone but Aulbach.

The answer by Adam Aulbach was soon forthcoming. He defended himself by stating that the two boys were both Irish. One was Joe Murphy, 16 years old and the support of his widowed mother and two sisters and a younger brother. This boy came to Wallace from the Comstock about a year and a half before. The other boy was Fred O'Donnell and was small for his age. Aulbach said that he would discharge him, but that he had more brains than half the members of the Mine Owners' Association. Freddy also had a widowed mother, a sister and a younger brother, and he contributed to their support. Aulbach added that both boys were healthy and that he was tutoring them in union principles. He closed his defense by stating that after the boys served their three years in the Press office, they could go to a town where there was a typographical union and join it.

By the end of April, the Association indicated it could afford $3.50 for all underground employees, but that it would not employ union men under any circumstances.

Late in April, the Coeur d'Alene Indians flocked to the surrounding area to cash the checks they received from Uncle Sam for their land. They averaged about $1,200 each and totalled about $600,000. Money was flowing like water near the reservation.

The Butte union assessed its members $5 per month in support of the unions in the Coeur d'Alenes. The Butte union claimed 6,000 members.

On the 25th, the local company of the National Guard elected its officers. W. E. Hood was elected Captain, J. B. Short, First Lieutenant, and A. D. McKinlay, Second Lieutenant. Captain Linn, Robert Short and E. G. Arment had resigned from Company A.

Aulbach figured that when the mines were operating, one-third of the wages paid to the miners went directly back to the employers for board and lodging. The companies made a profit on the other two-thirds in various ways. Some of the superintendents were financially interested in saloons, where checks were seldom paid at par; and then there were always the company stores to get back some of the wages. Aulbach's paper maintained a constant stream of anti-mine owner material.

The Northern Pacific had given orders to widen the gauge of its line between Wallace and Wardner, but the continued shutdown of the mines caused them to revoke the orders.

The Mine Owners' announcement that they would not employ union miners was a great help to the local unions. It brought assistance from unions everywhere.

President Tom O'Brien and Secretary J. F. Poynton of the Central Miners' Union were in Spokane late in April. Both had come from a trip to Butte and Missoula, where they arranged for help from outside unions. One of their aims was to purchase supplies for a large union supply store in Wallace, with branch stores in all the other nearby mining towns, for the members of the union. They felt it useless to strengthen the Mine Owners' Association by buying from their company-owned stores. They had received pledges of support from 33 labor organizations in Montana, and it was rumored that the Union already had $10,000 for its purposes on deposit in banks. Whether such items were entirely true would never be determined. Many news items were appearing in the papers for no purpose other than as propaganda, and it was difficult to sort the truth from the lies.

CHAPTER 30

MAY — 1892

May began with labor troubles still the major subject of concern. It was rumored that 300 men were enroute from Duluth to work in the Coeur d'Alenes, and that they had been sidetracked in Billings, when the locomotive engineer simply refused to haul them.

Campbell and Finch attempted to put five non-union miners at work in the Union Mine at Burke. The men were asked to join the miners' union, and three said they would, but the other two refused. These two men were escorted over the Glidden Road toward Thompson Falls.

> "When the two degraded mercenaries had got through talking, a community gave them a safe escort over the Glidden Road to the Montana line, where a blessing aided them on the lonely journey to Thompson Falls."

The Coeur d'Alene Miner reported that the miners in Burke fell into a trap when 35 of them escorted the two men over the hill into Montana. The Dunns claimed that their action laid a foundation for the Mine Owners' Association to appeal directly for federal authorities to protect them.

It was six months before the fall elections, but it was understood that there were already seven Democratic candidates for sheriff.

The Wallace trustees passed an ordinance placing a dance hall license at $300 per quarter in answer to the many complaints they had been receiving about dance halls in the business section of town.

The Supreme Court decision regarding the liquor license law, together with depressed conditions, caused eight saloons in Wallace to close their doors during the first week in May. There was only one saloon operating in Burke. Times must have been tough.

A. M. Esler, manager of the Helena and Frisco mine, arrived in Wallace and confirmed the report that the Frisco had been optioned to an English company for 60 days at a price of $1,500,000.

Since the closing of the district's mines, the smelters had been clamoring for lead. As a result there was pressure being exerted to remove the protective tariff of $30 per ton from foreign lead. It was starting to look as though the shutdown might hurt the Mine Owners' Association more than they realized.

Aulbach was to comment on the Court calendar:

> "Judge Holleman has for the first time in the history of the District nearly cleared the Court Calendar. Very few cases are left for the next term, but foolish mortals will get into trouble and in the fall another crop of litigants will have bogged up."

The *Anaconda Standard* reported that a circular was being distributed in the East, evidently by the Mine Owners' Association:

> "WANTED 500 to 1,000 miners for the west. Also a few timbermen and trammers. Company wages. Machine runners, $3.25 per day. Timbermen and miners, $3. Trammers, $2.50. Board, $6 to $7 per week . . . all to be ready to start from Duluth on Friday, May 6. Apply to Thomas G. White, Office at Union Depot, Duluth, or Captain Vivian Prince, North Star Street, Ironwood, Michigan."

A. M. Esler was interviewed by a Spokane reporter and declared the Association's position was still the same: No union men were to be hired; $3 per day to carmen and shovellers; and $3.50 per day to miners.

The union miners were fighting fire with fire. They petitioned Congress to remove the protective tariff on lead, which would cause the Association no end of difficulty if Congress were to do so. The Democrats in the House of Representatives were trying to abolish this tariff.

The two men who had been chased out of Burke toward Thompson Falls, William Pitkin and George Wolfe, filed affidavits stating that they had been taken from the Union Mine by 100 union miners to the union hall in Burke, where they refused to join the union, after which time they were chased out of town. They stated that they were refused food for the trip and that they had nothing to eat for the next two days. They further stated that in the parade out of Burke, they were called SOB's and "scabs," and the spectators beat on oil cans and cursed them.

The Dunn Brothers once again claimed that the union miners had fallen into a trap by chasing these two men from Burke. They said the Mine Owners' Association had followed a systematic course to obtain government protection in working their mines.

The Coeur d'Alene Mining and Concentrating Company obtained an injunction from the U. S. court in Boise, which directed the unions and others interfering with the operation of that company. The case title listed the four local unions and the central union as defendants, followed by a list of individuals. The first-named individual defendant was a C. L. Allison, the recording secretary of the Gem Union.

The complaint upon which the injunction was issued alleged that the plaintiff was the owner of the Bengal Tiger Fraction, Sherman and Union lode claims, and operated the Union concentrator. It charged the unions with conspiring to prevent that company from operating, except by meeting the union terms, and with union employees. The complaint set forth the secret oath and obligations that the miners took upon initiation into the union, which ended with an oath that the initiate swore never to work underground in Shoshone County for less than $3.50 per day.

The complaint further alleged that on April 21 the president of the Burke union, with two other union men, went into the plaintiff's mine and asked the miners if they belonged to the union and about the pay rate; also, that on April 28, certain non-union men were hired by the plaintiff, and that the defendants took these men from the mine while on shift to the Burke union hall, where the demand that they join the union was made. Afterward, two of the group were escorted from Burke towards Thompson Falls.

The plaintiff asked $50,000 in damages, and charged the union with placing advertisements in papers around Lake Superior to discourage laborers from coming to the Coeur d'Alenes to work. Albert Hagan and W. B. Heyburn were the attorneys for the plaintiffs, whose complaint was verified by Amasa B. Campbell, general manager and vice president of the plaintiff company. The union immediately employed Frank Ganahl and Walter A. Jones as attorneys to fight the injunction.

At about this time it was reported that three cases of guns and two boxes of ammunition were received by the express office for the Miners' Union headquarters in Wallace.

United States Marshal Pinkham came to the district on May 12 and served copies of the injunction on about 130 men, including Walter A. Jones, the attorney for the Union. The Marshal also delivered copies to Shoshone County Sheriff R. A. Cunningham and Adam Aulbach.

The serving of the injunction became a light-hearted matter, and the union officials helped the marshal make service in Burke and Gem; and the marshal "blew himself in" for about $20 in drinks for the union men before returning to Wallace.

Aulbach stated that Marshal Pinkham called at the *Press* office and presented his compliments and a copy of the injunction. Aulbach thereupon destroyed two pages of his paper which had already been printed off and which were devoted to a review of the labor troubles. His next issue had two blank columns which were captioned: "The Injunction Knocked This Column Out."

Aulbach did not take all this sitting down. He picked up his pen and wrote a blazing editorial entitled "The Press Gagged," in which he charged that the wealthy Mine Owners' Association could muzzle the free press and 150 others by posting a $2,000 bond and obtaining an injunction from the U. S. court.

Aulbach got in a couple more licks in that issue:

> "A. M. Esler, the mouthpiece of the Coeur d'Alene MOA, in an interview last Sunday, styled the Coeur d'Alene Miners 'Flannel Mouths, Molly McGuire's, and the worst element in this country.' We simply publish this as a matter of consideration, refraining from comment for fear of being yanked out to Boise."

Within a matter of a few days, news of the injunction spread across the nation, and the subject of Aulbach being enjoined in the printing of his papers was editorialized in the East. The *New York World* praised Aulbach and encouraged him to violate the injunction by publishing the facts, even if it meant going to jail, in the interest of a free press. This free press issue became hot quickly. The contention soon arose that Adam Aulbach had never been served with a copy of the injunction; instead it was contended that Marshal Pinkham had presented him with a copy for informational purposes only.

Captain Hood of the local unit of the Idaho National Guard had the company's guns and ammunition transferred from its frame armory to the vault in the Bank of Wallace Building. The next order of business for the district was the arrival of 73 men from Duluth, who went to the Union Mine at Burke, under guard of Joel Warren and about 60 guards, armed with Winchesters and other arms.

Aulbach headlined the story: "A Train Load of 'Scabs' and Hessians Arrive."

The men came in locked cars from Bozeman, Montana, and

were mostly timid Swedes, Finns and Italians. They arrived on May 14 on the Northern Pacific train. Sheriff Cunningham arrested Joel Warren on a complaint of James Graham, and brought Warren before Justice of the Peace Angel in Wallace. Warren was charged with impersonation of a U. S. Deputy Marshal. Bond was set at $1,000 which was posted by Sweeney and McAulay of the Mine Owners' Association.

McAulay went to see Secretary Poynton of the union to inquire of Warren's safety, and he was told that Warren would be safe. With this assurance McAulay invited the Union men to Cameron's saloon for a drink to a peaceful solution of the trouble in the mines. Not all members of the Mine Owners' Association could have done this. Several of the mine owners were pretty well despised by the union men.

Deputy Sheriff Jack Waite had warrants to serve on Joel Warren and others as they brought the labor train into the district. Waite had taken the Union Pacific train to Mullan to intercept the labor train, but it passed them on the way and proceeded to Wallace, and then up to Burke without stopping.

Large crowds protesting the arrival of the labor train formed. In Wallace, the president of the Central Union addressed the crowd and told them to keep cool and sober while the matter was tested in court. The crowd took the advice and returned to their homes.

The non-union train was originally scheduled to leave Michigan on May 6, but postponed its trip until the 12th. Seventy-three men filled the two cars and at Bozeman a car full of guards was added to the train. It was said that 16 men deserted the labor train before it ever got to the Coeur d'Alene district.

After the train arrived at the Union Mine in Burke, some of the men refused to work in view of the labor situation. Within a week 24 of these men had quit their jobs. The rule was that the men were free to leave the mine premises, but once gone they could not come back. Upon their leaving they were served with a copy of the injunction, by U. S. Deputy Marshal Harvey

Harris, who apparently was on duty at the mine at all times. About 120 men were on the Union mine property during the third week of May, and about one-half of them were guards.

The labor train consisted of the engine, baggage car, three coaches and a caboose when it arrived in the district. The engineer was Grinnell and the conductor was Joe Bradley.

The newspapers carried reference to "Palouse Hessians" from time to time. They were distinguished from "scabs," who were non-union men who took jobs of the miners on strike. The "Palouse Hessians" were the men employed as guards, who marched around the surface areas of the shutdown mines. The Hunter Mine fell into line with the Mine Owners' Association and closed its property on May 14. Its crew was paid off, and it was their first pay day in 4½ months.

Aulbach contended that there was an agreement among the members of the Mine Owners' Association that each was bound to remain in the control of the Association, under penalty of $5,000, until the first day of June. Aulbach contended they would be free to do as they each wished after that date.

"If this be so, the darkest cloud that ever spread over any mining camp will be removed."

Judge Frazer of Mullan was an ardent friend of labor. During the latter part of May he had deputized 47 special constables for the purpose of stopping any train bringing "scabs" into this district. At that time it was not unusual to see men in Mullan with Winchesters going towards the depot on the approach of eastern trains. Frank Ganahl, the union's attorney, stated that the judge did not have power to swear in special constables. After that time Frazer revoked his order and disarmed his special officers.

On the 26th, Governor Willey of Idaho arrived in Wallace to look over the situation. The Northern Pacific Railroad had asked for protection. . . . The Governor said it was merely a tour of observation, and there was no significance to his visit.

Jacob Heater, the constable at Mullan, came to Wallace and announced that he had been ordered out of Mullan. Later the same day, Heater was arrested in Wallace and charged with insanity. Judge Hollemen discharged him from custody after a short hearing was held regarding Heater's sanity.

Heater said that he had drafted a letter to the Governor setting forth that there were about 50 armed men in Mullan, sworn in as constables by Judge Frazer, and that they created considerable alarm in the town. He claimed that two parties came to his house and demanded the letter, and that his life had been threatened.

The charge of impersonating a federal officer was dismissed against Joel Warren, the Spokane detective, and he was re-arrested for bringing an armed body of men into Idaho for the purpose of suppressing domestic trouble. He was bound over to the Grand Jury under bond of $2,500, which was furnished by McAulay and Culbertson. Warren then went back to the Union mine.

Towards the end of May there were reports of non-union labor coming into the district every day and that these men were being hired. It was reported that 76 men were at work at the Frisco, and 35 at the Bunker Hill; 142 men, including guards, were at the Union Mine.

Every trainload brought in from six to 18 men. They were met at the depot by a delegation of the union men who used every argument to induce the new men to stay away from the mines. In some cases their efforts were successful, but most of the outsiders went through to the Frisco mine. . . . The mine owners were trying to import enough men to operate their mines and break the unions. . . . Adam Aulbach gave up trying to politely identify the labor importees, and his paper thereafter called them nothing but "scabs."

On May 28, there was quite a stir at the Union Pacific depot in Wallace, when the train was made up for the trip west. Many union miners were on the platform and they were angry. Fifteen guards came down from the Union mine, and the miners thought they were on their way out to meet another consignment of "scabs," but it was learned later that they had been discharged and were enroute to their homes in the Palouse. On the following day, five more guards came down and stopped in Wallace. They were looking for work and intended to go to Wardner and apply at the Sierra Nevada Mine or the Bunker Hill. . . . They were arrested in the afternoon on complaint made by Frank Ryan and charged with carrying deadly weapons. They were released on bail of $200 each until 7 p.m. that evening for trial. The case was postponed until 11 a.m. the next morning, at which time W. T. Stoll appeared for the defense. Each of the men was found guilty and fined $50.

CHAPTER 31

JUNE – 1892

Over a million dollars in wages had been lost and the railroads had lost a million dollars in freight, not to mention the loss in profits by the mine owners in the labor difficulties.

Starting a new tactic, the following notice was put up by some members of the Mine Owners' Association at their closed mines:

> "Not later than June 1, Union miners will be hired at this mine on condition they withdraw from the Union. This is the last chance, and if the old hands do not take it, outside miners will be imported and exclusively employed."

The Bunker Hill and the Helena & Frisco companies both obtained injunctions from the federal court preventing interference with their mining operations. The Bunker Hill injunction was partially based on an affidavit of T. H. Simmons, a miner who had been ordered out of the Wardner district in 1891. He apparently took the advice because his affidavit was signed in Grass Valley, California.

At the start of June, the Union Mill was running and there were enough men in the Union Mine to keep the mill going. Thirty-five men were working at the Frisco, but its mill was not operating. The Frisco employees were jeered by crowds for the first few days, but the Miner's Union stopped that sort of conduct. The Bunker Hill had about 30 men at work, and the Sierra

Nevada had 7 men working. It appeared more men would be imported.

Twelve Finns were imported from the East to work in the mines and their train was stopped in Mullan by union men. The Finns were induced to abandon their efforts to work in the Coeur d'Alenes. A hundred men met this same train when it later arrived in Wallace, only to find that the Finns were no longer on it.

Union men met a train in Missoula carrying from 40 to 50 men who were being imported to the Coeur d'Alenes. The union men must have used good arguments because they convinced the men they should not continue their trip. The union men had posted a picket on guard above Mullan to spot trains coming in from the east.

Adams and Carter, two miners working at the Frisco, were arrested on the 3rd for carrying deadly weapons in Gem. They claimed that their lives had been threatened upon several occasions by those who sought to prevent them from working at Esler's mine.

The Mine Owners' Association met in Spokane and resolved to continue their fight against the Miners' Union until the first of the year. However, it was to be noticed that some mines were offering employment to miners with no questions asked about union affiliation. This was understood to be a slight retreat from the Mine Owners' former freeze-out position.

At the Tiger mine, an offer was posted for miners at $3.50 per shift. The Union had a meeting and did not accept the offer because it was not cleared by their central union. A delegation went to Frank Culbertson, the superintendent of the Tiger, and asked him if he proposed to hire union men. He said,

"You ask no questions, and I'll ask none. We want competent men at $3.50 per day."

Bunker Hill was reported to be importing 250 men from California to work its mine.

The June 4 issue of the *Wallace Press* said the Mine Owners'

Association had been accused of putting two spies into the Miners' Union.

Thomas G. White and Co. of Duluth appeared to be the employment agent for the Mine Owners' Association, which was hiring men from that area. Although its membership was secret, the Mine Owners' Association had thirteen members early in June, 1892.

The Silver Bow Trades and Labor Assembly resolved that no Montana members of the Coeur d'Alene Mine Owners' Association should receive any patronage from organized labor, nor any votes for any position in Montana. The Montana group said that it would do all in its power to defeat the selection of Helena as the permanent capital of Montana at the coming election. This was apparently an attempt to put some pressure on A. M. Esler of the Frisco, who resided in Helena.

There was not much other news around the area. . . . High water downriver surrounded many of the ranch houses below the Mission; and a weekly newspaper was started in Harrison. It was called the *Ensign* and was pubished by H. L. Hughes.

Aulbach was always ready to offer some constructive criticism. He stated in early June that the Mine Owners' Association had made 12 blunders in the prior five months:

1. In organizing the MOA, a conspiracy contrary to law and against the peace and dignity of Idaho.
2. By employing two detectives to infiltrate the Miners' Unions.
3. In closing the mines over freight rates.
4. In issuing the MOA ultimatum.
5. In charging the Miners' Unions with an attempt to run the mines.
6. In hiring the *Wardner Barbarian,* a monthly paper, to write for them.
7. In closing the mines after the freight rates were settled.
8. In the systematic attempt by the MOA to provoke the miners to violate the law.

9. In the attempt by the MOA to ask the Governor to pro-
claim martial law.

10. In denouncing the civil authorities for their efforts to
enforce the law.

11. The MOA attempt to gag the *Wallace Press* and the
Mullan Tribune.

12. The ultimatum to keep the mines closed until January
1, 1893.

On the 11th of June, the Poorman and Tiger mines went
against the Association and announced they were going to work.
A celebration followed, but the Mine Owners' Association was
upset with Pat Clark and S. S. Glidden for their decision, saying
that it was a surprise and without proper notice to the Association.

A week earlier, the Governor of Idaho proclaimed that he
would declare martial law if any further threats of violence or
actual violence occurred. The local citizens were angry as they
did not think the situation merited such action. Protest meetings
were held throughout the county.

In Gem, Judge Pettibone fined two "gun carriers" from the
Frisco Mine the sum of $50 each and 25 days in jail. They ap-
pealed and their bonds were posted by members of the Mine
Owners' Association. Walter A. Jones acted as the prosecuting
attorney. Better times were in store for Mullan. Work was
starting up on the Morning concentrator, and 150 to 200 men
would soon be employed there. Neither the Hunter nor the
Morning belonged to the Mine Owners' Association.

The Gem mine was reported sold by Finch and Campbell to
an English syndicate for $920,000. Such reports were always
being made, but most of the transactions fell through. News of
the labor trouble had stalemated negotiation of sale of the Frisco
mine by Esler.

General E. J. Curtis, who came to Wallace with Governor
Willey, stated in Boise that he thought there would be trouble
before any settlement was reached. He added the Butte union

had shipped guns to the unions in the Coeur d'Alenes.

The Dunn Brothers editorialized that the Governor's threat caused no hardship to law-abiding citizens. They said there would be no martial law if the civil law was obeyed. They added that both the Mine Owners' Association and the miners' unions were wrong in some of their stands. The Dunns rapped the Mine Owners' Association for its announcement that it would not hire union miners, for the reason that unions were here to stay and the Association could not ignore them.

*   *   *

The townsite patent was finally issued to the town of Wallace on the 11th of June. The school authorities purchased six lots near Third and Pine Streets for $1,725, upon which to build a new school.

*   *   *

It was said that 2,500 men would be needed to reopen all the mines in the district; 180 woud be needed for the Poorman mine and mill when they once again were working at full capacity. The Poorman bought eleven Rand power drills for use in its mine. Burleigh drills were used in most of the district's mines. The Burleigh was operated by compressed air, and two men worked with them: the "Machine" (miner) and the "Chucker" (helper). The Burleighs drilled from 12 to 20 holes per shift. A hand miner was expected to drill about two holes per shift. There were about 15 Burleighs in the Gem mine alone. Some of the miners called them an enemy of the laboring class.

A resolution was passed at a mass meeting in Wallace to the effect that the Governor's proclamation did not present a fair statement of the existing situation, and that the issuance of the proclamation was not warranted. In a similar meeting in Burke, the citizens censured the Governor for issuance of his proclamation. They contended his inspection trip to the district consisted solely of meeting with the Mine Owners' Association in Wallace and Spokane.

A hearing was held in Boise on an order to show cause why

the injunctions should not be made permanent. Frank Ganahl argued that there was no necessity for such an injunction, and he presented affidavits from many men in the Coeur d'Alenes contradicting the allegations of the Mine Owners' complaint. Judge Beatty ordered that replies to the new affidavits be furnished by the plaintiff's attorney, and set the matter down for more hearings later in the month.

On the 11th, the Tiger and Poorman representatives submitted an offer to the Miners' Union, which provided:

1. That the companies could employ whomsoever they pleased; and
2. That no discrimination would be shown against union men; and
3. That the companies were to have the right to fire without union restraint; and
4. Union men were to support their union and hospital and provide benefits to sick or disabled members. Non-union men would have no rights to support of the Union or to receive Union benefits; and
5. That no discrimination would be shown against old employees because of the strike or their union affiliations; and
6. Day shifts were to be ten hours and night shifts nine hours long; and
7. The shift on Saturdays would be one hour shorter than on other days; and
8. The union was not to interfere with the management and vice versa.

The union spelled out some details which were immediately accepted by Pat Clark of the Poorman and S. S. Glidden for the Tiger. The news of their acceptance was received at the union headquarters in Wallace at 5 p.m. on June 11. The agreement had been signed by Thomas O'Brien and J. F. Poynton for the union, and Clark and Glidden for the companies.

When the news hit Wallace, "giant powder" was shot off, and the band played in the streets. A serenade for Pat Clark and Frank Culbertson at the Carter House was attended by a crowd of several hundred. The celebration lasted into the wee hours of the next day. The *Wallace Press* printed a special edition, and speeches were made from the porch of the Fuller House.

One prominent member of the Burke Union, Thomas Doyle, paraded through Wallace with the band—

> "He was dressed just as if he was going to take his shift at the Poorman, wearing rubber hip boots and a checked jumper, 2 candles in his hip pocket, a candlestick in his hat, a T.D. in his mouth and the Stars and Stripes in his hand."

A few days later the Mine Owners' Association held a violent and stormy meeting in the office of Finch and Campbell. Their talk could be heard out on the street, and you can bet there were people there to listen. Aulbach was prompted into an editorial over the split in the ranks of the Association:

> "Just remember! It is not a strike, but a mine owners' lockout. It has damaged the people several millions. Like a snake, the tail end of the MOA is wriggling itself to death. The head severed its connection from the body unceremoniously."

Except at the Tiger and the Poorman, the dispute was going on full blast. The Mine Owners announced during the middle of June that union membership would not prevent a man from being hired, and that all employees could live, eat and trade where they desired, but that their stand on the $3 pay for carmen and shovellers in dry mines was firm. There were then 267 non-union men in the Bunker Hill, 60 in the Sierra Nevada, 26 in the Last Chance, 70 in the Badger, 59 in the Gem mine, and 47 in the Granite mine.

At Mullan, neither the Morning nor the Hunter was ready to resume active work. Development work was being done in the

Hunter, but its mill was not working. One hundred fifty men were working in the Morning making outside improvements. At the Union mine, all of the non-union men were gone except four who were working on a contract.

On June 13, there had been a cave-in which closed the Union mine, and its non-union labor was divided between the Granite and Gem mines. Aulbach blamed the cave-in on sloppy work of the "scab" miners.

* * *

Other things were happening around the county and country. In Creede, Colorado, Bob Ford, the killer of Jesse James, was killed by a deputy sheriff. In Michigan, state troops were called out because of a strike in the region from which the non-union labor was being recruited for the Coeur d'Alene mining district. Markwell and Sons took over the Coeur d'Alene Dairy in Silverton.

Professor R. H. Wade was hired as principal of the Wallace school at a salary of $125 per month. There were two teachers on his staff, Mrs. Mary Foley and Mamie Phillips, who were paid $75 per month.

* * *

When Pat Clark made his speech at the Carter House, after the serenade, he advised miners to settle for $3 for carmen and shovellers in the dry mines. The Tiger and Poorman were wet mines. Clark had been a member of the Butte Miners' Union when he worked underground in that area.

Work resumed at the Tiger and Poorman on June 13; and it was a good thing. Business was so slow in Wallace that some business men were playing football in the intersection of Sixth and Cedar during business hours. The town fathers stopped this, so they took up pitching quoits on North Sixth Street.

Two non-union men, William Smith and Charles Erickson, quit the Frisco and demanded their baggage; it was refused them. They filed a suit against the Frisco for $100 in Justice Pettibone's court in Gem. A change of venue took the cases to

Judge Frazer in Mullan. Much interest was shown in this case as there were other non-union men who purportedly desired to leave as soon as they could get their baggage. A short time later the two miners were awarded $25 each from the Frisco by Judge Frazer.

P. J. Gorman, a non-union man, was arrested in Gem for carrying a concealed weapon. He was fined $100 or 50 days by Judge Pettibone. Mr. Finch appeared and stated that they would appeal. Justice Pettibone denied the right to appeal after the plea of guilty had been entered. It prompted Aulbach to comment that Judge Pettibone was acquiring quite an arsenal of Mine Owners' weapons.

On the next day, J. J. Monaghan, the foreman of the Gem mine, was arrested at Gem on a charge of assault with a deadly weapon. In an argument with a union man near the depot, he drew a revolver and pushed it in the face of the miner. Several bystanders disarmed him, but Monaghan struck one of them several blows in the face during the fracas. Judge Pettibone set bond at $2,500, and bound him over to the grand jury.

Five lodges of the Knights of Labor were organized in the district, each serving one of the towns.

Thomas Johnson, a union miner, was beaten at his cabin in Osburn. He claimed it was done by four "scabs" with clubs because he refused to work with them at the Bunker Hill.

Aulbach was still mad at Governor Willey, and hinted that the Mine Owners' Association was using him:

> "Let the Governor sit down quietly and see what an ass he had made of himself."

In mid-June, word came from Mullan that the Hunter was making arrangements to start up and would employ 100 men in their mine and mill. Martin Curran would be the Superintendent.

The Dunn paper stated that it had no favorite candidate for sheriff in the fall election, but that it desired to see a sober business man elected to fill the office, as it was one of the most important and best paying offices in the county. It was worth about $7,000 a year.

"We believe the time has come when someone can be elected Sheriff who does not devote his entire attention to drinking whiskey."

At the Granite mine, the lower tunnel was in about 1,100 feet, and this was 400 feet below the lowest of the old workings. The ledge had not yet been reached, but indications were that it was close. On the 16th, four union miners, who had been driving this long tunnel, quit and were replaced by four men who were described as "scabs" by Adam Aulbach. The Dunn Brothers' paper seldom used this word in describing non-union men.

The third week in June saw nothing new in the way of a settlement of the labor trouble. Payrolls were increasing, and ore shipments were on the upswing.

H. S. Davidson and John Rule were killed in a blast at the Bunker Hill on June 24. Rule came from California and was a cousin of John Hays Hammond, president of the Bunker Hill. Both were non-union men. Their bodies were embalmed, and it was planned to bury them at Wardner on the 25th. Their bodies would probably be shipped to California when the cool weather came later in the year. This was a common practice at the time. . . . Coroner Sims held an inquest, and the jury exonerated the company for blame in the deaths.

A. M. Esler returned to the district on the 24th and stated that no settlement between the Association and the Union had been reached. There were indications that the Mine Owners' Association had grown to 14 members. Esler also stated that all mines would soon be running, and that all Mine Owners except two members would refuse to recognize the Union and would favor hiring of non-union men. . . . Martial law was declared in the cattlelands of Wyoming about this time.

＊   ＊   ＊

In Murray, a flagpole 104 feet, 10 inches high was erected by members of the Republican Party at the corner of the Palace

Hotel. The Democrats got busy and put up one that was 111 feet, 5 inches high. The Mother Lode cleared $10,000 for its owners during the prior thirty days with a little five-stamp mill.

G. M. "Gabe" Dallas, Secretary of the Butte Union, was spending much time in Wallace at Union headquarters. Dallas planned to leave for Butte, but President O'Brien of the Central Union called him back on "important business."

Judge Clagett spoke at Utley Hall in Wallace and said that the smelters were out of lead ore, and unless the mines started up, Congress might remove the tariff from lead ores and lead, and the Mexican lead would flood the United States. The local miners said: "Let it come."

News from Wardner indicated that the Bunker Hill had imported non-union men from Grass Valley, California, to work the mine. There was speculation as to the number of men who came. Reports varied from 60 down to 12 men.

Florence McCarthy was one of the oldest prospectors on Canyon Creek, and he was an owner of the Belle Group of claims, which were south of the Gem mine. He started across the Gem property on his way up the hill to his claims and was confronted by an armed guard, who ordered him down the mountain. McCarthy decided it was wise to return to Gem. Armed guards had been stationed on most Gem and Burke mines ever since April 1. These armed guards drew the taunts of the townspeople, and it was "good sport" to have them arrested if they left the mines and came to town for a drink without taking off their firearms.

Lot jumpers were active in the Medimont and Harrison areas. About a dozen of them were arrested at Harrison and taken to court at Rathdrum. June ended with more hearings in Boise on the Mine Owners' injunctions, but no decision was announced.

Aulbach reported that nearly all "scabs" had quit the Granite mine, and at the month's end it was rumored that only three remained on the job. One of the Finns said he quit because of the food. . . . Esler was back at the Frisco. . . . Martin Kennedy

and Billy Hutchinson, foremen at the Frisco, were fired because
they sympathized with the Union miners.

❋   ❋   ❋

On June 29, in the afternoon, Syd Mills was traveling on the
divide between Dream and Fancy Gulches, two miles west of
Murray. He had cleaned up the sluice boxes at his placer in
Fancy Gulch and was taking the gold to the Bank of North
Idaho in Murray. He had done this several times a month for
previous three years. He was waylaid by two disguised men and
robbed of $2,000 to $2,500 in ingot gold. They ordered Mills to
return to Fancy Gulch, and they took off into the timber toward
Murray. Rewards totaled $850, and a search was soon under
way. Mills offered $500, the Bank offered $100 and the County
offered $250. It was speculated that if the men were caught,
their case would be tried by "Judge Lynch."

CHAPTER 32

EARLY IN JULY — 1892

Six months of shutdown and strike atmosphere had passed and things were still hanging together. Some of the seams had been strained, but the situation was still under control. As a matter of fact, the Shoshone County jail was empty on the first of July, 1892. Burke was peaceful, with the Tiger and Poorman working. In Wallace, the baseball fans donated money to send to St. Louis for a pitcher, catcher and extra man for the town team.

The First National Bank of Wallace was to open about August first. This bank was a new venture and did not grow out of the McAulay-DeLashmutt bank, which bore a somewhat similar name. F. F. Johnson was the president and Henry White, the vice president of the new bank. Horace Davenport would serve as cashier.

In Mullan, things were quiet, and the Morning and Hunter were working.

Aulbach entered July with mixed emotions. He was satisfied that the labor trouble was seemingly under control, but he was very upset with the Dunn Brothers and the Governor of Idaho.

In speaking of the Dunns, Aulbach said they started the *Wallace Free Press* about four years before, and that two years later he (Aulbach) sent Ed Tibbals over from Murray to buy it for $1,400. Then Aulbach came to Wallace to take charge and the Dunns soon started a competing paper, the *Coeur d'Alene Miner*.

Aulbach said the Dunns never had a dollar of their own until he paid them the $1,400. He closed his tirade:

"Place a beggar on horseback and he will ride to the devil."

Adam Aulbach considered the Dunns rather small pickings, so he turned his attention upon Idaho's chief executive, whom he chose to address as:

"His 'Accidental' Excellency, Governor Willey (by the forbearance of God and the stupidity of the Republican party, Chief Executive of Idaho)."

General E. J. Curtis, Adjutant General of Idaho, stated in his annual report that the state militia was in poor shape and not a single company was fit for service in the Coeur d'Alenes. Aulbach took this opportunity to accuse Governor Willey of shirking service during the Civil War.

Adam Aulbach took pride in pointing out that he was a member of the New York Typographical Union No. 6, and that he was a charter member of Typographical Union No. 21 of San Francisco, and that he was chairman of its committee on constitution and by-laws.

On the 1st of July, the Union Pacific brought in two cars of provisions, gaily decorated, from the Miners' Union at Butte. Their value was $2,400 and consisted of 10 tons of flour, 35 sacks of beans, 5 caddies of tobacco, 6 cases of tomatoes, 6 boxes of dry apples, 4 chests of tea, 3 cases of baking powder, 10 kegs of syrup, 25 boxes of codfish, 15 boxes of soap, 20 cases of coffee, 3 tons of bacon, 2 tons of sugar and 10 boxes of smoking tobacco. "Gabe" Dallas and Tom O'Brien returned from Butte on this train.

Early in July, the Granite, Gem, and Frisco were the only three mines left on the east end of the district employing only non-union labor. It was reported that almost all of them had left the Granite. The Gem had 55 "scabs" and 20 guards, and the Frisco had 50 "scabs" and 20 guards. Few of the non-union men were good miners, and this was also causing troubles . . . low production, mill breakdowns, etc.

The *Wallace Press* reported that the "scabs" of the Gem mine had secured an 80-foot pole and proposed to erect it on the Fourth of July in a separate celebration. Aulbach:

> "As most of the men belong to the realm of Queen Vic, they'll probably elevate the British flag."

Jacob Heater, the constable who left Mullan in a hurry, was reported to be working as a guard at the prison in Boise, through the recommendations of members of the Mine Owners' Association.

The Fourth of July would be observed in Mullan, and all towns on the South Fork were going there by special trains to celebrate. Mullan was in the best position to hold the celebration as its two big mines (Morning and Hunter) were working.

The Union Pacific reported that it might once again put on its regular passenger train. Since the shutdown in January, only a mixed passenger and freight train had been on the tracks. The beginning of ore shipments made entirely too much business for one train.

Under the dateline of July 2, from the nation's capital, it was reported that the Idaho Governor telegraphed the Idaho delegation in Congress to call on President Harrison and ask for U. S. troops to settle the Coeur d'Alene labor difficulty. The delegation called upon the President on July 2, and they all agreed that the statements made in the message did not justify the President's sending federal troops to the district. The President joined the delegation in the hope and belief that the differences would be settled within the law.

Adam Aulbach devoted considerable space in his next issue to roasting the Governor for having appealed for federal troops. E. J. Curtis, Adjutant General of Idaho, was a guest of Charles Sweeney and George B. McAulay on the Fourth of July, and Aulbach speculated that Curtis was on an inspection trip for the Governor:

"Governor Willey and the MOA formed an obtuse, odious, offensive, objectable, ominous, oppressive, omnivorous, obstreperous, onerous, obstinate, original oligarchy which deserves ostracism at the hands of an outraged public."

Trouble was brewing. . . . A prominent mine owner wired the Governor for a number of cases of guns for use by the guards at the mines working non-union men, as he feared an outbreak. Governor Willey replied that he had no arms available.

Early in July, 250 men attended a Union meeting in Wardner. G. N. Dallas of Butte, John Sweeney and Attorney Bushnell spoke. Although they contended that several union men had been beaten during the prior two weeks, miners were to refuse to be baited into trouble by "scabs." The union men were afraid to retaliate for fear of martial law by Governor Willey.

Charles Bonner, President of the Granite Miners' Union of Montana with 700 members, and Peter Breen, a member of the Montana State Committee of Miners' Unions, were in Wallace to look into the labor trouble. Breen had been an '84 pioneer on Prichard Creek. They expected to stay in the district until July 11 or 12.

The Bunker Hill tramway was still undergoing tests by its manufacturers. Some changes were made and it worked very satisfactorily; it easily moved 400 to 450 tons of ore in 10 hours. Work had begun on a long tunnel beginning in the vicinity of the Bunker Hill mill. This tunnel was designed to tap the ledges above Wardner at a very low depth, and it would be over two miles long when completed. Arrangements were made to enlarge the mill capacity to 750 tons daily, and about 300 men were employed early in July.

In Mullan, the big celebration was held on the Fourth of July in very orderly fashion. Round trip fare for visitors from Wallace was 35 cents. The horse race was easily won by a horse named Redbird. Very little money changed hands on the race, as Redbird was an unknown horse in the area. . . . One had to watch out for those "ringers" they would run into the races. . . .

Mullan displayed a new flag pole of 111 feet, and about midway up the pole were the emblems of the Miners' Union—crossed sledge, pick and shovel.

In Gem, a celebration was improvised for the Fourth, and W. A. Bradly was chairman of the event. Patriotic readings were made and songs were sung. The day closed with a grand ball in the evening. While this peaceful and patriotic celebration was going on, the Gem Mine force erected breastworks before the mill out of 3 by 12 inch lumber, with port holes for rifles; and Esler had 25 men with Winchesters parading up and down in front of the Frisco. War preparations on the part of the Frisco and Gem management did not seem to frighten the men, women and children of Gem.

Aulbach said Esler hoisted a broom above his U. S. flag at his home on the Fourth of July to celebrate his personal efforts in importing "scab" labor under armed guard. Adam scorched Esler for putting self-gratification above country. The Dunn paper set out a story, which may have been a slightly different version, to the effect that the non-union members of the Frisco erected a liberty pole on the Fourth, with a pick, shovel and broom on the top. They said the significance of this was not plain, but it made the union miners in Gem angry, and for a while it looked like trouble.

In any event, Aulbach published another attack on A. M. Esler in the July 9 edition:

> "Esler, the scab hunter and hounder of the Irish race, did not serve his country when his flag needed defenders, yet this blatant advocate of wage reduction wants the army of the United States to slap the glorious flag about his carcass and protect it with bristling bayonets."

Aulbach added that Esler would be known in the future as a "scab" hunter and no man had been more kindly treated by nature than Esler. Aulbach also charged that no man had done

more during the present trouble than Esler to provoke bloodshed.
Meanwhile, back at Wallace . . . The Dunn Brothers said:

> "Last Monday, the Fourth of July, was the dullest day in
> the history of Wallace. The town was practically abandoned.
> In the evening impromptu foot races were indulged in on
> Cedar Street. . ."

Most of the celebrants went to the St. Regis country or to Mullan
to celebrate the day.

The Morning Mine had a pay day on July 8, and the men received all their pay due until July 1. About $6,000 was put in
circulation. The shovellers received $3 per day, foremen of the
gangs $4 per day and teams $8.00. This was the second pay day
Mullan had had in the prior six months.

The Dunn Brothers, in publishing their weekly edition on
July 9, did not stress labor news from the district. Most of their
front page was given over to politics. A long article on an inside
page was entitled "Bullets and Dynamite," and it set forth stories
about the riots at Carnegie's Steel Works in Pittsburgh, which
were under fire for 13 hours on July 6. Pinkerton men were
playing a big part in the labor trouble in Pittsburgh. . . .

Also printed on an inside page was a letter from J. F. Poynton,
Secretary of the Coeur d'Alene Central Miners' Union, to the
Missoula Board of Trade, thanking them for their interest in the
labor troubles in this district and stating also—

> ". . . the organization which I represent is and always had
> been ready to meet the MOA more than half way for the
> purpose of adjusting existing difficulties. I trust that we will,
> by our strict observance of the law and order, continue to
> be entitled to your kind consideration."

Such were the first nine days of July, 1892. . . .

CHAPTER 33

GUNS AND DYNAMITE — JULY 1892

It had been apparent for more than a month that the only hope the union had to get the non-union men out of the Frisco, Gem and Bunker Hill mines was through violent means. Other forms of pressure had been exerted by the union, but to no avail. Meanwhile, these companies were gaining strength in their fight against the Miners' Union.

Both sides were well armed, and all that was needed was provocation to bring on the attack. Fist fights between members of the two factions were common, but they ended without any serious results. The non-union men became braver as their numbers increased; they fought back when taunted and abused by the union men. In early July, the non-union men were sometimes the attacking parties in these affrays, both individually and in groups.

On Saturday night, July 9, a guard at the Gem Mine and a discharged guard from the Frisco went to town and started drinking. They soon became offensive in their statements regarding the union men and expressed a willingness to fight and defied arrest. The union men then answered their invitation and attacked them. The Gem guard was almost killed, and the man from the Frisco escaped. John A. Finch, the manager of the Gem Mine, requested the Sheriff not to arrest anyone. Finch was trying to keep the pot from boiling over.

On Sunday afternoon of the 10th, a miner who kept a small

boarding house in the upper part of Gem had occasion to visit a family just below the Gem Mill. He passed the barricades and left the railroad track, stepping across what was known as the "deadline." One of Gem guards, named Putnam, warned him off. They had words, and finally a challenge for a fist fight passed between them. The guard pulled off his coat, and they went at it. Hundreds witnessed this fight, but no one from either side interfered. The miner whipped the guard severely and went home. After the fight the guard claimed that a rock had been thrown at him.

A half hour later three Gem guards, armed with Winchesters, were seen hurrying up the canyon. An alarm was given, and the union miners armed themselves and rushed up the canyon to protect their comrade. The guards ran to the Frisco and further trouble was avoided.

Subsequently a warrant was sworn out for the miner's arrest, charging him with assaulting the guard with a deadly weapon. This infuriated some who claimed the guard had voluntarily said he could whip the miner and then went beyond the "deadline" to engage in the fist fight.

These fights served to light the fuse, and later on Sunday, the 10th, union men, armed with rifles, shotguns and revolvers, began to gather at Gem. They came from Wallace, Mullan and Burke. This was no chance gathering.

From the Central Headquarters of the Union, at the corner of Fifth and Cedar Streets in Wallace, Thomas O'Brien, president of the Central Union, J. F. Poynton, secretary of the Union, "Gabe" Dallas, secretary of the Butte Miners' Union, and about a half dozen others left and passed through the principal business streets. They were on their way up Burke Canyon headed for Gem, some four miles distant, armed with rifles and revolvers.

All this preparation was under way in plain view of everyone, but, as yet, not a shot had been fired. The weekend fist fights were not the reason for events which followed. The cause was deeply rooted in the actions of the union men and the Mine

Owners for the weeks and months past. The Dunn Brothers were
to state:

"Armed union men had gone there to fight. . . . It was plain
that a bloody battle was about to take place."

Feeling was growing more intense all the time. Union men
claimed the "scabs" were antagonizing them. Learning of this,
John A. Finch, went to Gem on Sunday afternoon, directly into
town, and talked with the leader of the Miners' Union. He then
came back to Wallace.

Later than night, it was rumored that Esler had wired for
troops, and that the governor had ordered some to the Coeur
d'Alenes. About 9 p.m. that evening a special train from the
Union Pacific depot in Wallace left for the west, and it was
rumored that this train would meet soldiers at Cataldo. This
report spread quickly up the canyon. All the miners from the
surrounding towns, who could get arms, met at Gem.

Sunday night finally passed, and early on Monday, the 11th
of July, the men on the Frisco property could see groups of
armed men on both hill sides of the canyon overlooking the
mine. Superintendent Jack Howard had stationed a few guards
on the dump of tunnel No. 3. On the cliff just west of these
guards, in easy range, were a group of union men.

At about 5 a.m., firing commenced by the union men, both at
the men on the Frisco mine property and at the mill. The guards
stated later that they did not believe these first shots were intended to hit them, but to scare them out. One of the Frisco
men said that they did not return the fire until the bullets from
the union rifles came through the roof of the shed under which
they were standing. They returned the fire and were soon forced
to take cover in the mill. By this time, the shooting was general,
both sides aiming to kill.

Aulbach's version of the start of the battle was that a union
miner was walking from Gem to Burke, and that the Frisco
guards fired upon him as he approached the Frisco property.

He then ran back to Gem and gave the alarm, and the fight progressed.

One miner later said that there was no thought of blowing up the mill when the fight started, but that it arose as an incident of the battle. As soon as the miners came into view, the guards opened fire, but the range was long and no one was hurt. The miners scattered and an engagement followed. The guards were well-protected and could fire from hidden points and this forced the miners to go into the hills across the canyon. One man was killed and several wounded in the Frisco gunbattle. It was stated that about 1,000 shots were fired. The miners, seeing the guards had the advantage, circled the canyon and got above the mill.

Soon after the guards on the dump had been dislodged, the union men on the hill came down to the upper end of a sidehill tramway, which ran on tracks, placed several boxes of "giant powder" in the tramway car, and started it down to the mill. But the fuse was too short, and the powder exploded before reaching its destination. If the fuse on the load of giant powder and been properly gauged, both mill buildings would have been blown to kindling and the loss of life would have been very great. This explosion destroyed the tramway tracks, and other means then had to be devised to get powder into the mill. . . . This was soon done.

The men above the mill swung around and got to the flume where the penstock goes to the mill. Bullets whistled about these men, but they had only one aim—to get the boxes of powder down the penstock. The pipe was full of water, so holes were shot in it near the wheel. When the water drained out, the powder was sent down, and the last box of powder had a fuse attached. In the ensuing explosion, the entire old mill building seemed to rise bodily from the ground and then drop back, a mass of ruins. How many men were in the mill was not known; most of them had gone into the new mill after the first attempt to send down powder had failed.

This explosion caused damage of about $20,000, but did not

damage the adjoining buildings. A. T. McDonald was afterward found dead in the debris, while seven men were more or less injured.

Siringo claimed that many lives were saved because most of the 75 or more guards and non-union miners were at the far side of the mill building, shooting at the union men on the opposite mountain side from where Pettibone and his small gang were doing their work.

Meanwhile the shooting on both sides continued, but the Frisco men began to realize that theirs was a hopeless cause. In a short while, they showed a white flag, and the firing ceased. About 60 of the Frisco men then began filing out. It was claimed later by the non-union men that after they had come out un-armed they were fired upon and one of their number fell dead. The union men denied that anyone was killed after the surrender. . . . Siringo praised Peter Breen for standing up and giving the order that no more Frisco prisoners were to be mistreated.

The captured men were formed into a line, with a guard on each side, and then marched to the union hall in Gem, where they were held until later in the day. The union hall at Gem presented a strange spectacle. The seats along the sides were crowded with the prisoners from the Frisco, while on the benches lay the dead and the wounded men.

It was said that not more than half the Frisco men had rifles, and they were heavily outnumbered.

✿   ✿   ✿

Shortly after the fight began at the Frisco mill, there was a general outbreak near the Gem Mine. The non-union men at the Gem mine had erected barricades of lumber and cord wood. Portholes were left, and riflemen could fire through these port-holes towards the rear of the buildings fronting on the main street of Gem. The Union Pacific railroad tracks and Canyon Creek were between the town of Gem and the Gem Mine.

The night shift was coming out, and the day shift was going in when the fight at the Gem mine began. Two of the Gem

men, Dick Lang and Ivery Bean, left the mill to go to the boarding house in the town of Gem. When they were on the bridge
crossing the creek, the report of a rifle was heard, and Bean fell
dead. Lang ran back, and then the non-union men opened fire
on the town, and firing became general from the union men.

The union men claimed Bean was shot by the non-union Gem
guards, who responded that Bean was killed by a shot fired from
the town of Gem by union men. Siringo claimed Bean was shot
by Web Leasure.

Volley after volley was fired into the heart of Gem from the
barricades. Daxon's saloon, a hangout for union miners, was rid-
dled with bullets. Billy Daxon was in bed upstairs in the saloon
when the first shot was fired. He hurriedly got up and ran
downstairs. These stairs were in the rear of the building and in
plain view of the barricades at the Gem Mine. Daxon had to
run through a hail of bullets. How he escaped was a mystery.
The door and frame showed 10 bullet holes, and the back end
of the building showed about 30 bullet holes.

At the Gem Mine bunkhouse, which stood on a little elevation
overlooking the town, men pulled out mattresses and from behind these a deadly fire was poured into the town of Gem. When
the trains went up the canyon from Wallace that morning they
were stopped by the Gem guards. No one was allowed to pass
them on the railroad tracks. The Sheriff was on one of the
trains, and he took the mail on his shoulder, and as he came
within the "deadline" a dozen rifles were pointed at him, but
they were lowered when he was identified. An hour later the
trains were allowed to pass on to Burke.

Gem women and children had to be moved several times to
places of security. Most of them had gone either to Wallace or
Burke, during the previous night. Some traveled on foot.

Three union men were killed and a number wounded in the
Gem Mine battle, before a white flag was sent up from the
union side. Firing ceased and Ed Kinney, who was in charge
of the non-union men at the Gem mill, went out to confer with

the union leaders. Kinney was told the Gem men and the company property were at the mercy of the union, and Kinney was asked to surrender. Kinney refused, and stated he had come to protect the interests of the company by whom he was employed and that he had no authority to surrender.

At about this time the Shoshone County Sheriff, the District Attorney and deputy United States Marshals arrived in Gem, and a truce was declared in the hostilities.

A short time later, Inspector General Curtis, of the state militia and Colonel Hammell arrived. Another conference was held and it was agreed to submit the matter to A. L. Gross, who was in Wallace. Gross was the only member of the Gem management in the district. The men on the Gem property had only 20 or 25 guns and not a great deal of ammunition, and it was evident that they could only hold out for a limited time against the larger union forces. At noon, after considering these facts, Gross agreed to surrender and withdraw his men from the mine, which was done. . . . It was said that Peter Breen gave A. L. Gross 20 minutes to decide whether to surrender or lose the Gem Mill. Breen pulled out his watch and Gross took all of the 20 minutes to make up his mind. When Breen called "Time's up," Gross surrendered the Gem.

The terms of the surrender of the Gem mine were reduced to writing:

Wallace, Shoshone Co., Idaho

The representatives of the Gem mine agree with Messrs. Breen and Bonner, representing the parties engaged in hostutilities against the employes of the Gem mine, as follows:

The Gem employes are to surrender their arms to a committee of four citizens of Shoshone County, two of said committee to be chosen by Mr. Ed Kinney, of the Gem mine, and two to be chosen by the parties engaged in the hostilities. The employes of the Gem mine are to peacefully leave the mine and the town of Gem, and Messrs. Breen and Bonner, as such commissioners, guarantee said employes safe conduct and to protect said employes from any act of violence.

And Messrs. Breen and Bonner further agree that all the property of the Milwaukee Mining Company shall be fully protected and saved from harm of any kind.

> A. L. Gross,
>   For Milwaukee Mining Company
> Chas. Bonner,
> Peter Breen,
>
>   On behalf of citizens.

Dated July 11, 1892.

The guns from the Gem Mine were turned over to the committee referred to in the surrender agreement. However, it was made up of two men, not four. The Gem mine selected Captain W. C. Human, Deputy United States Marshal, and the union selected a man named Harris, of Burke. They started to take the guns to Wallace to put them in a bank vault.

About this time, the non-union men from the Frisco, who had been held prisoner, were released from the Gem Union Hall. The guns and about 2,000 rounds of ammunition were placed on a hand car and started down the track. Jesse Sears of Gem went with Human and Harris. When they neared the Granite Mill, they were stopped by about a dozen men. Sears made an effort to hold them off, while Harris took the ammunition from the hand car and started toward the Granite Mill. The group of men overtook Harris and took the ammo away from him. The guns on the car were taken from Sears at gunpoint. There were 27 Winchesters from the Gem Mine, and 37 Winchesters had been taken from the forces at the Frisco. When the fracas was over in Gem, over 100 union miners boarded the Northern Pacific train there and came to Wallace. They were met at the depot by hundreds of union sympathizers. The train carried three union and two non-union dead men. The crowd, with over 200 armed men, followed the wagon which carried the three union dead to the undertaker's. Afterwards the crowd went to the Miners' Union headquarters.

On the 11th, after the trouble in Gem, the Wallace town trustees held a special meeting. They feared the union men would come in a mob to Wallace. The trustees issued an order closing all the saloons in Wallace, and the town marshal served the order that afternoon. Some of the saloon keepers refused to close on such a busy day, so finally all of them stayed open. . . . On the following day, the union officials were concerned about the behavior of some of their men and asked the Wallace saloon owners to close. This request was immediately complied with.

Later in the evening of the 11th, as darkness fell, squads of men were seen leaving town down the tracks toward Wardner. Some were armed. A wagon carrying guns left Wallace in that direction. A short distance below Wallace, the men boarded two Northern Pacific freight cars and released the brakes. With the down grade, the men were soon in Wardner Junction.

After a brief march, they arrived at the Bunker Hill concentrator, which they soon took into their possession. Many miners placed themselves on the mountain overlooking the Bunker Hill Mill. A ton of "giant powder," taken from George Crane's powder house, was placed under the mill. Victor M. Clement was then given his choice whether to send his non-union miners from the country or see his mill blown up.

Clement was given until noon of the next day to get his men out of town. By Wednesday, troops from Fort Sherman were camped at Cataldo, and Clement hoped that they would arrive in Wardner in time to protect the Bunker Hill men and property. But the troops did not arrive in time, and the non-union men were sent on their way.

The troops were held at Cataldo under threat if they moved on to Wardner, the Bunker Hill and Gem Mill would both be blown up. No troops came. The Sierra Nevada force was evacuated pursuant to the union's request.

The news of troops on the move set the union men into a frenzy. About 150 of them, mostly armed, appeared at Wallace at sundown on Tuesday. They came from Gem and Mullan, and climbed the mountains around Wallace to secure advantageous positions. Their rifles could sweep the railroads and the streets of Wallace.

The next day, it was learned that these men intended to detain Negro troops coming in from Missoula, at the risk of a battle with them. A piece of track was blown out above Mullan, and a bridge was destroyed west of Mullan. The colored troops arrived in Mullan at 2 A.M., on Wednesday the 13th, and remained there until 9 A.M. At that time they received orders to return to Missoula, rather than to proceed the last seven miles to Wallace. The union men harassed traffic on the Northern Pacific all week.

Earlier on Tuesday morning, the county commissioners and sheriff wired the Governor for troops. He replied at 5 P.M. by instructing the sheriff to first exhaust his civil power. Upon receipt of the telegram the sheriff issued a call for a posse. He summoned about 20 Wallace men and 20 from Murray, and he intended to get 50 from Wardner. The Wallace men were to respond at 10 o'clock that night and go to Wardner on a special train. Only one man from Wallace answered the call to duty— George Crane, a carpenter. Every Murray man responded by coming over to Wallace. The Sheriff went alone to Wardner where he found himself powerless in the midst of all the miners.

When the union men were finished in Wardner they returned to Wallace and their homes in Canyon Creek. A lot of them boarded the Northern Pacific train bound for Gem and Burke. When the train had traveled but a short distance, the conductor found that only a few of the union men had tickets, and the rest refused to pay. The conductor was not about to be unduly pressured; he had the engineer back the train to the depot and compelled all the free riders to get off the train.

That afternoon, after the miners left Wardner, Sheriff Cunningham sent a wire to General Carlin at Cataldo, where the troops were quartered:

"The miners have disbanded and gone to their respective homes. There is not trouble in Wallace or Wardner."

It must have taken a lot to excite Sheriff Cunningham.

The Tiger and Poorman mines in Burke were closed from July 10 until July 15 because not enough men appeared to work them.

Meanwhile, on Tuesday, nearly all the non-union men from the Gem and Frisco mines took the train from Wallace to the outside world. Some private citizens of the district who had incurred the wrath of the union were also among those being deported. The group, which numbered about 130, traveled to the Cataldo Mission, where they left the train to wait for the boat to take them to Coeur d'Alene. Most of these people were unarmed. The non-union men had been paid that morning by the companies. The boat was delayed until 1 A.M. the next day because it had been engaged in transferring troops across the lake.

In the early evening, while they were waiting, a group of union men or their sympathizers came into sight on horseback and began firing on the non-union men. Being unarmed, the non-union men ran. Some of them went across the meadow and others went into the river. The next day, 17 men, most of them wounded, were picked up along the river. Only 15 of the group returned to take the boat at 1 A.M.; the rest had fled.

It was suspected that some men were killed in this affair, but no bodies were ever found. Ed Kinney of the Gem mine was one of the group, but he was not injured. James Monaghan, foreman of the Gem mine, was believed to have been killed in this fracas, but he turned up in Spokane two days later after a lot of swimming and walking. A young man named Abbott was shot.

Some of the men fled over Fourth of July Canyon and walked 30 miles into Coeur d'Alene. A large number of those waiting

for the boat were robbed of all they had. Aulbach reported that
the members of the union maintained that no union man had
anything to do with the "Mission Massacre."

Charles Siringo stated that Abbott, the wounded man, who
was hidden in the tall grass, said he saw the "union men" rob
several dead bodies, then cut open their stomachs so they would
sink and then dump them in the river.

* * *

The casualty list for the events of July 11 and 12 was as
follows:

3 non-union dead:

Ivery Bean..........................Killed at the Gem mine
John Stanlick......................Killed at the Frisco
A. T. McDonald................Killed at the Frisco Explosion

3 union dead:

James Hennessy, Gus Carlson and Harry Cummings; all
were killed at the battle at the Gem mine.

9 non-union wounded:

J. W. Gaukroger................Shot in left hip
R. K. Adams.......................Fractured rib
Frank C. Wilcox................Shot in left jaw
Samuel Carkhuff................Internal contusion
S. C. Collins.......................Shot in left thigh
L. L. Abbott.......................Contusion of left leg
John Whitty.......................Shot in calf of leg
M. F. Halcrow...................Shot in left jaw
Charles E. Peterson...........Fractured skull

3 union wounded:

John Ward and James Nicholson....Not seriously wounded
George Pettibone................................Seriously injured hand

Most of the wounded were not shot, but instead were injured
in the explosion. Aulbach reported that 16 or 17 men were
wounded in all.

Wallace had two undertakers and two hospitals in 1892. The Miners' Union dead were taken to Worstell's Undertaking Parlor, and Ward's Funeral Parlor made arrangements for the non-union dead. The Holland Hospital cared for the non-union wounded, and the Miners' Union Hospital cared for two of the union wounded. George Pettibone fled to the hills, and therefore did not receive immediate care for his injured hand.

The funeral for the three union dead took place at 1 P.M. on Wednesday, the 13th. Over 500 men were in the procession, which was led by the Wallace band. The burials were in Nine Mile gulch at the Miners' Union cemetery. The funeral services were conducted by Reverend J. E. Staunton, assisted by Father Keyzer, who preceded on foot the three wagons containing the bodies. The wagons were followed by carriages. In the first carriage sat a young lady who had been engaged to marry August Carlson. Carlson was a Protestant; and the other two dead were Catholics.

Shortly after the funeral for the union miners, the burial of Bean and Stanlick, the two non-union men, took place. There were two wagons, two handsome coffins, the drivers of the wagons, and the Episcopal Minister Staunton. No mourners. No procession to the graveyard. Alone they were taken to their last resting place, where Christian burial services were read over their remains. An hour or so after the burial, Bean's relatives wired undertaker Ward to ship his body to New York City for burial.

Ivery Bean was a member of the Knights of Pythias in good standing, and it was reported that they were going to handle his burial until they were warned off by the union men.

A. T. McDonald's body was not found in the debris of the Frisco mill until July 13, and then it was brought to Wallace. He had been killed by falling timbers during the explosion. McDonald's funeral took place during the afternoon of July 14, a day after the other burials.

Some seventy-four years later, Ben Oppenheim told of his

remembrances of the funeral procession which took the union dead through Wallace on the way to the graveyard. He was a young boy at the time and had watched the procession from the balcony of the Arment Hotel. Ben Oppenheim described the town of Wallace as being so tense that no one spoke above a whisper on the day of the funerals.

*   *   *

Two heavy explosions were heard on the evening of the 14th in Wallace. It was first believed they had come from Canyon Creek, but it was learned the next day that someone had blown up two telegraph poles in order to disable the line between Wallace and Mullan.

Within a very short time, the non-union men who had been driven out of Wardner returned to resume work at the Bunker Hill. About 15 union men called the returnees "scabs" as they started up the hill toward the mine. The name callers were arrested for their actions.

*   *   *

On the 13th day of July, Governor Willey proclaimed that Shoshone County was in a state of rebellion and insurrection. Copies of his proclamation were soon posted all over the district. Governor Willey cited that the Shoshone County authorities had declared they were unable to cope with the situation. He directed General J. F. Curtis to proceed to Shoshone County and to protect the railroad and telegraph and arrest all wrongdoers and keep the peace.

By the 15th, Companies B, C, D, E and F, 14th Infantry, from Vancouver Barracks, consisting of 194 enlisted men and 11 officers, were stationed in Wallace. Lt. Col. Thrakes was in command of this group.

Wardner had three companies from Fort Sherman, three companies of 4th Infantry from Fort Spokane, three companies of 25th Infantry from Fort Missoula and three companies of the Idaho National Guard. There were over 500 troops in Wardner. Mullan had eight companies of the 20th Infantry from Fort

Keogh in Montana, consisting of about 250 men. Gem had one company of the 4th Infantry from Fort Sherman, and two companies of Idaho National Guard men. Two companies of cavalry were standing by at Fort Walla Walla awaiting any call which might be made for their services.

The first United States troops came to Wardner on Wednesday, the 13th. The next day, trouble broke out at Wallace about 11 A.M. Some miners from the Granite mine were having difficulty with a mob. The troops hurried up from Wardner, and all was peaceful upon their arrival 30 minutes later. By Saturday morning, on the 16th of July, several companies of soldiers were stationed in Burke, and there were over 1,000 soldiers in the district.

By Friday, the 15th, Coroner W. S. Sims assumed the duties of Provost Marshal of Shoshone County, and under his direction a detachment of soldiers began making arrests. Their first stop was the Miners' Union supply store, where all arms were seized and a guard was placed over the building. Sims assumed the office of sheriff by the appointment of the military authorities. Sheriff Cunningham had been ousted from his office on the 13th of July, by the declaration of martial law.

From the time of the surrender on July 11 until the troops took possession on the 15th, the Gem Mill was under strict guard by the Miners' Union men, who would allow no one to approach the premises. Everything was left as it was found on the 11th. The barricades and wood piles for the riflemen were still intact. Gem townspeople said there was never any threat or effort to burn or destroy the Gem mill, and that no excitement prevailed in Gem after the evening of July 12.

The Granite Mill was located a half mile below the Gem Mill, and the miners had not removed a board from it during the week. It was untouched during the trouble.

The town of Gem was placed under guard by the troops on the 15th. The soldiers presented quite a curiosity to the children. An appeal was sent by wire to senators and members of Congress for a congressional investigation into the troubles of the Coeur d'Alene mining district. It was sent by Peter Breen of the Butte Union, Attorney Bushnell of Spokane and 100 others.

President Thomas O'Brien and Secretary J. F. Poynton of the Central Union, together with Thomas Heney, president of the Mullan Miners' Union, were arrested and placed in the guard house. A company of soldiers were stationed at Sixth and Cedar Streets in Wallace, and many arrests were made.

Siringo described President O'Brien thusly: "He was not a bad man at heart, but his head had gone wrong through taking the advice of such men as Joe Poynton and "Judge" Pettibone. . . . I shall never believe that nature intended Mr. O'Brien to wear prison stripes."

Elsewhere in the West, the schoolhouse served as social centers for their communities. Not necessarily so in Wallace. . . . The schoolhouse on west Bank Street was converted into a guard house to hold the union men who were arrested. Among the better known prisoners housed there were: Attorney Walter Jones, Robert Neill, Mike Conway, M. J. Donnelly, Thomas Whalen and Thomas McMullen. Many lesser known parties had also been arrested. The same situation existed in Mullan, Gem and Wardner.

A lot of the union men took to the hills to escape arrest. The troops were intensely interested in capturing George Pettibone, Peter Breen and Gabe Dallas. It was reported that Hugh McGee and Billy Daxon were arrested, along with 15 others, in Gem on the 15th. Some others were arrested over in Murray. . . . Siringo described Gabe Dallas as "a one-eyed, two-legged Irish hyena from the Butte City, Montana, Unions."

Feelings were high all over the district, and the furor caused many opponents of the unions to leave. Van B. DeLashmutt, an owner of the Granite, Sierra Nevada and Stemwinder Mines, and A. L. Gross were special targets of union animosity, but they stood their ground and refused to leave the district during the trouble.

Secretary of State A. J. Pinkham was in command of the Idaho State militia, and he was stationed in Wallace. In Boise, Judge Beatty of the United States Circuit Court ruled that the injunctions previously issued against the Coeur d'Alene Miners' Union would be made permanent.

James F. Curtis, the colonel commanding the Idaho National Guard, issued two orders on July 15. The first was to his troops, and he ordered them to shoot anyone found in the act of blowing up railroads, bridges, mills or other property. The second order was to the union men:

> Headquarters,
> Wallace, Idaho.
> Idaho National Guard.
> July 15, 1892.

To the officers and members of the Coeur d'Alene Miners' Union whether permanent or temporary: You are hereby commanded to surrender yourself and your arms to the commanding officers or troops at your respective localities. Protection under the law will be guaranteed. All good citizens of this county are requested and commanded to aid in identifying and arresting those who do not surrender.

> Acting for the Governor,
> James F. Curtis, Col.
> Idaho National Guard, Commanding.

The Dunn Brothers had a field day writing up the events of the week, in their issue of July 16. Editorially, they pronounced: "The Miners' Union of the Coeur d'Alenes is Dead." In this issue, the Dunn Brothers demonstrated their position in the labor-management problem clearer than ever before. Their articles were sympathetic to the Mine Owners' Association, and the union was written in a poor light. Their headlines included such interest-getters as:

"GUNS AND DYNAMITE"   "Death and Destruction"
"The Miners' Union at last shows its true colors."

"At the Frisco and Gem Mines . . . An Armed and Blood Thirsty
Mob in Control of the County."

"Martial Law has been proclaimed and the United States
Troops are in Complete Possession."

"Leading Union Men Under Arrest."

They made one terse observation:

"The Winchester has taken the place of argument and giant
powder has been substituted for arbitration."

Adam Aulbach featured the following headlines in his edition
of July 16:

"Peace and War" The Cd'As Suddenly Plunged into Chaos . . .
Six men killed and about seventeen wounded . . . A
dastardly and fiendish deed at the Mission.

Shoshone County Placed under Martial Law and Several
Regiments of Troops in the South Fork Valley."

Aulbach's coverage of the events of the week differed in some
respects from that of the Dunn Brothers. Things had been moving so quickly, some differences as to factual matters could be
expected. Other differences between the two publishers can be
attributed to the prejudices and sympathies. Truly Aulbach was
sympathetic with the Miners' Union, but he did not condone
their unlawful acts:

"Last week peace, this week war. However bitter the controversy between capital and labor may be, labor always
gets a further set back by resorting to arms and bloodshed.
Those who live by the sword shall die by the sword, is an
old proverb, and labor is not trained in that school."

Wallace was bristling with newspapermen by the end of the
week. The town was visited by representatives of the *San Francisco Examiner, Boise Statesman, Butte Miner, Anaconda Standard, Helena Independent, Missoula Gazette, Western Democrat,
Chicago Herald, New York World, Spokane Review, Spokane
Chronicle, Spokane, Spokesman* and the Associated Press. They

kept the telegraph wire warm and wore out the operators—
McCandlish and Ross. The telephones were also kept busy up to
their capacity. Twenty thousand words were sent out to the
various newspapers on some days, and 50,000 would have been
forwarded daily if the facilities would have allowed it.

Coroner Sims drew up a jury, and said that it would investigate the shooting at the Frisco and Gem mines. The jury was to
attempt to fix responsibility on the side which fired the first shot
in the trouble. It was to commence on July 16, at 9 A.M. Nothing ever came from this effort.

Some of the people in the district expected the military force
to leave the area within a week, as nearly all the miners would
be under arrest by that time. Their expectations were certainly
in error, and the troops were to be around for quite some time.

There was some confusion between the local civil authorities
and the military commanders. Some felt the local officers were
barred from doing anything, while others contended that the
miiltary was not in the district to punish those responsible for
disorders that occurred before their arrival. These same parties
contended that the military was present merely to restore the
peace so that the civil authorities could enforce the law. This
confusion continued to some degree as long as the soldiers
stayed, but it was to lessen with the passage of time. Within a
few weeks, the local authorities started to exercise jurisdiction
over criminal and civil matters.

The events of the week ending July 16 were too momentous to
pass without A. M. Esler having released a press statement. He
stated that on the 10th he and Finch chartered a special train
from Wallace to Gem to look things over. He said his men were
very nervous and asked for more guns. He had seen men about
Gem and Burke with guns, and a week before he asked Governor
Willey for about a hundred stand of arms and was told that none
were available. Esler then wired Portland for two cases of guns.
While on the chartered train to Gem, Esler asked the conductor
to run them back down to Wallace, where they found the rifles

had arrived and were in a freight car. Esler took them back to the Frisco Mill on the special train, and he said his return inspired the men, and they told him they would hold the fort. (Aulbach reported that A. M. Esler left Wallace for Spokane at 10 A.M. on July 11.)

Esler continued that his men at the Frisco then had about 40 rifles in their possession, and he had directed the boss to take everyone out of the mine and concentrate on defending the mills. He left about 80 men in the mill in charge of U. S. Deputy Marshal Harris, and instructed them not to fire unless they were first attacked. . . . Esler said the first shot fired on the 11th was at the Gem Mill. (This last statement does not seem to conform with any of the many other versions told.)

Esler reported that the iron penstock at the Frisco Mill was 16 inches in diameter, and about 600 feet long, with the upper end 290 feet above horizontal, and that it conducted the water to the wheel in the mill. He said the union men had torn up the flume above so that they could put the giant powder into the penstock.

All these events served to almost obliterate the fact that Clarence R. Pebbles, an electrician at the Poorman Power House, 2 miles above Burke, was killed on July 12 by electrocution. He was an employee of the Edison Company.

Lastly, Adam Aulbach reported that the week's news included a discovery of 5 feet of rich ore in the lower tunnel of the Custer Mine on the 15th. Pete Porter said the ore strike was the biggest so far at that mine. The development work at the Custer was carried on by contract, and the mine was practically unaffected by the troubles in the Coeur d'Alenes, although it was within three miles of Gem.

Noah Kellogg was not distracted from his matrimonial troubles by the big blowup at the Frisco. Mr. Kellogg filed suit for divorce on July 12. Seven months later the divorce was granted, and his wife received a $5,000 cash settlement for her property rights.

CHAPTER 34

UNDER MARTIAL LAW — JULY 1892

Although ten days had passed, since the open warfare in Gem, no man had yet surrendered in accordance with the terms and inducements and efforts of the Governor and the military authorities. About 400 men had been arrested, but a lot of them were released on July 22 because no positive information on their activities had been obtained.

About two-thirds of the prisoners were from Gem and Burke. Nathan Wittner, a cohort of Peter Breen, was arrested by the troops in the Sunset Peak area. Martial law had scarcely been proclaimed in Wallace when Wittner applied to the commanding officer for a permit to leave town. Someone had filed a protest against the passport being granted. His request was promptly refused and he took off for the hills.

Captain Bubb scanned the mountains surrounding Gem with a pair of field glasses and when he saw any sign of a miner on the sidehill he would send a detachment up on the mountain to make a "drag." During a routine "drag" of the mountain, on July 20, Captain Bubb and a squad of his state militia soldiers captured one of the "most wanted" union men. Their prisoner was George Pettibone, the Justice of the Peace at Gem, who was said to have aided in sending the powder down the penstock into the Frisco Mill. The capture was made near a cabin in a heavily timbered draw on the mountain west of Gem. When Pettibone was approached by the soldiers and put under arrest, he demanded that papers be produced to show that his captors were authorized to arrest him.

Pettibone was then taken into Gem, and Captain Bubb wired the news that George Pettibone had been captured. At seven o'clock that evening, Captain Human and Sheriff Sims went to Gem on a special train to bring their prisoner to Wallace, where he was put in the town jail as an extra precaution to prevent his escape. Pettibone's hand was in bad condition, and he was sick to his stomach much of the time coming to Wallace on the train. It was not known whether he had been shot in the hand or had hurt it in the explosion at the Frisco.

One story was that after the powder had been sent down the penstock, a long time passed without any explosion. It was said that Pettibone was at the top of the penstock and that he grew curious about the cause for the delay. Pettibone then looked down into the penstock to see what had happened; the explosion finally occurred, blowing him up the mountain into a tree and severely injuring his hand.

Things were settling down; on the 20th of July wives and sympathizers of prisoners brought food to the guard house, where a big feast was given the prisoners. Another faction raised money to feed the soldiers at the guardhouse something besides bacon and hardtack, which had been their military rations.

The Gem Mine resumed operations on July 20 with about 100 men on the payroll. Some of the non-union workers had returned to their jobs. A. M. Esler was in Helena, Montana, and he stated that the Frisco Mill would be rebuilt in the very near future. The troops at Mullan were having trouble capturing the union men, who had fled into the hills toward the Montana border. These men came back into town at night for supplies and were proving to be quite elusive. The soldiers would not cross the Montana border in pursuit of the miners.

The Dunn Brothers reviewed the recent troubles and raised their list of wounded in the Gem gunfights to twenty. They added that about 600 men were chased from the district by the union miners during their rampage, and added that a Mrs. Robinson of Gem was deported by the Union on July 11 for having washed clothes for the non-union men. Their paper also carried an article on the Pinkerton detective agency, but no mention was made of their playing a part in the local labor trouble.

The Mine Owners' Association decided to drop their boarding houses and supply stores, and their miners were free to trade where they pleased. The wage scale was still the same, $3.50 for miners, and $3.00 for carmen and shovellers in dry mines, and 50 cents more for them in wet areas.

All the provisions in the Miners' Union stores were to be distributed to the union men and their families in accordance with a system set up by the Idaho National Guard.

On the 22nd of July, General Curtis issued an order modifying the order declaring martial law so as to allow civil and criminal cases to proceed in regular fashion, so long as they would not conflict with proper enforcement of military law by the military authorities. The County officers were to proceed with their duties.

At Wardner, the Bunker Hill tramway broke down again. A bucket lost its grip on the cable and jarred 5 or 6 others loose, one of which fell to the ground, striking the same house which had been struck in a prior accident. William Stoll, a lawyer close to the Mine Owners' Association, had left the area shortly before the trouble at the Frisco. He arrived back in Wallace on the 23rd with his bride.

Two Swedes found it convenient to return also. They had been among the employees of the Gem and Frisco mines who were attacked while waiting for the boat at the Mission. These were not "Dumb Swedes," for when the attack started they hid their purses which contained about $200 each. - - - They returned to recover the purses from the hiding places at the Mission.

Things were settling down; on the 24th of the month, the Wallace town team played baseball with the Fort Keogh team; the score was 12 to 11, in favor of Wallace. But all was not quiet for Adam Aulbach. He served as a correspondent for the Associated Press in the district. The *Portland Oregonian* refused to print his articles on the trouble at Gem, because they felt Aulbach was too sympathetic with the miners' union.

General Curtis and General Carlin both were upset with Adam Aulbach, who had been defying them in a quiet way; possibly he tempted them to arrest a member of the press. General Curtis lost his temper and said,

"Mr. Aulbach, you are a murderer."

No matter how one looked at it, Adam was having trouble in Wallace. Perhaps this was what prompted him to sell the *Wallace Press* to R. E. Brown, who had formerly edited a publication called the *Barbarian*. It was rumored that Aulbach was going to Mullan to take over the *Mullan Tribune*, which he already owned.

In any event, Adam Aulbach's last issue of the *Wallace Press* had been published on July 16, and it was a journalistic masterpiece. He had covered a subject of national interest, and upon which he held intense personal views. However, his coverage of the events of the week of July 9-16 was factual and quite objective, all things concerned.

The other item of big news during the week following the blowup of the Frisco concerned a murder in Murray on the 16th. Frank Reed, the owner of several gold properties, became embroiled in an argument over a property line with George Trask, a surveyor. The argument got hot, and Reed took a shot at Trask, but the bullet missed its target and struck Robert Stevens, who was reading across the saloon with his back to the fracas. - - - Lynching was talked, and 80 men so inclined were in front of the jail on the next morning, but they did not have a leader. A troop of soldiers went to Murray to protect the prisoner and they returned him to Wallace.

At a later date Reed was convicted of the crime and appealed the decision to the Idaho Supreme Court. One of the grounds for his appeal concerned the fact that the jury which heard his case was furnished liquor during the trial by the bailiff. The Idaho Supreme Court held that the mere fact that the jury was furnished a quart of whiskey each morning, under the direction of the District Judge, and that beer was served them, did not in itself constitute grounds for a new trial, unless there was some reason to suppose that the liquor was drunk in such quantity as "to unfit the jurors for duty." . . .

> "At the same time we must express our decided disapproval of the practice of allowing jurors to indulge in intoxicating liquors while in the performance of their duties, except in cases of actual necessity." - - -

The court never saw fit to spell out what might constitute "cases of actual necessity."

The end of July saw 400 to 500 soldiers still in the district. Some of the others had returned to Fort Missoula and Fort Keogh, and all soldiers had been removed from Mullan.

By the end of the month, 127 prisoners had been arrested in Wardner. In Butte, a policeman had to shoot William Black in the leg in order to capture him. Black was arrested as a fugitive from the troubles in the Coeur d'Alene.

A Pinkerton detective, Charles A. Siringo, had posed as a miner under the name of C. Leon Allison. After the union men were captured and place in the guard house, Siringo returned to Wallace for the purpose of identifying some prisoners. He went into the guardhouse and the union men closed in on him with a threatening manner. Siringo was forced to pull his gun to keep them at bay.

On the 25th of July, 25 prisoners were taken from Wallace to Boise for trial. They arrived in Boise, under escort of Company A of the Idaho National Guard, and were met by 2,000 curious people. They were placed in the county jail, and Patrick Reddy of San Francisco, and Hawley and Reeves of Boise, were retained as their lawyers.

The prisoners who were taken to Boise were: Ed Boyce, F. E. Dean, Quinn Sullivan, Dave Cosgriff, Joe Davis, N. Nelson, all of Wardner; and Thomas Eaton, Hugh McFadden, Joseph Poynton, H. Robinson, Tom Whalen, Dave McGee, E. A. Mangurson (sometimes referred to as Andrew Magnuson), John Nicholson (sometimes called Thomas Michelson), Dan Harrington, William Gaughan, Hugh McGee, Tom O'Brien, Gus Peterson, George Smith, Thomas Heney, S. H. Brockman, Thomas Doyle, John Fitzgerald and Pat Kennedy.

The Gem, Granite, Custer and Sierra Nevada mines were shipping ore again by the end of July. All of them, with the exception of the Custer, employed non-union men exclusively. The Tiger and Poorman were having a difficult time with production because of the arrest and confinement of a large number of their underground crews.

Fifteen to twenty men were cleaning up the ruins of the Frisco Mill, and they found that some of the "jigs" could be repaired. This work was being done in advance of the rebuilding of the mill.

Wardner mine owners announced that their employees could board and buy supplies where they pleased. The Mine owners could receive no orders, nor protect anyone on their payrolls, and they would pay "full and honest money for honest labor." This announcement was issued over the names of V. M. Clement, George B. McAulay and Chas. Sweeney.

CHAPTER 35

AUGUST — 1892

August saw the release on bonds of a number of the prisoners who were arrested during the prior month. Their bonds varied in amounts from $300 to $5,000, and they were set by United States Commissioner Hoffman.

Judge Frazer, an ardent supporter of the Miners' Union, had the distinction of having a $5,000 bail set for him. He had been a prisoner in the Wallace guardhouse some three weeks before his release. Upon bond being posted, Judge Frazer returned to Mullan where a band and several hundred people met him at the depot. His was a hero's welcome.

Peter Breen, the Montana legislator, was captured and brought to the Wallace jail by Deputy Marshal Human. Dallas was still loose and efforts were made to locate him. It was announced in Mullan that the *Mullan Tribune* had suspended publication. Adam Aulbach was the owner of that newspaper, but it was edited by others.

Sheriff Cunningham was out of office inasmuch as George McAulay, Alex Monk and James Doherty withdrew from his official bond. Colonel Curtis appointed Dr. W. S. Sims as sheriff to replace Cunningham on August 5. Earlier Sims had been appointed provost marshal of Shoshone County when martial law was declared; this was considered to be the chief executive office of the county.

In Wallace all of the saloons closed at midnight every night by

order of the military. Apparently enough money was being saved
by this measure to justify the establishment of the First National
Bank of Wallace, which opened for business on August 8.

Everyone was striving to organize. The miners and the mine
owners had their organizations. Now the Shoshone County
druggists organized a pharmaceutical society, which they hoped
would form a nucleus for a state organization. The Wallace
town fathers announced that the townsite deeds were ready to
be picked up, and the cost would be $8.50 per lot claimed.

On August 4 some of the 25 prisoners went on trial in Boise
upon a charge of having violated Judge Beatty's injunction of
May 28. The attack on the Frisco Mill was the subject of the
violation. All of the men pleaded not guilty. Their defenses
were either that they had not been served with a copy of the
injunction or that they were not in the attack on the Frisco property. The men charged with violation of the injunction relating
to the Bunker Hill property were to be tried later.

During the course of the Frisco Injunction Trial, a long list
of witnesses testified against the union men. The list of witnesses
included: Colonel W. W. Hammell, Deputy Marshal; Frank Esler,
an owner of the Frisco; Harvey Harris, Deputy Marshal on the
Frisco payroll; Mrs. O. J. Shipley, a Gem lodging house operator;
Van B. DeLashmutt, an owner of the Granite Mine; Percy Summers, a non-union miner; Ed Kinney, the man who refused to
surrender the Gem mine property; W. C. Human, Deputy Marshal; A. L. Gross, an owner of the Gem mine; John A. Finch, an
owner of the Milwaukee Mining Company; Frank L. Higgins, a
Gem Mill watchman; Phillip Stansbaugh, foreman of the Milwaukee Mining Company; James Monaghan, Superintendent of
the Gem Mine.

Perhaps the most important witness of all was the Pinkerton
detective who inveigled himself into the good graces of the union
men, and was elected the Recording Secretary of the Gem Union.
He was known in Gem as C. Leon Allison, but acquired national
fame under the name of Charles A. Siringo. The union men's

defense was that the union did not start the fight, but instead the union men acted in self-defense.

Deputy United States Marshal W. C. Human testified that he was in Gem on the morning of July 11, and that he was present when the guns were turned over for transportation to Wallace. He told of the handcar loaded with guns being stopped by 20 or 30 armed men, who had thrown a railroad switch and stopped the car. He named Tom Heney, president of the Mullan Miners' Union, as the leader of the gang. Quite a few years later Heney was elected Sheriff of Shoshone County.

A man called John Kneebone testified that 15 or 20 men were in the band that raided the group of men waiting at the Mission. A few years later this same John Kneebone was to meet his death at the hands of union men in labor difficulties.

Frank Esler testified that he had been up all night prior to the commencement of the fight at the Frisco, which he stated began about 4:30 A.M. At that time he was near the mouth of the No. 3 tunnel as a general lookout. A half hour later he left this spot for the old Frisco Mill, and he just arrived inside the door when the mill was blown up. He was stunned by the concussion for a time, and when he recovered he went to the new mill, after which he went into a "hole" which he had made, and he remained there until 10:30 that night. Esler said he had prepared a "retreat" six weeks before. On the night before the fight 18 rifles had been distributed among the mill empoyees at the Frisco, and these were in addition to the twelve already in their possession. A man named Abbott commanded the armed men on the Frisco property. Esler stated that his retreat had a door, but no windows, and that when he came out that night he went to Wallace. He stated that he fired 6 or 8 shots during the battle, but he did not think he hit anyone.

Ed Kinney testified that Ivery Bean was killed by a shot fired from the direction of Daxon's Saloon in Gem. He also identified William Black, a Gem miner, and one DeMoville, a union man from Gem, and Robert Dawson, a Gem miner, as being among the gang who raided the non-union men at the Mission.

Mrs. O. J. Shipley said that she saw 12 or 15 armed men in front of her place, a lodging house and fruit stand, on July 11. She spoke to some of them, and they told her it was safe to remain there if she stayed in her own house and attended her own business. She identified certain men, including Andrew Magnuson, as being within that group. This woman was a good friend of Charles Siringo.

Harvey Harris testified that he was a United States marshal in the employ of the Frisco people. On the evening of July 10 he saw many armed men coming into Gem. He slept in the Frisco Mill that night and awoke to the sound of gunfire in the morning. He saw an ore car start down the tramway to the old mill, but its cargo exploded before it reached the mill. Later he saw men fooling around the head of the penstock that led to the old Frisco Mill. He stated that when the mill blew up, the men at the head of the penstock were knocked over by the blast of air that was forced up the penstock by the explosion. Harris saw George Pettibone walking through the bushes near the Black Bear Mill, coming from the direction of the the Frisco flume a short time later. He said that Pettibone's hand was injured.

Harris happened to comment that he was armed while on the witness stand, and the Judge told him to go into the Marshal's office and leave his weapon there. The Judge added that he wanted no person, save officers of the Court, to bring arms into the courtroom.

Siringo was called to the witness stand, and he testified that he had been a resident of Gem since September, 1891. In October, he was told by George Pettibone to come to an empty saloon building in Gem, and there he became a member of the Miners' Union. Later Siringo was elected recording secretary of the Gem Miners' Union. On July 10, in the morning, Siringo told Sheriff Cunningham there was going to be trouble. Siringo rode from Wallace to Gem on that day and saw crowds of men, some of them armed with Winchesters, running up the creek. He climbed on a fence and saw a crowd of men who had just finished beating up Putnam, a guard at the Gem mine.

On the previous night, Siringo said he heard union miners say that they were going to kill the guards. He claimed that he heard nine miners plot to do away with Barber and Putnam as soon as the lights at the dance hall had been put out. Later, after the lights went out, Siringo said the union men began insulting these two non-union guards.

Siringo then secured his rifle and went to the Gem Mill and told Supt. Monaghan that the union men in Dutch Henry's Saloon were about to finish some of his men. Almost immediately, word came in that Barber had been nearly beaten to death. Siringo then went to Wallace and sent a doctor to Gem.

On the 10th, after Putnam was beaten, the union men started to congregate in front of Hugh McGee's Saloon. Some of them went into the saloon and left their rifles there. The crowd grew bigger, and the excitement became greater. Siringo testified that a union man then came galloping in from Burke, left a message at McGee's Saloon and then returned to Burke. Shortly thereafter, Burke union men started to arrive in Gem, and others came in from both up and down the gulch.

Siringo said he heard Poynton call John A. Finch a "S. O. B." and say that Finch had gone there to kill them and their families. Poynton told Finch he had better move on. Finch responded by leaving. (At about this time, Siringo had been identified as a detective by certain union men, but this knowledge was not yet known to all of the union men.) Siringo stated that a union man who did not know him said that a fellow named C. Leon Allison had been spotted as a traitor and that blood was to be shed. This man told Siringo that rifles and cartridges were coming in by a secret route and there would be trouble that night.

Siringo's testimony continued by stating that union men were stationed behind White and Bender's Store and that he crawled under a platform to watch the movements of the union men. A short time later, Siringo went to Superintendent Monaghan's house and told him that danger threatened the non-union men. Monaghan began to prepare for defense. At 3 A.M., Ed Kinney came to the Gem Mill and said he thought trouble was at hand.

At daybreak (on the 11th) Siringo slipped back into the town of Gem and went to his room and looked out a window. He saw Gabe Dallas with a shotgun on his shoulder and others carrying guns. He soon heard shots fired near the Frisco Mill, and then the shooting became general. Siringo started to run to the Gem Mill, but he was told by a company man not to go further, as there were 50 union men hidden at Daxon's Saloon.

Siringo testified that he then saw a Gem Mill guard coming from the mill and that this guard was warned by someone to go back. Just then a shot was fired and the guard, Ivery Bean, fell dead.

Siringo then went to Mrs. Shipley's room, in back of her store, and sawed a hole in the floor through which he might escape. A trunk was pushed to cover the escape hole. Siringo had been beneath the floor of Mrs. Shipley's building when the Frisco Mill blew up. Mrs. Shipley told Siringo that she had been told that his life was in danger. He began wriggling along under the building until he found himself underneath the wooden sidewalk in front of Mrs. Shipley's building. There he heard union men cursing their rifles for their poor shooting quality. Siringo was under the sidewalk when he heard someone remark about a traitor being discovered, and that he should be burned at a stake.

Siringo then crawled under the sidewalk until he came to Sear's Place. He then could see the mob stop at the Shipley building. Siringo continued crawling along, and he came to Harrington's Saloon, and he crawled under this building, and a moment later started running to the Gem Mill where he joined the non-union forces. When the Gem Mill was surrendered later in the morning, Siringo took to the hills behind the mill. Siringo's testimony indicated that Ivery Bean had been nearly facing the union men when he was shot, and that Bean's back was toward the Gem Mill. The bullet had entered Bean's chest.

Siringo reflected that Dan Harrington had told him on July 1 that there would soon be bloodshed, and that Thomas Eaton, acting president of the Gem Miners' Union, had appointed a committee to work secretly against the non-union men. Siringo also testified that Eaton also ordered him to mutilate the books of the Gem Union which contained the minutes of a meeting at which Sweeney, a union man, asked the Gem Union men if they would stand up with the Burke union men in the event the latter pulled the pumps in the Tiger and the Poorman mines. Such contemplated action would flood these properties.

Under cross-examination by Lawyer Reddy, Siringo testified that he came to Idaho from Denver and that he had been a Pinkerton detective since 1886, and that he was paid a regular salary. At Gem he went to work as a miner and soon became a member of the union. Siringo stated that when the oath of membership into the union was administered he did not repeat it, allowing the remainder of the group to take the oath. There was no doubt but that Siringo's testimony was crucifying the union men. A prolonged effort by the defense attorney to tangle the witness in his testimony proved unsuccessful. Siringo had been hired to do a job, and he did it well. In his book, *Cowboy Detective*, Siringo wrote that he was hidden on the mountain south of Wallace when the troops arrived in town.

On August 11, Thomas O'Brien, Joseph Poynton, Thomas Eaton, John Fitzgerald, Daniel Harrington, Hugh McGee, John Nicholson, Gus Peterson, H. Robinson and Thomas Whalen all were found guilty. Each of them received jail sentences, varying from four to eight months; the majority were for six months.

Judge Beatty announced that he would start the trial for those charged with violating the Bunker Hill injunction on August 12, and that he would hold a term of Federal Court in Coeur d'Alene on August 28 for the purpose of trying some local parties who were charged with conspiracy.

Back in Wallace, things were moving along. All the men injured in the blowup of the Frisco Mill were reported getting along well. Some had been released from the hospital. Abbott, the man shot at the Mission, was improving and was able to be up and around the hospital. . . . Mining was getting back to normal. James H. Smith was killed when he drilled into a loaded hole at the Granite mine early in August.

The Northern Pacific announced it would resume passenger service over the Montana divide on August 28, and 1,317 names were signed to a petition for removal of the county seat to Osburn. The names were printed in the Wallace newspaper with the request that W. S. Haskins, chairman of the Wallace County Seat Committee, be notified if any of the names were not entitled to vote on this question. Among the signers were H. L. Day of Wardner and C. L. Allison of Gem.

Three hundred men, mostly Californians, were working at the Bunker Hill and sixty at the Sierra Nevada by the third week in August. Arrangements were being made to start the Stemwinder, and the Last Chance would soon be shipping ore.

*   *   *

Over on the St. Joe River, settlers were anxious that the outlet of Coeur d'Alene Lake be lowered 4 or 5 feet so that it would drain and reclaim much valuable agricultural land. Beginning at the mouth of the St. Mary's River, every foot of ground was occupied far beyond the head of navigation by farm houses, barns and hay sheds. Hay was the principal crop. Captain J. M. Daggett was one of the first settlers on the St. Joe and he owned a fine ranch at the mouth of the St. Mary's. Judge A. K. White, who lived on the St. Mary's near the mouth of the Santa, cut 8,700 pounds of hay from one acre of his land. Daggett said he cleared $70 per acre from potatoes in 1891, and that he sold most of them to Wallace merchants.

Many prospectors were looking over the upper St. Joe, and it was fine country for camping. The main river was described as

having so many fish that they almost crowded each other out of
the water:

> ". . . and deer, bears, elk, mountain sheep, to say nothing of
> grouse and pheasant, abound in great numbers. Along the
> lower level, on the reservation, there are plenty of ducks and
> geese."

General Curtis was not concerned with hunting and fishing for
the moment, however. On the 20th he closed down the Tiger
and Poorman mines. He also ordered every saloon in Burke
closed until further notice. He had closed all the saloons in
Wallace on the 17th, and there was no sign that he would rescind
the order. General Curtis did not give any explanation for his
orders, but it was thought that he viewed these saloons as the
meeting places of the union miners, who were still rebellious.

General Curtis ordered the Wallace Marshal to have the streets
and alleys of the town cleaned. The citizens of Wallace were
slow in responding to outside authority, and on the 19th General
Curtis removed Thomas Argyle from the office of Marshal, and
declared it was the duty of the Shoshone County Sheriff and his
deputies to enforce the law in the towns of Wallace and Wardner
in place of the town marshals. This Special Order #56 made
sense to the General because he had already appointed Sims to
serve as Sheriff of Shoshone County.

A smart fellow from Boise, Calvin Cobb, the publisher of the
Boise Statesman, came to Wallace a few days later and stated:
"Wallace is the cleanest, neatest and best behaved town in Idaho."
He proposed that Boise and Spokane should be put under martial
law until such times as their streets and alleys were thoroughly
cleaned.

By the end of August, some of the people in the district were
wondering as to the whereabouts of Judge W. H. Frazer, who
was still out on $5,000 bond. He was not in the district, and
some of his Mullan bondsmen were becoming concerned.

Walter Jones, the union lawyer, was arrested for contempt of court. He had become abusive over a matter in a local justice court, and he did not cool off after having a $10 fine for contempt levied on him. The Justice then ordered his arrest. Jones had been arrested once before since the arrival of troops in the area. The first arrest was for interfering with the military arrests.

Toward the end of August, Frank B. Crossthwaite, special agent of the Department of Justice, came to Wallace from the nation's capital. He checked on conditions and treatment of the prisoners in the district, and wired an immediate report to the Attorney General. He was satisfied that things were about as well as could be expected under the circumstances.

Adam Aulbach was not publishing in either Wallace or Mullan in August of 1892. Later, he returned to his former home in Murray, where he printed the *Murray Sun* until 1912. Even after that date, Aulbach wrote articles which other papers published, and he did some writing of historical nature.

The Dunn Brothers estimated that the union men had 400 Winchesters and 400 other rifles and six shooters, plus 75 guns captured from the non-union men or stolen from the government. They called attention to the fact that none of these weapons had been surrendered as demanded by the proclamations of General Curtis and the President of the United States.

The Bunker Hill added 65 men to its payroll during the last week in August. Other mines in the district were getting back into production.

G. M. Dallas had still not been captured, and it was said that he was not in the Butte area. Peter Breen was refused freedom on a writ of habeas corpus. He was charged with murder, and his bail was set at $20,000. It was said the Larabie Brothers, Butte bankers, were making arrangements to put up bond for Breen's release.

Both Adam Aulbach and General James F. Curtis were leaders, but General Curtis had the advantage of being on the winning team. Curtis had a background of two years as chief of police in San Francisco, during the 1850s; in 1865 President Andrew Johnson appointed him brigadier general. Curtis came to Idaho in 1885 to examine possible routes for the Union Pacific railroad, and he thereafter became active in Idaho politics.

Aulbach's departure from Wallace was without fanfare. His "followers" were temporarily disbanded, and Aulbach could not fight the Army and the Mine Owners Association all by himself. After the declaration of martial law, the game of "freeze out" against Adam Aulbach was accelerated, and he was "frozen out" in the summer of 1892. . . . The silencing of the "voice of labor" was a tremendous victory for the Mine Owners Association.

CHAPTER 36

SEPTEMBER AND OCTOBER — 1892

Early in September, Governor Willey indicated that martial law would continue in Shoshone County for an indefinite time. The Butte Union had instructed the union miners in the Coeur d'Alenes to work at the rates recently offered by the Mine Owners' Association—$3.50 for miners and $3.00 for firemen and shovellers in the dry mines, with a fifty-cent extra pay allowance for firemen and shovellers in the wet mines. It appeared that the local union men had decided to take orders from the Butte Union inasmuch as the local unions were in trouble.

In Gem, Will F. Read took over the building formerly occupied by Mrs. O. J. Shipley. He continued the confectionery and newsstand business which had been operated there. It appeared that her testimony at the contempt trials in Boise got her in trouble with the community.

William T. Stoll announced in public print that he was no longer one of the Democratic Party and would henceforth be a Republican. He was upset at the Democratic Party platform, which was sympathetic to the action of the miners in the Coeur d'Alenes.

Peter Breen was still in jail. The $20,000 bail proved quite difficult for him to raise. If Breen raised the money for bail, he would probably have been arrested on other charges. In Burke, Ben E. Thayer, the new manager of the Poorman mine, arrived in that town.

Captain W. C. Human, the Deputy U. S. Marshal, took 16 prisoners to Coeur d'Alene for trial on the 8th of September. He transported every prisoner with the exception of Peter Breen, who was scheduled to be tried first in the state court. The conspiracy trial which was scheduled for Coeur d'Alene included Peter Breen in its title, but he was not to stand trial in the Federal Court at that time. Human, accompanied by Lieutenant Brooke and a detail of ten soldiers, took the prisoners by way of the Union Pacific to Coeur d'Alene.

The prisoners were: Charles Trimble, Robert Bradley, John McGowan, William Lettrick, Theodore Tillington, Charles Anderson, Charles F. Flynn, Richard Thomas, Daniel Tobin, Dennis Shea, George Dolan, M. Godfrey, Theodore Warner, Joe Davis, Robert Jones and Web Leasure. One man was specifically detailed to look after Web Leasure, as there were graver charges against him, and every precaution was taken to bring him to trial.

The Morning Company announced that it would build a four-hundred ton mill, which would be the second largest in the Coeur d'Alenes.

W. Y. Williams, of Wardner, announced that he would try for the Republican nomination for Sheriff. He had been mining in the Coeur d'Alenes since the early days. For years he was superintendent of the Sierra Nevada, Stemwinder and Granite mines, and was held in high esteem by both the employers and employees of the district.

In Gem, the new Frisco Mill started up on the 19th of September. By the middle of September, five more companies of soldiers left. They returned to Vancouver, leaving seven companies of soldiers still in the district. General Curtis stated that martial law would probably last for another month. He recently had been in Boise visiting the Governor.

A local union man, Samuel Black, who was in charge of the miners' supplies, stated that the strike in the Coeur d'Alenes was not over. The Butte Union was not able to help the local miners because Butte had two or three thousand miners idle in their own district.

The Tiger and Poorman mines reopened during the middle of September and were adding to their employment rolls each day. The *Wallace Democrat* was first published on September 16, with P. J. Holohan as its managing editor.

During 1892, Murray had been the most prosperous town in the district. There was more money to the man in Murray than in any other town simply because there was no transient population there. About every man was a worker and had some substantial interest to hold him in Murray. The business in that area had increased from that of former years, as 200 men were employed in the vicinity of that town.

Elsewhere in the West, cheap silver had made thousands of miners idle in Arizona, Colorado, Utah and Montana.

The Hecla mine in Burke had ten men on its payroll in mid-September, and they were mining a good grade of ore from an ore body which gradually increased in size, as depth was obtained. The newspaper noted: "The Hecla is a promising property."

At Wardner, the monthly payroll of the Bunker Hill was $43,000. There were about four hundred men employed, and fifty men would be added in the near future. The Stemwinder, Last Chance and Sierra Nevada also employed large forces, and there were innumerable smaller mines working. Wardner would shortly have a payroll of $100,000 per month. In Wallace, round steak was selling at 3 pounds for 25 cents, pork chops at 2 pounds for 25 cents and chuck roast at 6 cents per pound.

On September 21, the grand jury was called in Judge Holleman's Court. James H. Hawley was the attorney for Peter Breen and Web Leasure, and Frank Ganahl was the attorney for Frank Reed. The attorneys challenged the entire grand jury on the grounds of irregularity in drawing the names. The attorneys further claimed that the military authorities had no power to remove Richard A. Cunningham as Sheriff and that at the time of the drawing of the panel, Cunningham had not been removed from office by the county commissioners, and that Cunningham should have been present at the drawing of the jurors' names, instead of Sims, who assumed the duties of the office. Captain Ballance acted in the capacity of Assistant Judge Advocate General, and he helped District Attorney O'Neil against the challenge of Hawley and Ganahl. Judge Holleman overruled the objection, and the grand jury stood as originally drawn.

The County Commissioners purchased fifty patent iron booths for election purposes. The purchase of these booths was made necessary by the use of the new Australian Ballot System.

At Coeur d'Alene, on September 20, Charles A. Siringo took the witness stand. He testified at length but was not cross-examined by the defense attorneys. Siringo named George Pettibone as the first president of the Miners' Union, and his testimony was quite similar to that given by him in Boise earlier, except that it did not deal with the events of July 11 at Gem. Siringo testified that he first went to Gem about September 5, 1891.

By the 24th, the conspiracy trial of Coeur d'Alene was almost over. The prosecution had presented sixty-seven witnesses and took twenty-one days to present its case. The defense countered with thirty witnesses and took one and a half days to present its case. Arguments to the jury began on September 26.

On September 28, the jury returned verdicts of guilty on George Pettibone, Mike Devine, Charles Sinclair and John Murphy. Pettibone was sentenced to two years in prison, Murphy was given fifteen months and the other two were given eighteen months in Federal prison. The other defendants charged with a conspiracy to violate the Bunker Hill injunction were acquitted.

Judge Frazer of Mullan was one of the men acquitted in the Coeur d'Alene trial on the 28th, and on the same day he was nominated by the Shoshone County Democratic Convention to run for the Idaho Legislature. The Dunn Brothers were incensed by his nomination and stated that Judge Frazer had lowered the United States flag in Mullan to half mast when the troops came into the district.

The end of September saw Adam Aulbach's return to Murray, where he planned to revive the *Murray Sun*, his old newspaper. . . . On the 30th of September, C. L. Allison signed a criminal complaint charging a John Doe with use of abusive language and with threatening to kill Allison. These threats were made during a train ride from Gem to Wallace earlier in the day. A man was arrested upon these charges. The Wallace newspaper did not explain what happened to the defendant nor why Charles A. Siringo was still using the name of C. L. Allison.

Work was going on at the Vienna and International mining claims, which had been located by John D. and A. B. Livingston, Nick Miller and J. H. Graham. The claims were about four miles from Wallace up Placer Creek. . . . On the corner of Sixth and Pine Streets, Joe Camia erected a new building which would house a saloon known as the Chicago Club.

On the 6th, Coeur d'Alene Jack, a pioneer dog of Eagle City, died in Cameron's Saloon in Wallace of general debility. The dog was buried after proper services on the following day. "Coeur d'Alene Jack" pulled the first toboggan over the Trout Creek Trail into Eagle City in the winter of 1883-84 and relieved the hungry miners.

William Black was sentenced to five years with assault to commit murder in Butte. He was the fugitive from the riots at Gem and had been shot while being arrested. Police Judge Angel joined with Sheriff Sims to introduce the use of the ball and chain in Wallace. Prisoners refusing to work were given bread and water. Those working had been sawing wood, and would work on the streets in town. Pettibone, Murphy, Sinclair and Devine would serve their sentences in the Detroit, Michigan, prison. They left from Boise on the 3rd of October.

On the 6th, the Shoshone County grand jury brought in forty-two indictments on the recent riots. So far George Dolan and William Lembke and John Shanahan had been arrested. Some of these men had already been arrested on other charges. Frank Reed was indicted for first degree murder. . . . Thirty-one of the indictments were against the former Sheriff, R. A. Cunningham. These indictments charged the ex-sheriff with failing to pay over to the county treasurer certain license fees and sheriff's fees which Cunningham was supposed to have collected. The charges accused him of retaining more than $10,000 of county funds.

The Grand Jury found that the Sheriff at that time employed ten paid deputies and these were no more than were absolutely needed to preserve order. In addition, they found that many criminal cases were being sent up to District Court by Justices of the Peace which were of such trifling nature that they should have been decided in the lower courts thus saving the county needless expense. It was rumored that there was a "black list" of about three hundred names of men, who the mines in the area would not hire because of their union activities. . . . Peter Breen finally posted bond and was released.

The Northern Pacific Railroad had eighty Chinamen working on its grade on the Idaho side of the Montana Border. This was the first time Chinese worked in the Coeur d'Alene District. The Dunn Brothers called attention to the fact that the Northern Pacific Railroad was taking advantage of the presence of soldiers in the district.

During the middle of October a sudden flurry of hostility presented itself in the district. A few union men threatened to blow up the Gem mine and to injure certain hated individuals. On the 15th, an armed masked man entered a Gem saloon and shot at a man named Graham, hitting him in the hand. Graham was rumored to be a detective. This new terror caused a few of the non-union men to leave the district.

The Northern Pacific announced that it would take the Chinese off the job on the summit when the work was completed. The railroad said it had difficulty in keeping a white crew on the job so it had to resort to hiring Chinese labor.

The District Court in Murray granted a change of venue in a number of the cases charging murder and riot, and these cases would be sent to Rathdrum, in Kootenai County, for trial. C. L.

Allison sold his lodging house in Gem and other property interest to H. M. Davenport. Allison was scheduled to remain in this area until after the trial of the rioters in Coeur d'Alene. Allison's lodging house property was on a lot twenty-five feet wide between the Gem Hotel, owned by Jerry Savage, and a saloon owned by Costello. Allison received fifteen hundred dollars for the sale.

On the 26th, a dance was given in Burke for the benefit of the families of certain prisoners confined in the Murray jail. It was a financial success and a special train carried a very large crowd from Wallace. In Wallace the business climate was improving all the time. Gem had nine saloons and room for about eleven more. Every idle mine in the district would probably be working within the next thirty days.

CHAPTER 37

NOVEMBER AND DECEMBER – 1892

November marked the opening of another school term in Wallace. Miss Annie Angel took charge of the first kindergarten in the Coeur d'Alenes. Children from three to seven years were admitted to it for three hours per day, from 9 a.m. until Noon. It was held in a room in the new schoolhouse. . . . The 127 older children were divided into three different classes, as distinguished from grades. Those children working in the first and second readers were entered in the Primary Department; those in the third and fourth readers were in the Intermediate Department; and those in the fifth reader and higher were placed in the Highest Department. This system was merely temporary, and in a few days each pupil was to be assigned a grade in the school. . . . Apparently the differences in their earlier opportunities for education made this arrangement necessary to ascertain the proper grade for each student.

The big news early in November was the Presidential election. The Dunn Brothers printed Republican praises in every issue, and they took special delight in opposing Adlai Stevenson, the Democrat candidate for Vice President. They accused him of shirking duty during the Civil War and of being anti-labor.

Election day came on the 8th, and Grover Cleveland was elected president of the United States. An editorial compared the quiet election just held with the secret Australian balloting to the prior ones under the former system in the Coeur d'Alenes.

Apparently there had been quite a bit of chicanery at the earlier polls. The Dunns were prompted to report:

> "Ben Hill looked lonesome last Tuesday. The Australian system robbed him of his occupation. The bruiser and bull-dozer at the polls is a thing of the past."

Wallace may have had a quiet election, but charges of ballot box stuffing arose at Bonners Ferry.

One of the political advertisements in the local campaign for offices in the 1892 election read:

> "You may never meet a mysterious death, but if you should and Dr. Bruner was coroner, he would give you a square deal at the inquest. Vote for him."

Judge Frazer, the Democratic candidate for the state legislature, was beaten in his attempt for office. . . . The vote to change the county seat from Murray to Wallace did not come out to the satisfaction of the Wallace people. Their town got 1,232 vote, while Murray received 652. It was necessary for Wallace to receive a two-thirds vote in order to get the county seat, and Wallace lacked 24 votes.

November was a bad month for newspapermen. R. E. Brown was no longer with the *Coeur d'Alene American,* the paper that replaced Adam Aulbach's *Wallace Press.* . . . F. K. Jerome, formerly of the *Mullan Tribune,* was in the Wallace jail upon a charge of forgery. Will Taylor, who ran the *Mullan Tribune* earlier in the year, committed suicide in Spokane on the 17th.

Web Leasure, Archie Kerr, Charles Trimble and Thomas Tall-entire were taken to Rathdrum for trial on the 19th. George Dolan, Henry Lempke, John Shanahan and Anderson, who were out on bonds, appeared for the trial and it was expected that Peter Breen would also show up for trial. Leasure and Breen were charged with murder. Leasure's case, which involved the death of Ivery Bean was to start on the 25th. George Dolan was released almost immediately after his appearance for lack of evidence.

General Order No. 9 of the military authorities, dated November 18, revoked the proclamation of July 13, which declared that Shoshone County was in a state of rebellion. Martial law ended at noon on November 19. The military authorities also restored Thomas Argyle to his position as marshal of Wallace. The Dunn Brothers indicated that martial law was administered so mildly during its last days that the only change expected was the absence of blue coated soldiers. . . . It may not have made much difference to them, but one can be sure that there must have been a lot of relieved union miners in the district.

Mr. Argyle resigned as town marshal soon after his reinstatement and he was replaced by R. L. Duncan. Dr. Sims returned to the practice of medicine in Wallace on November 12, after about a six months' absence while he served as the provost marshal and sheriff of Shoshone County.

The Dunn brothers, searching for news by the end of November, wrote an article describing the Pioneer Sampling Mill. It was situated 1½ miles west of Wallace between the Union Pacific and Northern Pacific tracks, and was managed by George D. Potter. The ore from the Poorman, Sierra Nevada, Mammoth, Black Bear, Custer and Hecla was sampled there. Its purpose was to give an independent sampling of the ore, giving its weight, moisture, assay value and New York value on the day of sampling. Its certificate was taken as correct by the smelters. The Mill charged 75 cents per ton for sampling ore, and it anticipated reducing this charge to 50 cents per ton after the first of the year. It had 12 men on the payroll, and they could sample 200 tons a day.

The beginning of December saw Judge Angel "floating" several men from Wallace for being known thieves and having no visible means of support. . . . Judge Angel was one of the very few men who occupied positions of authority during the labor trouble of 1892, who maintained the respect of both the miners and the mine owners. Neither the Dunn Brothers nor Adam Aulbach ever criticized him, even though the two publishers had covered almost everyone else with the acid of their pens.

The troubles of the year no longer occupied everyones' minds, and there was a shifting of the population. It was necessary for hundreds of union miners to leave the district because of attitudes that prevailed in the hiring halls.

The Helena and Frisco Mining Company filed a claim for about $50,000 against the Shoshone County Commissioners on the theory that the Shoshone County law enforcement agencies had a duty to protect their property, and they had failed. A. M. Esler retired from personal management of the Helena and Frisco mines, and he was working toward buying the Argentine Mine 2½ miles west of Wallace. Pat Clark, formerly with the Poorman, was following mining in the Slocan District in Canada.

The Leasure trial for killing Ivery Bean had started late in November in Rathdrum. Lawyers Reddy and Hawley appeared for Leasure, and Lawyers O'Neil, Heyburn and McFarland appeared for the prosecution. A witness named Higgins stated that Bean was on the bridge leading to Savage's Hotel in Gem, and that he was killed by the second shot fired. He said that Leasure was in a group of 5 or 6 men behind Daxon's saloon, and that when Bean fell, Leasure's rifle was smoking. Then he said the big fight broke out. Higgins was one of the non-union men who were escorted from the Gem mine on July 11.

The trial continued late in December, and the Wallace newspaper, dated December 23, reported that the case had probably gone to jury, but the results were not yet known, as Rathdrum had no telephone, and the telegraph wires were down. A few days later, news of Web Leasure's acquittal reached Wallace.

Jack Waite, who was defeated by D. R. Cameron in the last election for sheriff, waited until December before he protested the election. Waite, a 34-year old former professional fighter from Montana, charged the election judges in Kellogg were drunk. In addition, he said Noah Kellogg, an election judge, had several bets riding on Cameron. Not content to stop there, Waite said Robert Cheyne, an election official, was not a citizen of the United States. Waite charged them with further acts of vote marking and miscounting.

The Poorman Mine continued to make news. It produced 700 tons of concentrates monthly. Its shaft sinking operation was 10 feet from the 500-foot level during the middle of December. One of its mill employees, William Roach, was killed in a mill accident. The Poorman crew was made up of 110 miners, 20 millmen and about 30 working as blacksmiths, machinists, carpenters and outside men. During the month, a chunk of galena, practically clean ore and weighing 4 tons, was taken from the Poorman Mine and sent to Chicago to be placed on exhibition at the Chicago World Fair.

The Poorman used nine Rand Drills in its mining operation. These drills were operated by air from a steam-driven air compressor. At one time or another, in the Poorman's early years, it used water, steam and electricity as sources of power to run the machinery. Their efforts were satisfactory to the shareholders, who had received $310,000 in dividends by the end of 1892.

Burke was undergoing the throes of progress. Negotiations were being made to secure a resident minister. The Dunns commented:

"It would doubtless be an excellent field for missionary work, as it is practically virgin territory. . . ."

A. M. Esler wanted Adam Aulbach's scalp. . . . Esler filed a $15,000 libel suit in Federal Court against Aulbach for an article in his newspaper, which included the passage:

". . . such an excitor of riots as the black-hearted and lying A. M. Esler."

Aulbach was successful in later getting this suit dismissed; Esler never collected anything on his claims against the county and Aulbach.

The Frisco Mine had attained a depth of 700 feet, and it had started to raise and stope on 100 feet of open vein from the 700 foot level. The ore averaged a width of 7 to 8 feet, but in some places it broadened out to 40 feet. The Frisco's crew of 100 men shipped two cars of concentrates every three days in December.

The year 1892 was ending at Wardner, which had grown considerably since the arrival of the troops. Its newspaper, the *Wardner News*, was edited by Jack Langrishe, of Western comedic acting fame. The paper was started by Adam Aulbach, on June 11, 1886, and was the first newspaper in the South Fork drainage of the Coeur d'Alene River.

Up and down Wardner's narrow canyon some 850 men were employed, with the Bunker Hill hiring about half this number. Its aerial tramway ran about 10 hours a day, and carried about 500 tons of crude ore. The largest ore body found in the Coeur d'Alenes until that time was being mined out of the Bunker Hill in a stope 400 feet long and 100 feet wide. The drilling was done almost entirely by hand, and the holes were put down sometimes to a depth of 10 to 12 feet.

The big Bunker Hill stope was on the Reed Tunnel level, which was about 1,000 feet below the level of the first workings of the mine. The output of the Bunker Hill was practically limited by the capacity of its tramway at the end of 1892.

At the Last Chance, 75 men were in the mine and mill. The mill turned out about 24 tons of concentrates daily. Idaho was growing elsewhere too. The new town of Harrison had a population of 350 by the end of 1892, and the University of Idaho boasted an enrollment of over 100 students. . . . But all was not progress; 50 pounds of opium was seized in a smuggling raid at Bonners Ferry.

Christmas weekend 1892 saw the temperature drop to 3 degrees below zero in Mullan. . . . This prompted Colonel C. W. Moore, of the Mullan Hotel, to say the lowest temperature ever reached in Mullan was during the middle of January, in 1888, when it fell to 37, 39 and 41 degrees below zero for three consecutive days.

Seventy-three men were employed in the Gold Hunter Mine,

and about 15 more worked there as carpenters, blacksmiths and laborers. The mill required 15 or 17 men when in full operation. Seven Burleigh drills were used in the mine, and they drilled by compressed air with a pressure of 200 pounds to the inch. The power for the compressors was furnished by steam, and the concentrator was run by water power. This was reliable at all times, except during the cold weather when the flumes were liable to freeze and cause a shutdown.

The severe cold toward the end of the year caused several of the mines to close down for a few days, but they reopened as soon as it got warmer. Pottsville, famous during the railroad construction days for its tough characters and big fights, was a ghost town by the end of 1892. It produced a lot of wood for the mines, and thirty cords were taken from there daily.

Employment was up all over the district. Sixty men were at work at the Sierra Nevada and 100 men at the Stemwinder. The gold property on Elk Creek was working about 15 men.

At the Last Chance Mine ore was being hauled out through the Sweeney tunnel in trains or horse drawn cars. This mine was open by three main levels. The third and lower one was generally known as the Sweeney tunnel, and it was about 10 feet wide in the clear and six feet high, allowing for a double-car track. This tunnel went into the mountain 2,450 feet, and drained everything in the area; a stream of water averaging 80 cubic feet per minute was then flowing from it. Seventy men were employed in the Last Chance mine and mill. The mill was run by water power, and much of the water came from the Sweeney tunnel.

The Providence (Miners' Union) Hospital in Wallace ended 1892 in the charge of Sister Superior Joseph. Sister Peter was the druggist, and Sister Loretta was the bookkeeper. Sisters Rosalia and Mary Louise had charge of the kitchen, and Sisters Josephine and Harmen did general work about the building.

The children of Holy Trinity Church and their friends assembled at the church at Christmas time. Lawrence Worstell and Glen McKinlay had brought a tree in from the mountains, and these boys sat with a bucket of water and a sponge to guard against fire from the many lighted candles with which the tree sparkled. The Rector gave the children a short explanation of Christmas and Santa Claus, and then distributed presents to all. Besides a present, each child received a Bible, candy, an apple and an orange. This was followed by an hour of games and then the chilly but happy trip home.

A hard year was coming to a close. Times have not always been easy in the Coeur d'Alene Mining District, but seldom has a year ever held a candle to 1892 for its trials and tribulations. The State of Idaho issued reports at the end of the year stating that its costs in the recent labor trouble in the district amounted to $21,150.52.

Things were under control at the end of the year in Wallace, however, and the Dunn Brothers proclaimed:

> "Poker is the most popular gambling game in Wallace now. Though times are hard, there have been a number of games recently where over $1,000 was on the table at one time."

CHAPTER 38

JANUARY, FEBRUARY AND MARCH – 1893

The year 1893 was to start on a note similar to that of 1892. The mine owners were having trouble with the railroads over the freight rates again; they claimed the rates were excessive for the Coeur d'Alene mines as against the rates charged for the Butte mines. Wesley Everett was arrested on January 5 and charged with threatening to blow up the Bunker Hill Mill. He was jailed on a $2,500 bail. The Black Bear Mine began the year with seventy men on its payroll. It had first been located in 1885 by John Bartlett and William S. Haskins.

In Gem, a wife was beat up by her husband early in January, and town sympathy was soon extended to the woman. The townspeople took up a collection and sent her to her home at Wilbur, Washington. The trainmen and others helped her pack her trunk, and the departure of the train was delayed until such time as she had finished packing her possessions.

At Burke, Father Keyzer held services at the Miners' Union Hall to a large attendance. The Dunn Brothers waxed poetic:

> "At any rate it is good even for a little while, to deflect the thoughts of men from worldly things, such as craps, stud poker, fusil oil, etc., and the women—ah! woman, thy name is frailty."

It was rumored that the Miners' Union at Burke would soon be reorganized. During the middle of the month, the Mine Owners' Association announced that it was having little luck with the railroad companies in getting them to reduce their freight rates.

George Allen was killed in a fall sixty feet down a chute in the Gem Mine on the 15th. Winter was in full swing and miners, carrying their blankets on their back, were a very common sight. Changes in employment seemd to be quite frequent, resulting in a large floating population which was present one day and gone the next.

A new compressor had been ordered for the Helena and Frisco mine which would have a capacity of sixteen No. 3 Rand drills. These were made almost a necessity by the very hard ground in the stopes. Four and one-half feet of hand drilling per day was all that could be accomplished at that time. The Tiger and the Poorman mines were forced to close down late in January because of the cold weather. The water in the flumes froze solid. They would reopen as soon as the temperature rose.

West of Wallace, the Argentine Mine employed fifty to sixty men, and stoping was in progress on two levels. About six cars of ore were shipped daily to the Union Mill for concentration. Their vein was about sixteen feet wide in the deepest workings. It was expected when they got along a little further they would be able to take out about one hundred and fifty tons of ore per day.

On January 27, the south side in Gem burned to the ground. The fire started about 4 a.m. in a shed at the rear of the Miners' Union Hall, and it was believed to have been set. Many business buildings burned, including the Union Hall and Billy Daxon's Saloon.

A special train took men up from Wallace immediately to help out. During the fire there was much drinking, followed by looting and fighting. The drinking got so bad that the deputy sheriff closed the saloons in Gem, and several men were deputized as special constables to quell the trouble.

While the fire was raging, the occupant of Siringo's building, Will F. Read, carried his wife's trunk across the street and put it on the porch of Samuels' store to keep it safe from the fire. Samuels was a strong union sympathizer, and did not like Will Read because of his friendship with Charles Siringo. Giving vent to his feelings, Samuels kicked the trunk into the street. Read then went into his burning building for his shotgun. Their argument grew hotter and Samuels was knocked through the window in his store front by Read. Samuels took a couple of shots at Read with a pistol, but missed. Read responded by shooting Samuels' right arm off at the shoulder.

Will Read took off for Wallace, where he gave himself up at about 5:30 a.m. Read was placed in jail, but the Sheriff left the jail door open, giving Will Read access to a Winchester rifle and 100 rounds of ammunition. Soon a mob of Samuels' friends from Gem came into sight, but Read lay on top of the jail with the rifle, ready to do battle. Web Leasure stopped the mob by pleading with them to let the law take its course. It became necessary for Leasure to point a cocked gun at the leaders and threaten to kill the first one who stepped forward. . . . Within a short time a preliminary hearing was held on the shooting affair before Judge Angel, and Will Read was freed.

❁ ❁ ❁

A new telegraph line was put through Fourth of July Canyon between the Mission and Coeur d'Alene. The old government telegraph wire, put through the Coeur d'Alenes years before, had been in constant service for the telephone company through the canyon. It was replaced with good copper wire, and there would be a new line put in between the South Fork and Murray.

A severe storm on the Lake caused the sinking of the *Corwin* and the *Volunteer*, two small steamers, and caused the *Georgie Oakes* to break from her moorings, doing much damage to her. The latest quote for lead was $3.95 per hundred pounds. This was the highest price for lead in three months.

Thomas Wakely was killed in a blast at the Morning early in February. During the middle of the month, John Mullan and Anton Scheffler were killed by falling rock at the Bunker Hill.

Charles Smith met his death by a falling timber in the Bunker Hill at the end of February.

On the 21st, the Wallace town trustees met and discussed a petition from twenty-five ladies and heads of families. It asked for more strict law enforcement on the subject of children being allowed inside saloons, and "to partake of the enjoyment there provided." The Idaho statute provided that it was a misdemeanor for a saloon keeper to allow children between the ages of five and sixteen years to frequent or enter a saloon.

New freight rates went into effect on February 15, and they were lower. It appeared that V. M. Clement of the Bunker Hill and A. L. Gross of the Morning had gone back East to represent the Mine Owners' Association in negotiation with the railroad.

Toward the middle of February, several of the prisoners who had been confined in Boise because of the difficulties of the previous July returned to the area. A large number of union men came down from the canyons to meet the men who were returning home.

By 1893, at Wardner the Stemwinder Mine had an aerial tramway extending from Wardner Junction, some two miles to its mine, which employed 76 men.

The Peter Breen case had been continued until the summer term of court at Moscow.

The Northern Pacific had side tracks sufficient to accommodate 75 standard gauge and 50 of its narrow-gauge cars. Daily service consisted of one passenger and one freight train on the narrow gauge, two mixed trains on the Burke branch, and a passenger and a freight train on the Missoula cut-off. The trains on the Missoula cut-off were double headers, so that there were seven train crews running in and out of Wallace daily for the Northern Pacific in 1893.

The Union Pacific had eight side tracks in Wallace, which would hold 275 cars. It had two main-line passenger trains daily and two freight trains; also an up and down passenger train on the Burke branch. In addition to the crews of these, there were three other crews of men operating from Wallace. One of these divisions extended to Burke, one to Mullan and one to Osburn.

February ended with the Bunker Hill announcing that it would shut down its mine for an indefinite period because of low prices for lead and zinc, and primarily because of the high freight rates. The mine was to close on February 28, and rumors were about that the Bunker Hill might be sold.

Manager Bradley said that the Bunker Hill's mining expenses for mine, drill and concentrating were $4.55 per ton on the crude ore or about $30 per ton on the concentrates. The railroad and smelting charges amounted to $25.50 per ton. These expenses did not include the cost of taxes and insurance, and administration, and legal expenses. On concentrates assaying 58% lead and 29 ounces of silver per ton, there was little money left for the owners of a mine.

A crew of 50 to 75 men would be employed for a couple of weeks after the shut-down to clean up the ore already broken in the stopes and the reserve that was in the bins at the mines.

On the 2nd of March, eighty tickets were sold by the Union Pacific station at the Wardner Junction, and at least half of them had San Francisco as their destination. The depot platform was crowded with miners, their trunks and bedding. Sixty-one of the discharged men chartered a special train for Portland, from where they would proceed to San Francisco by boat. Elsewhere at Wardner, the Stemwinder Mine put on a night shift and announced that its ore was richer than at any time before.

✽ ✽ ✽

Flags were raised and bonfires were lit in Gem on March 6 when the news reached there that Pettibone and the others had been released from the federal prison. Scarcely had this news been received before the miners were celebrating another event —Former Sheriff Cunningham was not convicted at his trial as the jury could not agree. It would be summer before he could be tried again, and it was getting more difficult all the time to convict those on the side of the union men.

Jack Waite's contest of the Sheriff's election was dismissed by the court for lack of his showing of fraud. Wallace was finally to elect a "genuine" mayor. Under a new law, Wallace was then a City of the second class and no longer a town. Up until that time it had had a Board of Trustees headed by a Chairman.

In the suit between Tyler Mining Company and the Last Chance Mining Company, which had been on trial since February 22, before Judge Beatty, a verdict was returned on March 5 for the Tyler Company. This case involved the same vein that the Bunker Hill and Stemwinder mines were on. The case was tried in Boise the previous winter and the Last Chance won there, but the Circuit Court of Appeals at San Francisco reversed that decision and ordered a new trial. The case involved a question of who located on the vein first and also took into account the apex law. After the trial, the Last Chance people chartered a special train to Spokane while the Tyler people started holding a big party. It was presumed that the case would be appealed. Charles Sweeney, principal owner of the Last Chance, said: "It is only horse and horse."

On March 13 a jury in Burke refused to hand in its decision until they were paid. Judge Buree refused to be coerced and told them they must hand in their verdict first. He fined each juror two dollars for contempt of court. None of the jurors seemed to mind this until their supply of whiskey was exhausted. They then hurriedly paid their fines and turned in their verdict so they could be paid. In Burke it was announced: "J. P. Flanagan is assuming autocratic airs since he joined the church."

The Morning Mine in Mullan shut down for an indefinite period because of low metal prices and high freight rates. Exploration work within the mine continued. Although the Bunker was shut down, there were about 60 men doing development work on that property. The Alma and Nellie Wood gold property on Elk Creek was working between 25 and 30 men. The stamp mill there was running full blast day and night. At Burke, Steve Blake was promoted to night clerk at the Tiger Hotel and now wore the regulation collar and diamond pin.

On March 23, the Mine Owners' Association met in Spokane to discuss freight rates with a representative of the railroad.

Thomas O'Brien and Joseph F. Poynton were ordered released from the Ada County jail by United States Judge Beatty on the 20th of March. Their full term of eight months would have expired on April 12. They were the last of the prisoners held for violating Beatty's injunction. On the 28th, all remaining cases against rioters and labor troubles were dismissed in Rathdrum upon motion of District Attorney O'Neill. This included the case against Peter Breen and Joel Warren. O'Neill said that he had insufficient evidence in these cases.

Meanwhile, the Mine Owners' Association and the railroad people were still holding meetings in Spokane with no results. The Mine Owners were asking for a $4 per ton reduction. A reduction of $2 per ton would save the Bunker Hill about $50,000 per year. . . . Among the mines belonging to the Mine Owners' Association during March of 1893 were the Stemwinder, Sierra Nevada, Granite, Bunker Hill, Gem, Standard and Union, Morning, Poorman, Last Chance, Custer, and Mammoth.

The Wallace newspaper always noted progress:

> "Hereafter no smoking will be allowed in Justice LaGrande's Courtroom while in session. This is a move in the right direction. If the Judge will now order that there shall be no spitting on the floor, it will be another advance."

CHAPTER 39

APRIL AND MAY — 1893

The Wallace city election was big news early in April. W. S. "Billy" Haskins had been elected mayor. He favored municipal ownership of the water system. His election prompted the water company to offer the city water for fire protection, free of charge.

Thomas O'Brien, President, and Joe Poynton, Secretary, of the Coeur d'Alene Miners' Union, returned from prison in Boise to Wallace, on April 4. They were met at the depot by a crowd of friends and a brass band, which headed a parade that marched through the streets of Wallace, after which the band serenaded various business men known to be in sympathy with the released men. In the evening, O'Brien and Poynton were guests of honor at a banquet held at the Hanley House restaurant in Wallace. The celebration lasted far into the night.

"Wednesday (April 5) was a gala day among the members and friends of the Miners' Union (at Gem). About 4:30 a procession was formed to go down and meet Thomas O'Brien and Joe Poynton, who were coming up on a hand car. The boys unhitched the immortal mule and proceeded to pull the load themselves. Nearly half the town turned out to meet them. After being hauled through the town, they returned to where their old home stood, and amid cheering, Mr. O'Brien in choice language thanked his friends for the reception tendered him. In the evening Sivart's restaurant was the scene of special merry-making and dancing, which made many think of the good times that took place before the trouble."

The Coeur d'Alene Bank in Wallace closed its doors on the 7th of April. The only owners known locally were George B. McAulay of Wardner and Van DeLashmutt of Portland. The Miners' Exchange Bank at Wardner was owned by the same two men, and it also closed its doors on the same day.

Times were growing difficult, particularly in Wardner. First, the Bunker Hill had closed down, and then the Last Chance was closed by court order; now the bank had failed. Nine saloons closed during the last week in March rather than buy a license for the second quarter. Three more closed at Wardner Junction. Yes, a depression had come to the area, but not one of the more than thirty saloons in Wallace closed its doors. The Wallace population had grown to 1,961, according to a census taken in April.

No official notification had been received in the district regarding a reduction of freight rates. It was rumored that the Northern Pacific was willing to grant a $4 per ton reduction, but that the Union Pacific refused to go along with this.

At a meeting on April 13, the Mine Owners' Association negotiated further with several important railroad men, who represented both the Union Pacific and the Northern Pacific. No immediate announcements were made from this Wallace meeting, but it was felt that some decision was soon forthcoming.

Ten days had passed since their return, and O'Brien and Poynton had been given an ovation in every camp in the Coeur d'Alene since their return home from jail. Wardner was the last to greet them, and it threw a social dance in their honor, which drew a large attendance from all over the area.

The Nellie Wood and Alma claims on Elk Creek were operated, in the spring of 1893, by the Pandora Mining Company, which employed 30 men. Clarence Cunningham was the superintendent. It was a solely gold proposition, and was run as one of the oldest mines in this area; Jim Wardner was the original owner. They were working at a depth of 200 feet, on a level which had been driven a distance of 700 feet. The ore was free milling, and ten stamps were employed in the treatment of the ore, which averaged about 12 ounces of gold to the ton. Jim Wardner had worked this property with varying success for a time.

The wages paid the mine workers were still a subject of great concern. On the 20th of April, the Mine Owners' Association met with representatives of the Knights of Labor, who were serving as intermediators between the Association and the Miners' Union. At this meeting the Mine Owners proposed a sliding scale of wages tied into the prices of metals.

The Knights of Labor were represented at this meeting by M. T. Wight of Mullan, M. J. Donnelly of Wallace, Conn of Burke, Charles Tremble of Gem and A. J. Devlin of Wardner. The Knights of Labor asked that $3.50 per day be paid to all men underground regardless of their duties.

The Mine Owners' Association refused to meet this demand, and said they were paying at the present time $4 per day to the miners sinking shafts, and in some cases the timbermen were getting $4 per day. The Association insisted upon the right to grade their labor inside the mines. Both sides agreed to meet further in regard to the wage question.

Near Burke, the Standard Mine was owned by Finch and Campbell. It was located about ¾ of a mile from the town of Burke, and 16 men were on the payroll in April of 1893. Its new tunnel was six feet ten inches high by four and one-half feet wide at the bottom and three feet ten inches wide at the top. Pear-shaped tunnels were common in smaller properties in the district. They had to be wider across the handles of the wheelbarrows than across the ears of the miners.

*   *   *

At 1:30 in the morning of April 20, a fire blazed in Wardner which was to destroy 80 buildings. The Wardner water supply was inadequate to stop the fire, which had started in the bedroom of T. L. Lawson, at the rear of his clothing store.

Many business houses were burned to the ground, together with a number of residences. All the buildings on both sides of Mill Street for a distance of two blocks were burned. The Wallace City Council held a meeting early that day to provide emergency aid to the Wardner people. There had been no time to take up donations, but the Wallace stores gave supplies and trusted for payment at a later date. A large shipment of bread, butter, coffee, ham and bacon was quickly sent to Wardner by train. More supplies were to be sent later. It was a simple matter . . . a need existed, and it was fulfilled.

A week after the Wardner fire, new buildings were being erected amid the ruins. A prominent Wardner citizen, Henry Loren Day, had been placed in personal charge of the money and provisions sent to the Wardner people from the surrounding area. About a week later, Day reported that 45 or 50 people had been given provisions thus far as they had needed them. He pointed out that the Bunker Hill and Last Chance shutdowns, plus the bank failure, followed by the Wardner fire, had left many Wardner families absolutely destitute. Henry Day said that some of these people had not and would not accept any aid.

Winter was coming to an end. On the 26th, the Murray Stage made its first through trip of the year on wheels. . . . With the advent of spring, Richard Foley, the Burke Constable, attached the fire hose to the water main and washed out the town jail. It was something that was badly needed, having been neglected for years past.

The Mullan correspondent for the Wallace newspaper furnished some mining news:

"J. F. Ingalls resumed work on the Lucky Friday lode this week. The discovery of this property is located on the spur of the hill running down to the Hunter Concentrator, the location notice on the dump showing that it was made November 1, 1889. The only work done on the property consists of a shaft 80 feet deep at the point indicated. The ore on the dump is more or less decomposed and copper stained, with very little lead present. Selected specimens have assayed as high as 175 ounces of silver per ton. It is Mr. Ingall's intention to sink the shaft deeper and possibly to drift on the vein in a short time. The vein is conveniently located for development, should further exploration prove it to be a paying mine."

The Mullan reporter visited Judge Maher, who held court in a room that served three purposes: 1. general store, 2. saloon and 3. courtroom. On the day of the visit, Judge Maher was busy transferring bottled ale from the cellar to the main part of the building, which prompted the reporter to write:

"At the time in question, the judge stated that a jury trial was on the docket for that day and that it was only proper that suitable provisions should be made to the jurors in order to secure, as far as possible, a perfect administration of justice."

The case referred to was entitled James Gleason vs. John Wilson. Gleason was suing for $290 stumpage on a wood contract at Pottsville. Later in the day the case resulted in a hung jury so a new trial was ordered.

On the following day, a new trial was held. Gleason wanted either the wood that Wilson cut or its equivalent in cash. . . . Judge Maher, besides being the Court and Counsel for the prosecution, was a creditor of the defendant in the sum of $37. . . . The jury decided in favor of the defendant, after deliberating about 15 minutes. . . . The situation demanded rash measures. . . . Judge Maher set aside the verdict and ordered that a new trial was to be held on the next day. . . . The Judge was reported to have said: "If necessary, it will go to the Supreme Court of the United States."

By this time Wilson had learned a lesson; Judge Maher was not to hear his case again. The case was transferred to the Probate Court at Wallace, where Judge Gregory presided. The trial was to be held on May 6, and Judge Maher drew up the complaint, which was so interesting that it was published on the front page of the Wallace paper.

When the 6th of May came, Judge Gregory dismissed the much tried case for the reason that the defendant had not been served with a copy of the Summons and a copy of the Complaint. To add insult to injury, Judge Maher was arrested on the same day for selling liquor without a license. His case was to come to trial on the 25th.

The Morning Mine resumed operation early in May. Little discrimination was used in choosing their miners so far as union membership was concerned. Their primary concern was to hire experienced underground workers.

On May 7 and 8, some damage was done in Wallace, Canyon Creek and in Burke Canyon by high water. Printers' Creek in Wallace overflowed, and water ran down Bank Street and across Fifth Street. The Nine Mile Road washed out just north of the cemetery and the Northern Pacific line had a small washout just below Gem.

At Wardner, Milo Creek apparently ran strong during the flood, but did little damage: "It cleaned out the filth and that fact should atone for all the alleged transgressions and eccentricities of Milo Creek."

During the middle of May, the whole district suffered from high water. The railroad tracks in Wallace were covered by water and the Union Pacific depot was virtually an island. Some bridges were blown out and others were washed away. The White and Bender warehouse in Gem was washed away, as were the gardens at the Providence Hospital. Damages to the railroads in Canyon Creek amounted to between $10,000 and $30,000.

The Union Pacific lines below Kellogg were under water during the week and were tied up for a few days after the flood was over. Much damage was done at Wardner and Kellogg, but no lives were lost.

During the flood, Gem's beer supply was exhausted. Jacob Lochman came to its aid, by bringing a horse drawn cart full of beer up the tracks to Gem. From such things, heroes are born.

D. C. McKissick's wholesale liquor business failed during the middle of May. No reason was given, but it could not have been for a lack of liquor consumption in the district. He must have been the victim of outside competition.

Thirty criminal cases were set on the criminal calendar for the court session to begin May 31, and Richard Cunningham, the former Shoshone County Sheriff, was the defendant in each and every one of them. He had been brought to trial in March but the jury failed to agree. . . . In the June 1893 trial, the jury was once again unable to agree, and the case was never tried again. The charges against Judge Maher for bootlegging were dismissed on May 26, inasmuch as he bought a license to sell liquor after he had been arrested. He had to pay $36 court costs, however.

Michael Maher was born in Ireland in 1846 and came to America when he was 21 years old. Time was to take him to California and then to the Comstock in Nevada. Later, he moved on to Oregon, and 1884 brought him to Murray, where he ran a general store for two years. The new town of Mullan attracted him in 1886, and he was to make it his home until 1897, when he moved to Burke for the rest of his life. In 1920 he passed away and was buried in the Miners' Union Cemetery near Wallace.

May ended in Wallace with renewed hope for the miners. . . . The news had come to town. The Western Federation of Miners, a new union, was formed on May 15 at Butte, Montana, after the miners of six states had banded together in one body. John Gilligan was elected president, and the next annual meeting was to be held in Salt Lake City in May of 1894. One provision of its constitution made it unlawful for any local union to strike without a 75% vote of approval of its members.

The birth of the Western Federation of Miners may have occurred in Butte, but it had been conceived earlier in the minds of union men from the Coeur d'Alenes serving time in prison cells.

CHAPTER 40

JUNE, JULY AND AUGUST — 1893

When June arrived, there was at least one man in the area who did not have his mind on labor troubles . . . a lovesick Swede, Charles Challenge, was arrested on a complaint by Joe Camia, proprietor of the Chicago Club. The Swede was charged with disturbing the peace after he endeavored to lead one Louise, an inmate of the Chicago Club, back from a life of wantonness and ease, to the path of rectitude and honor. To accomplish this, he offered the young lady his hand and heart which she promptly declined. He still pressed his case, however, to the annoyance of Louise and also of the other occupants of the building. He was for this arrested and fined $15 or fifteen days. His new headquarters were at the Wallace Jail.

During May of 1893 there was more ore shipped from Canyon Creek than had ever been taken out of that area in one month. Rumors were prevalent that the Bunker Hill would soon resume operations. At the time, there were about 1,400 men at work in all the mines in the district. The prices of lead and silver and the differences existing between the Miners' Union and the Mine Owners were causing a depression.

About 9:00 P.M. on June 7, several shots were heard near the corner of Fifth and Cedar, and at the same time the fire bell was rung. Evidently someone misunderstood the reports of the pistol for a fire alarm, and one of the hose carts was promptly on the spot. Howard B. Johnson was found lying wounded. He was probably the best known colored man in Wallace. Johnson had been about to enter his room, and he had keys in his hand. Suspicion at once rested on Ella Tolson, the colored girl who had signed charges of seduction against Johnson during the previous week, but she had since withdrawn these charges. Ella was later apprehended, and she confessed that she had indeed shot Johnson. Johnson's clothes were torn by three bullet holes which never touched him, but he was wounded by two other shots. Ella Tolson was to appear in court on the 10th.

Pete McCloskey tipped the scales at 282 pounds, and the Dunn Brothers commented that he was a fine illustration of the good food to be found at McCloskey's restaurant. At Burke a new bridge over the creek at the west end of town was nearly completed. The old one had been washed out by the recent spring flood. The new bridge would be quite an improvement for that town; it had guard rails for the safety of children and Burke drunks.

Fred Witts ran the Morning Boarding House at Mullan, which served over 170 men, and his kitchen crew consisted of eight men at all times. The newspaper reported the boarding house used: 300 pounds of flour a day and 1,500 to 2,000 pounds of sugar a month, 100 dozen eggs a week, half a beef every two days, mutton and other types of meat, 750 pounds of ham per month, a sack and a half of potatoes every day.

James Herrington, about 60 years old, was shot three times with a .38 caliber revolver by Robert A. Cunningham in Gem in an argument over a dog bite. Herrington was a man with a reputation as a gunman and had killed a number of men in bygone days. He served seventeen years in a Nevada prison for one killing. It was announced that he would survive the shooting. The wounded man stated without reluctance that his injuries were solely due to the fact that his own pistol failed to work properly, thus preventing him from killing Cunningham. His reputation as a handyman with a pistol was far more precious to him than the legal punishment of his assailant.

Further down the river, the Yankee (a Sunshine Mine property) on Big Creek had been a producing and paying property for the previous three years. It was about three miles from the mouth of the creek and was rich in silver. The ore vein was only four to six inches in width, but did not require concentrating. Only three men, including the Blake Brothers who owned the claim, worked there, and they shipped a car of ore every two months. The ore ranged in value from $75 to $400 per ton.

*　*　*

Ella Tolson, the colored woman who shot Howard Johnson, appeared in Court, and she was released on her own recognizance to appear before the Grand Jury at a later time.

At Kellogg, Doctor T. R. Bussey moved across the valley to McAulay (Sunnyside), and he moved half a building with him. It seemed that he owned a half interest in the building, which was sawed exactly in two to satisfy the owners, who went their separate ways.

All indictments against the labor rioters of 1892 were quashed, except those against George Pettibone and G. M. Dallas. - - - And time was to erase these charges from the court docket. Neither Pettibone nor Dallas were convicted of these charges.

V. M. Clement, formerly of the Bunker Hill, left Chicago for South Africa about July 10. He was employed as general manager of extensive mining operations at a salary of $20,000 a year, plus expenses. He was accompanied by John Hayes Hammond, formerly of the Bunker Hill.

The Idaho Board of Education, in session in Boise, granted a state diploma to Miss Eleanor B. Day of Wallace, the same being for life and the highest the Board could issue. Miss Day was born in Nevada in 1867 and received her advanced education in California. Her investments in the Hercules Mine brought her financial security after the turn of the century. She later married Edward Boyce, who was to rise to the presidency of the Western Federation of Miners.

On June 21, freight rates were once again reduced. It was not stated what immediate effects the reduction would have on ore shipments, because there existed the possibility that ore shipments would be handled by separate contracts. The rates had been dropped 39% in the last four months. The price of lead was $3.50 per hundred, and silver was 81¼ cents per ounce. These were the lowest prices ever on silver, and the price for lead was a 12-year low.

The carmen and shovelers at the Frisco Mine went on strike for a 50 cent raise to $3.50 a day on the 20th of June. Joseph McDonald, superintendent of the Frisco, laid off all employees, as the mine could not operate without the carmen and shovelers. Finch and Campbell, of the Gem Mine, feeling that their mine would be next, also laid off their mine crew on the afternoon of the 20th. Not all men were for the strike because of the low prices for lead and silver.

On the evening of the 20th, after giving Mr. Culbertson three days' notice, Al Richardson and John Duncan, the engineers (hoistmen) on the Tiger hoist, quit work because they considered twelve hours too long to work at an occupation of that kind. The shaft at the Tiger was being sunk, and this fact greatly increased the danger that might result from inattention on the part of the engineers. They requested that their time be reduced to eight hours per day, thus making three shifts per day instead of two. Culbertson did not see fit to grant this request. Consequently, operations of the Tiger Mine were suspended.

On June 22, in the evening, a man named Merrill shot James "Limber Jim" Allison at George McKinniss' place at Wardner Junction. They had been disputing over a piece of ground, and Allison was shot in the thigh. Merrill was arrested soon thereafter.

With a depression in the Coeur d'Alenes and tough times prevailing over most of the West, it was estimated that there were no less than 2,000 prospectors scouring the hills in Canada's Slocan country during June.

Later in the month, a landslide occurred at the Spokane

Hydraulic Company property near Murray. The slide was over 125 feet high and 50 feet deep with a width of 60 to 70 feet. It killed Fleming Goolsby, the night foreman, and crippled another man.

Eleanor B. Day was hired to teach the intermediate department in the Wallace School. She had finished two years of teaching in Wardner, and prior to that time she taught in Spokane.

On the 27th of the month, an underground robbery occurred at a prospect between the Standard and Mammoth mines. G. Ericson and Jake Headman were robbed by two armed masked men who came into their tunnel about midnight. Ericson lost $38 and his partner lost $440. The culprits were never captured.

By the end of June, nearly all the mines in the Coeur d'Alenes were shut down due to the strikes and the sudden fall in the silver market. The government of India announced it would stop the coinage of free silver, and this broke the price on that metal. On the 27th, silver fell to 77 cents an ounce, and the following day the price fell to 69 cents. The outlook for silver was very dim.

The falling silver price caused the Morning mine to close down on June 28, and the Standard, Black Bear and Mammoth mines followed suit on June 29. The Tiger closed down on June 30. The effect on all kinds of business in the district was disastrous. A number of families and miners were leaving the district every day. Some of the smelters declined to buy any more ore under the existing circumstances. The end of the month saw the Frisco and Gem companies engaged in boarding up the windows of their mills. Very few mines in the district were operating, and they were small mines. It was predicted that a large portion of the state of Idaho would be looked over thoroughly for gold in 1893. It was one of the only industries not seriously affected by the recent drop in metal prices.

News of this Silver Panic caused many businesses to shut down immediately. There were three saloons left running in Mullan shortly after the 1st of July. Two newspapers in the county folded the same week, leaving but three survivors: The *Coeur d'Alene Miner, Wardner News* and *Murray Sun.*

The Dunn Brothers announced that the *Coeur d'Alene Miner* would be cut in size from an eight-page weekly to four pages. It chose to weather out 1893's financial storm in this manner. The entire staff of one of the closed newspapers took off for the St. Joe country to prospect for gold.

The Northern Pacific and Union Pacific railroads again announced lower freight rates on ore from this district. They would charge $12 per ton from Wallace to eastern terminals upon ore of a value of $45 or less per ton. Ore having a value of less than $65 per ton would be hauled at $14 per ton, and that ore being worth more than $65 per ton would cost $16 per ton for freight. This represented a substantial decrease in freight rates.

On the 3rd of July, the Alma and Nellie Wood gold mine and mill of Elk Creek, started up again at full capacity. It was being worked on a cooperative plan, and there were 18 men on the job.

The Helena and Frisco Mining Company filed suit against Shoshone County for $100,000 in damages done by the riot during the prior summer. The suit was filed in Federal Court at Moscow. District Attorney O'Neill filed his demurrer to the complaint, which raised the question of law as to the liability of the county.

Tough times or not, the 4th of July was celebrated in grand style in Wallace. The events started with loud blasts of dynamite and ended with fireworks in the evening. Special trains brought visitors from all over the district into town, and patriotic speeches were made.

In the competitions, double-hand drilling was the feature of interest. Pat Welch and Tom Gaffney of the Poorman were on one side and T. J. Ferguson and John Dunphy of the Standard were on the other side. Gaffney and Welch drilled 33¾ inches to their opponents 22½ inches. First prize was $100 and second prize $50. Gaffney struck an average of 53 blows a minute.

Other contests of the day included boys' drilling, men's foot race, bicycle race, tug of war, horse race, trotting race and a single-hand drilling contest. C. A. Tooley drilled eleven inches in seven minutes to win the single-hand drilling contest.

The horse race had spectators from Sixth Street to the Holland Hospital. The conditions were the best two in the three heats. Follett's Redbird, Peter Bernier's Pinto and W. S. Harris' Buckskin were the horses.

The first run did not count because of a false start. At the end of this run, Pinto and Buckskin threw their riders and departed for the hills. They were caught later, however, and the next two heats were run in good order. Follett's horse, Redbird, ridden by Joe Tilley's little boy Hal, came out ahead in both heats, and therefore a third race was not run.

*   *   *

The Miners' Union erected an eight-foot granite monument to Cummings, Hennessey and Carlson, the Miners' Union dead of July 11, 1892. The monument was placed at the Miners' Union Cemetery in Nine Mile. On July 11, 1893, about 400 union men paraded from Wallace to the graveyard to commemorate the first anniversary of their deaths. Addresses were delivered by Peter Breen, Bushnell and Thomas O'Brien. About half of the men wore Miners' Union badges. Miners' Union Day was observed for several years thereafter by similar proceedings.

The inscription on the monument, which still stands, reads as follows:

"Erected by the Coeur d'Alene Miners' Union to the memory of Cummings, Hennessey and Carlson, who were killed in the cause of freedom and justice, at Gem, July 11, 1892. Dead, but their memory still lives in the hearts of their friends.

James Hennessey, aged 40 years.
Harry Cummings, aged 36 years.
Gus Carlson, aged 30 years."

The Dunn's newspaper carried an open letter from William K. Smith to Fred Dean of Wardner:

> "I was on hand to take part in the sword contest with you, as arranged between us at the Fuller house, but for some reason unknown to me you failed to appear."

The same newspaper carried an announcement that Doctor Ignatz Mayer, Eye, Ear, Nose and Throat and Eye Glasses Specialist, was coming to town on July 20 for ten days. He published a list of his references, and they were all from the Moscow area and included Governor McConnell and President Gault of the University of Idaho.

Mining news of interest included the following items:

The gold property on Elk Creek had discovered another four-foot vein which was free milling and looked good. Their stamp mill was run full blast. . . .

In Pine Creek, 40 men were employed at the Antimony mine and smelter. . . .

Andrew Lind, who was injured in the Hunter Mine three weeks ago, died in Spokane on July 25th. . . .

Trout were selling in the local butcher shops at 15 to 20 cents a pound. Times were looking pretty bad by the end of July: "Nearly everyone has gone fishing or are laying in a supply of wood for the winter, but dollars are as scarce as raisins in a boarding house pudding."

These and many other articles indicated that during the mine shutdown there wasn't much to do in the district except for fishing and picking huckleberries.

The Palouse country was flooded with men who desired to work in the fields at the rate of $1.50 per day and board. In many cases, they would have to wait until the grain was sold before they could collect wages as most of the farmers were without money.

On July 25, Joe Camia was arrested for keeping a disorderly house. A complaint had been filed against him by a Finlander from Pottsville, who claimed that he had been robbed of $20 in the house by one of the female inmates who occupied an apartment in the upper story. The case was tried before a jury in Judge Lichtenstein's court. It was difficult to determine just exactly where the money went, and the case was therefore dismissed.

From Murray it was reported that a wagonload of fish, which had been blasted out of the river, left the North Fork for Wallace early in August. It was further claimed that the bottom of the North Fork was covered with dead fish from the blasting.

At the beginning of August, four or five of the principal mine owners expressed their willingness to start back to work within a few weeks at a scale of $2.50 per day for all men working underground, regardless of the capacity in which they were employed. They also proposed to reduce board 75 cents per day. This offer was made in the hope of bridging the difficult times ahead, and it would grant immediate employment to over 1,000 men. Not all of the mines in the district could resume work even at these reduced prices, but some of them would be able to make it. No immediate response was forthcoming from the miners.

Lead was quoted at $3.20 per hundred, which was the lowest price since May of 1879. The highest price in prior years had been $6.50 per hundred in October of 1873. The average price for the previous 22 years had been $4.96.

The mine situation was precisely the same as it had been earlier. No men had gone to work at the wages offered, and no meetings had been held between the Mine Owners' Association and the unions. A mass meeting was held at Utley's Hall on August 8. Parties came from all over the mining district to discuss the problem of welfare for the less fortunate people in the district.

The St. Joe Valley was becoming a favorite camping ground during the summer. Steamers traveled up the river every other day, and the Union Pacific had erected a drawbridge across the river. During the summer of 1893, it was a common practice for local miners to pack into the head of the St. Joe River via Mullan and Stevens Peak trails.

On the 17th, John A. Finch returned from Chicago and other eastern cities where he represented the silver producers. He stated that the eastern newspapers were almost unanimously against any proposals for the free coinage of silver. He added that the eastern cities were plagued with unemployment.

The Poorman Mine announced that it hit its finest body of ore on the 800-foot level. The vein of galena was five feet wide. One hundred ten men were still on the payroll at that mine. A slight accident at the Poorman Mill during mid-August caused a breakdown and duplicate parts were ordered. The mill and mine were shut down in the interim. It took about a week to repair the mill, but there seemed to be no indication that operations were soon to be resumed at the mine and mill.

It was rumored that the Poorman was likely to close down permanently within a short time because of the low metal prices. This would mean an expense of over $1,500 per month to keep the water pumped out unless the company decided to pull the pumps and allow the mine to fill up. It was hoped that this would not be done because it would take so long to reopen. The Poorman offered its miners a promise of continued employment if they would agree to a cut in wages. The union held a meeting that night, and on the next day the union announced the men absolutely refused to go to work for reduced wages.

Patrick Clark, the general manager of the Poorman, said the mine could not continue at the existing wages. He then proposed that a sliding scale be adopted based on the average price of lead and silver for each month. The scale would be based upon a wage of $3.50 per day when one ounce of silver and 100 pounds of lead would sell for a combined price of $4.50 at New York quotations. For every raise of 5 cents in the value of these two metals combined, the wages were to be advanced 5 cents per day, and for each decline of 5 cents in their combined prices, the wages were to be lowered 5 cents a day. These wages were to be paid to all men underground except the timbermen who were to be paid 50 cents extra per day. Clark further proposed that each side was to have the privilege of withdrawing from the agreement to work for these wages, upon fifteen days' written notice to the other party.

Taking the then existing quotations of silver and lead, 74¾ cents and $3.20 respectively, the wages offered by the Poorman would compute to be $2.95 for all men working underground except the timbermen who would get 50 cents a day more. Applying the sliding scale proposal back to the average price for 1892, the offer of the Poorman would have meant $3.92 per day for underground workers.

The Spokane Hydraulic Company at Murray quit for the season late in August. Their operations were hampered by the lack of water during the last few weeks.

On the 25th, the Granite mine offered the Miners' Union $3.00 per day for underground work. It was considered doubtful that the Miners' Union would accept. It is interesting to note that all of these proposals for reduced wages were first offered to the unions. The past practice by the mine owners of ignoring or bypassing the union seemed to have ended.

The Italian element in Kellogg gave rise to the following news items: On August 23, Justice of the Peace George A. Barnard performed a marriage between Jensen Pecards of Kellogg to Miss Catalina Sala, of Borca, Italy. . . . On the same day Mr. and Mrs. Peter Albinola were parents of a daughter, and Pete was setting them up for everybody. Peter Albinola had been busy blowing out stumps on his lot on Milo Creek where he planned to erect a home.

The *Spokane Review* of the 24th announced the marriage of Bledso Johnson and Ella Tolson. This was undoubtedly Howard B. Johnson and the woman who took several shots at him a few months before. Apparently this also ended the legal affairs involved in the shooting.

August was ending, and the Miners' Union had been wrestling with the Granite mine's proposition to pay all men $3.00 per day. Their deliberations went on for a week, and it was rumored that the Gem Union voted almost unanimously to accept the terms offered and go back to work. Their approval, however, was subject to further approval by the Central Union at Wallace.

From Murray came the report that the air was filled with smoke. Unless rain soon came, they were going to have serious fire difficulty.

> "The smoke resulting from the forest fire has been growing denser for the past few weeks until it now hangs like an immense pall over the whole district. . . ."

> "The smoke from the burning timber has become so dense within the past 24 hours as to obscure the surrounding hilltops. . . .

The Bunker Hill offered to let certain portions of its mines go to contractors. The company proposed to pay so much a ton for the ore mined and sacked and placed on the wagon platform at the mine. The amount to be paid was to be determined by the assay value of the ore. The Company was asking for bids on the various grades. Wallace miners were looking into this proposal.

CHAPTER 41

SEPTEMBER THROUGH DECEMBER
1893

The month began with the Poorman Mine resuming operations. All men would get the old wage of $3.50 for working underground. The pumps had been pulled out earlier, and this necessitated a delay of some days before the mine was clear of water. By the 4th of the month, nearly 200 men were on the payroll.

Montana Governor Richards granted a pardon to William Black, who had been in trouble during the Frisco riots and was serving a five-year sentence at Deer Lodge for assault with intent to kill. He was the fellow who had to be shot in order that he be arrested in Montana after he fled from Gem. Black was still suffering from a wound in his hip and was in bad shape. The Governor pardoned him on the condition that his friends would not allow him to become a public charge of any county in Montana. Thomas Heney, President of the Mullan Miners' Union, promised to post a bond for his release, if needed, but this turned out to be unnecessary. Sister Joseph of the Providence Hospital had written to Black that the doors of the Providence Hospital would be open to him should he return to the Coeur d'Alenes. Black was well known in this area, having lived in Mullan for some time and worked at the Gem previous to the labor trouble of 1892.

In Wallace, Joseph Peila had refitted and repaired the St.

Louis Beer Hall near the Northern Pacific bridge. The upper story was fitted for sleeping rooms and was very convenient for those wishing to take the early trains.

Manager Bradley of the Bunker Hill announced that if silver and lead prices continued to improve, they would put on a limited number of men in their best stopes. These were presently being contracted out, and about 20 men were working under contract taking out ten tons of ore per day. Early in September the Granite Mine resumed operations with a force of about 50 men. The Mammoth was still idle. Over the entire district many miners were returning to work, but more men were available than there were jobs. At Mullan, the Morning and Gold Hunter were both closed down without any indication of reopening, and a large number of Mullan men had left the district.

Bradley announced on September 14 that the Bunker Hill would resume operations as soon as they could get it ready. They would employ about 200 men on a one-shift basis, and they were paying about $3 per day for miners. The Bunker Hill management contended that its mines were different from the mines in Canyon Creek and that the Bunker Hill Mine was perfectly dry. This, as a rule, saved the miners the expense of rubber clothes.

The Dunn Brothers were prompted to write an editorial which included the passage:

'There is no longer any doubt that the panic is over."

The section men of the Union Pacific and Northern Pacific railroads of this area struck. They had recently had their wages reduced. They had been getting $2 per day and then were cut to $1.75. Early in September their wages were dropped to $1.40 per day. The last reduction was too much for them, and they refused to work. They had not been replaced, and it did not appear they would be.

On September 12, the Wallace City Council heard a petition from the citizens praying for the removal of the woman "Arkansaw" from her present location on the alley east of Sixth Street

to some less centrally located part of the city. The Chief of
Police was instructed to remove her and other obnoxious characters from the alley east of Sixth Street and report the results to
the next council meeting.

During the middle of September, the Dunn Brothers wrote an
editorial advocating the acceptance of the Poorman's offer for a
sliding scale of wages. It cited that under the present prices of
lead and silver, to-wit: $3.80 for lead and 74¾ cents for silver,
the present wages would be $3.55 for every underground miner
at the Poorman. The wage question was still unsettled throughout the whole district.

Posters bearing the following notice were distributed all over
the Northwest during mid-September:

"Notice—KEEP AWAY FROM THE COEUR D'ALENES.
Working men and miners are requested to keep away from
the Coeur d'Alenes, as the trouble is still unsettled and the
country is flooded with idle men.

"By order of the executive board of the Miners' Union.
W. J. Wilson, President.

"J. F. Whalen, Secretary and Treasurer, Wallace, Idaho,
September 16, 1893."

On September 18, posters appeared in Wardner warning miners not to accept the $3 per day offer of the Bunker Hill:

"Notice—Hall of Knights of Labor, L. A. No. 2462, Wardner,
Idaho, September 17, 1893, to the working men of Wardner
and vicinity:

"You are hereby notified that organized labor of Wardner
and of the Coeur d'Alene District in general refuses to
accept the scale offered by the Bunker Hill and Sullivan
Company and call upon all working men—union and non-
union—to resist this outrage. Other mines, working under a
great deal more adverse circumstances are paying the scale
asked for by organized labor and claim to be making money.
Is the Bunker Hill and Sullivan entitled to any more con-

sideration than other companies? Three dollars now means Two dollars next year; history proves this. Take your choice LIBERTY OR SERFDOM.

"By order of the Committee."

This caused some of the men who were at work at the Bunker Hill to quit their jobs.

On September 24, a notice was posted by the Bunker Hill offering $3 for carmen and shovelers and $3.50 for miners. Meetings were shortly held by the Knights of Labor, which resulted in acceptance of these terms. Late in September, there were about 175 men working at the Bunker Hill. The Wardner storekeepers had ordered new stocks of goods in anticipation of a good winter trade. Business there was looking up. Earlier the Bunker Hill had posted a notice in its bunk house which reduced board to $6 per week and room rent to $1 per month per man. The bunks on the third floor of the boarding house were free.

In Gem, the miners refused to go to work for $3 and $3.50 per day. There was no change in the conditions there late in September. They were holding out for $3.50 per day for everyone, and they refused to recognize the action of the Knights of Labor at Wardner. It was the desire of the union men in Gem that there be only one wage standard throughout the entire district.

The Dunn Brothers started off October by chastising the local union men for not accepting the offer of $3 for carmen and shovelers and $3.50 for miners. The Dunns were favoring the companies' position more openly than in prior months. Possibly this was because the unions did not have a paper in the district at the time that could respond to their editorials.

At the end of the first week in October, the Bunker Hill had 280 men on the payroll. The town of Wardner was becoming more settled, and the miners there had absolute freedom as to where and how they should board and trade. The Bunker Hill no longer had any interest in any store or inventory in that area. The employees were given the option of paying their $1 for hospital fees to the Wardner Hospital or to the Providence Hospital in Wallace.

October 7 saw the union men still holding out for $3.50 per day for everyone in Burke Canyon. Three prominent members of the Butte Union came over, and numerous secret meetings had been held in Gem, Burke and Wardner. It was reported that the Gem and Burke unions voted to refuse the offer and that the Wardner union voted almost unanimously in favor of continuing work at the Bunker Hill at the rate they had accepted two weeks previously. The Burke and Gem unions justified their stand by saying that carmen and shovelers were exposed to the same risks as the miners.

The Dunn Brothers criticized the union men from Butte as encouraging the local men to hold out for the $3.50 per day all around. They cited that the market value of silver and lead combined had fallen about 25% since 1887, but that the price of necessities had fallen fully 33% within the same period.

Tension regarding the wages built up all through the county. On October 9 many of the Knights of Labor in the surrounding camps were at Wallace and met with the Mine Owners' Association. The Gem and Frisco mines made an offer of $3.25 per day all around, and the union took some time to think it over. Three days later this proposal was rejected. Both the Gem and Frisco desired to start up during the middle of the month, but their plans were hopeless unless the question of wages could be settled. The situation was changing from day to day.

On the 13th of October, businessmen and miners held a mass meeting in Wardner, and some were in favor of working for 25 cents per day less in hope of inducing the Bunker Hill to keep the mine running. Most of the men refused to do this. The Bunker Hill laid off 40 men during the week because of another decrease in the price of lead. It was feared that if the price fell more, further reductions would be made. Not everyone was concerned with the wages however. Jerome Jacobs took the opportunity to present a window display in his saloon on Sixth Street of items of curious and historical nature.

By the third week in October, the Gem, Frisco and Mammoth mines resumed operations. Even though lead had fallen to $3.20, which was the lowest point yet reached, it was felt that the price could not go much lower. All of the mines, with the exception of the Bunker Hill, were paying $3.50 per day to all of their employees. At the Tiger there were but twelve men on the payroll, and they were doing development work preparatory to resumption of operations, which would be about the 1st of November unless lead dropped clear out of sight.

*   *   *

Wesley Everett, of Mullan, and August Doyle met a bear and two cubs on the hills near Mullan. Everett wounded the mother bear, who attacked him and knocked his gun from his hand and then grabbed him. The mother bear then fell dead from the effects of the bullet. The animal weighed 500 pounds. The wounded man was brought to the Providence Hospital and soon released after his injuries were treated.

On October 21, O. C. Otterson was held up in his store during the evening about 7:30. Two masked men came in while he was sorting clothes near the back of the store, and they leveled revolvers at him. He was ordered to open his safe, and did so. The robbers left by the back door and a general search of the town and area was begun. Sheriff Cameron formed a posse which searched for a couple of days before giving up. . . . The loss from the safe amounted to $895.94. The getaway was complete, and the robbers were never captured.

November came to Wardner and found a half dozen men working at the Sierra Nevada doing development work. Eight men were working under contract or lease at the Stemwinder. About four men were doing development work for the Last Chance. The Bunker Hill was working only one shift per day.

Times were improving; three saloons had reopened in Wallace during the first week of November.

Woods and Keats took an ad in the newspaper and advertised their groceries: Potatoes, $1 per hundred; creamery butter, 35 cents per pound; 13 pounds of sugar for $1; 95 cents for a sack of flour; 20 pounds of navy beans for $1; 7 cans of tomatoes, $1; 5 cans of Eagle milk, $1; 5-gallon keg of syrup, $1.75; ten pounds of crackers, 90 cents; dried apricots, peaches, plums and prunes ran about 6 pounds per $1; 3¼ pound package of sealed tobacco, 50 cents.

It was rumored that the Miners' Union would open a Miners' Store at one or more points in the Coeur d'Alenes, providing that proper arrangements could be made. The U. S. Congress, feeling the effects of the silver panic, passed a law stating that no assessment work need be done on mining claims for the year 1893 in order to hold the same.

In Burke, the Poorman was putting out more concentrates during the past month than ever before. Its production was 2,000 tons and during October they had put out more than three cars of concentrates per day.

The Last Chance Mine was waiting for a decision of the appellate court and was presently working twenty men. When the decision was handed down it favored the Last Chance over the Tyler Mining Company. The Bunker Hill was putting out about 50 tons of concentrates a day. W. H. Bailey and Son of Wardner Junction supplied 24 cords of wood daily and three carloads of stulls every week to the Poorman Mine.

All through the district things started to appear more prosperous. While times were not good, they were not as bad as before. Payrolls were increasing and a time of stability appeared to be at hand.

Early in December, the Tiger mine resumed operations and added 25 more men to the 18 who had been doing development work. All of the principal mines in Canyon Creek were in operation.

The Weber Bank of Wardner filed Articles of Corporation with the Secretary of the State of Idaho. The directors were John

H. Weber and P. P. Weber, Lucy Weber, W. N. Morphy and H. C. Desilets.

At the end of the first week in December, the Poorman Mine shut down for improvements and repairs. They were having some trouble with the hoisting equipment, and it was necessary for them to lay off all but thirty men to make repairs. It was predicted the Poorman would be closed down until spring or perhaps longer. Its management complained about low prices of lead and silver and the fact that they could not make any profits under the existing prices.

Within a week the Tiger's payroll had grown to eighty men, and the Poorman was busy putting in a new air compressor which would handle twenty drills. Lead dropped to the price of $3.10 per hundred.

It was understood that the post offices of Kellogg and McAulay were to be discontinued and the post office at Wardner Junction was to handle their mail instead. No official notice had been given of this change as yet. . . . George E. Bent was the Superintendent of the Bunker Hill, where Jack McGee was killed in a cave-in on December 19.

Owing to low prices of lead and silver, the Gem Mine laid off about 50 men effective at the end of December. The mill would continue to run for a week or so to clean up the ore on hand, and then a small force would be kept to keep the mine in repair.

All during 1893, there were many robberies and break-ins throughout the district. A newspaper in mid-December reported the theft of $500 from a resident in Burke, where the money was in a satchel which had been hidden. All these reports reflected that there were many people out of work who were traveling in and out of the area. Each notice that a mine was going to resume operations started a flood of miners in from everywhere.

Just before Christmas, several miners got into a brawl in Gem, and at least three men received severe injuries. Those injured were Scandinavian miners from the Frisco. No arrests were made, and the affair seemed to have been caused by the exuberance and drinking of the evening. Bottles and pistols were frequently used in these festivities.

The Wallace City Council met late in the month and reduced the police force to one man. They cited the low condition of the city's treasury as their reason. The one man was to act as night watchman from 7:00 P.M. to 7:00 A.M. at a salary of $75 a month.

The year ended, and there was no further reduction in payrolls at the Tiger, Frisco or Bunker Hill, and there were no rumors that these mines would lay off any men. Things seemed to be going all right on these properties, but their continued operations depended mainly on the metal market.

The year had provided many hardships, but the future appeared brighter to the people of the Coeur d'Alenes. . . . A mining camp is an excellent breeding ground for such things as faith and hope. . . .

CHAPTER 42

A SUMMARY, BUT NOT A CONCLUSION

For the most part, the preceding stories were about people and their successes and failures. By the very nature of things, such stories do not necessarily come to immediate or conclusive ends. The first ten years of the Coeur d'Alene Mining District illustrated the cycles through which a mining camp lives.

The most basic of all cycles is that of life and death. The foregoing stories were of the birth of the Coeur d'Alene Mining District and the very early stages of its life from exploration into the early stages of production of silver, lead and zinc. The life cycle for gold mining in the Coeur d'Alenes appears to have been shorter and completely unrelated to that of the other metals.

Basic to mining and all other extractive industries is their quick and immediate economic connection with the general business trends of the United States and the world. The cycles move up and down quickly without advance notice. The mining game, by its very nature, can be discreetly labeled speculative, or it can be more plainly called gambling. . . . There can be no winners without losers; and, as many have learned, once a winner does not mean always a winner.

In the Coeur d'Alene Mining District, there have always been the two classes: labor and management. Each serves its own masters and quite often finds itself in conflict with the other.

Each and every cycle worked independently of each other and caused great friction and hardship on the miners and their families. For the most part, these men had no control over economic conditions, the finding of ore, labor troubles and difficulties with government. Unemployment was rampant and there could be a long time and distance between jobs.

The Coeur d'Alenes offered other things over which the miners had little or no control, including fires. . . . Its climate presented distinct seasons and brought severe winter weather. Snow, cold and ice endangered their lives, homes and jobs, and sometimes curtailed their food supplies. . . . Of course, as one old-timer put it: "It all balances out; the rich get their ice in the summer and the poor get theirs in the winter."

It was not enough that men came to the Coeur d'Alenes and found ore. To be sure, the presence of ore was a necessity, but so was the combination of other factors: beginning capital, water, management, labor, transportation, a demand for the metals and a market price that allows for a profit to all concerned in the operation. . . . From time to time, this combination broke down and difficulties ensued.

The foregoing paragraphs paint a dark and dreary picture, and sometimes such was the case. . . . However, the basic drive for "riches" provided the power to keep the whole process in operation. Thus far it has overridden every breakdown in the system.

❋   ❋   ❋

Enough of hardships. . . . The people involved in these stories of the Coeur d'Alenes have gone to their rewards and they deserve more than the small recognition these tales provide. . . . Who is to say which were the "important" stories, and which were not? To those involved, each was significant.

Hardrock mining breeds a special type of men. They have borne many labels: strong, hardy, bold, independent, irresponsible, stubborn, cantankerous, devil-may-care, gamblers, drinkers, shiftless, renegades, good men and bad men. The foregoing list is not meant to be all inclusive. . . . If the truth be known, most hardrock mining men incorporate a majority of these characteristics in their makeup, give or take a couple extra now and then.

Of course, nothing holds true for all men, but miners do seem especially independent and rebellious towards authority, be it management or government.

It has been said that nothing is new and that everything has its counterparts in the past. Recognizing this as basically true, perhaps something can be learned from what has happened.

*   *   *

There is a *camaraderie* among the people of the Coeur d'Alenes; past and present. It is built on a foundation of many things including hardrock mining, hard living, hard drinking, and just plain hardship. The pride of a miner in his work provides the glue that holds it together, and the miners' sense of humor is the softening agent that keeps it from drying out and breaking up—

> "This old woman . . . she's a mining camp, she is. Nothin' more, and nothin' less . . . She's one of the last of a bygone era . . . She's old enough to have quite a past, but young enough so she won't tell all. . . ."

INDEX

A

Abbott, L. L., 226, 227, 249
Abeling, Otto, 45
Adams, Gus, 162
Adams, Mr., 199
Adams, R. K., 227
Aerial Tramways: Bunker Hill, 123, 127-128, 165, 170, 172, 213, 238, 265
    Custer Mine, 125
    Last Chance Mine, 85, 126
    Morning Mine, 70, 94, 105
    Stemwinder Mine, 43, 156, 271
Albinola, Peter and Wife, 293
Allen, George, 269
Allison, C. Leon, (See also Siringo, Charles A.) 161, 191, 240, 243, 245-249, 257-259
Allison, James, 286
Alma Gold Mine, 273, 276, 288, 290
American House, 133, 138
Amott, S. D., 170
Anderson, Charles, 254, 261
Anderson, Theodore, 28
Andrews, James, 123
Angel, Annie, 260
Angel, Judge A. E., 84, 97, 153, 194, 257, 262, 270
Antimony Mine, 290
Arastras, 77, 87, 152
Argentine Mine, 95, 142, 172, 269
Argyle, Thomas, 250, 262
Arment, E. G., 33, 187
Arment's Hotel, 24
Associated Press, 233, 239
Aulbach, Adam, 32, 72-73, 75, 78, 85, 91, 95, 109, 115, 118, 131, 137, 145, 156, 161, 173, 175, 178-179, 183, 186-187, 192, 195, 196, 200-201, 206, 214, 218, 233, 239, 251-252, 257, 264-265

B

Baby Fraction Mine, 70
Badger Mine and Mill, 70, 170, 204
Baer, Harry F., 18-19, 83
Bailey, W. H. & Son, 301
Bair, Professor, 126
Ballance, Captain, 256
Bank of Murray, 28
Bank of Wallace, 101, 113-114
Banner Mine, 141, 153
Barber, Guard, 246
Barnard, George A., 293
Barnard, T. N., 67, 136
Barry, J. J., 185
Bartlett, John, 268
Baseball, 51, 67, 74, 93, 143, 210, 238
Bathing facilities, 42
Bayard, (See Burke, Idaho)
Bean, Ivery, 221, 227, 228, 244, 247, 261, 263
Beatty, Judge, 203, 232, 243, 248, 274
Beaver, 111
Beaver Creek, 12
Beaver Mining District, 67
Beaver Station, 57
Belknap Trail, 14
Belle Claims, 208
Bender, Charles E., 155
Benner, E. W., 127
Bent, George E., 302
Bernard, Henry, 50, 73
Bernier, Pete, 108, 289
Billy Miller Claim, 87
Bitterroot Mountains, 7
Black Bear Mine and Mill, 16, 65, 70, 110, 135, 138, 139, 151, 262, 268, 287
Black Cloud, Idaho, 113
Black Cloud Mine, 16, 66, 153
Black Hills, 13, 90
"Black listing," 183, 258

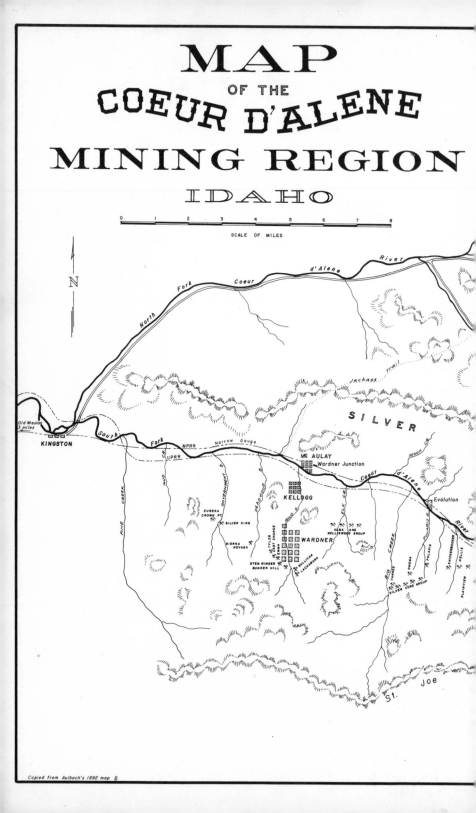

MAP
OF THE
COEUR D'ALENE
MINING REGION
IDAHO

0 1 2 3 4 5 6 7 8

SCALE OF MILES